STRATEGIC THOUGHT IN THE NUCLEAR AGE

Books by
LAURENCE MARTIN

Peace Without Victory
The Sea in Modern Strategy
Arms and Strategy

General Editor

HOSSEIN AMIRSADEGHI

Strategic Thought in the Nuclear Age

Editor

LAURENCE MARTIN

Vice-Chancellor
The University of Newcastle upon Tyne

Contributors

Coral Bell
Louis-François Duchêne
John Garnett
Klaus Knorr
Laurence Martin
Robert E. Osgood
Henry S. Rowen

The Johns Hopkins University Press
Baltimore, Maryland

Manufactured in Great Britain

The Johns Hopkins University Press, Baltimore, Maryland 21218
Library of Congress Catalog Number 79–2979
ISBN 0–8018–2330–7
Library of Congress Cataloging in Publication Data
Main entry under title:
Strategic thought in the nuclear age.

Includes bibliographical references and index.
1. Strategy—Addresses, essays, lectures.   2. World
politics—1945–   —Addresses, essays, lectures.
I. Martin, Laurence W.
U162.S774   355.4′307   79–2979
ISBN 0–8018–2330–7

Contents

Contributors

LAURENCE MARTIN
Laurence Martin is Vice-Chancellor of the University of Newcastle upon Tyne; he was formerly Professor of War Studies, University of London, Professor of International Politics, University of Wales, and Associate Professor of European Diplomacy, the Johns Hopkins University. His books include *Peace without Victory* (1958), *The Sea in Modern Strategy* (1967), and *Arms and Strategy* (1973).

LOUIS-FRANÇOIS DUCHÊNE
Louis-François Duchêne has been a journalist on the *Guardian* (1949–52) and *The Economist* (1956–8 and 1963–7). A former personal assistant to Jean Monnet, he was from 1969 to 1974 Director of the International Institute for Strategic Studies. Since 1974 he has directed the University of Sussex European Research Centre. He has published a full-length study of W. H. Auden (1972), and many articles and chapters on European and security affairs.

KLAUS KNORR
Klaus Knorr is Professor of International Affairs, Woodrow Wilson School, Princeton University. He is also the editor of *World Politics*. His recent publications include *The Power of Nations* (1975), (ed.), *Historical Dimensions of National Security Problems* (1976), (ed.), and *Economic Issues and National Security* (1977).

ROBERT E. OSGOOD
Robert E. Osgood is Dean of the School of Advanced International Studies, and Christian A. Herter Professor of International Studies at the Johns Hopkins University. His books include *Limited War: The Challenge to American Strategy* (1957), *NATO: The Entangling Alliance* (1962), *Force, Order, and Justice* (with Robert W. Tucker) (1967), and *New Era of Ocean Politics* (with Ann L. Hollick) (1974).

HENRY S. ROWEN
Henry S. Rowen is Professor of Public Management at the Graduate School of Business at Stanford University. He was President of the RAND Corporation for six years. In the Kennedy and early Johnson

administrations he was Deputy Assistant and Secretary of Defense for International Security Affairs, and later Assistant Director of the Bureau of the Budget.

CORAL BELL
A former member of the Australian diplomatic service, Dr Coral Bell is now Senior Research Fellow at the Australian National University, Canberra. She was formerly Professor of International Relations at the University of Sussex, and Lecturer at the London School of Economics, the University of Sydney, and the University of Manchester. Her books include *Negotiation from Strength* (1962), *The Debatable Alliance* (1964), *The Conventions of Crisis* (1971), and *The Diplomacy of Detente* (1977).

JOHN GARNETT
John Garnett is a Senior Lecturer in Strategic Studies at the University College of Wales, Aberystwyth, and a Consultant at the National Defence College. He is also a member of the Foreign and Common-wealth Office Advisory Panel on Arms Control and Disarmament, and British member of the United Nations Advisory Board on Disarmament Studies. He is the editor of *Theories of Peace and Security* (1970), *The Defence of Western Europe* (1974) and co-author of *Contemporary Strategic Thought* (1975).

Foreword

Informed debate about international political, economic and strategic issues is an important basis for stability and security. It is with this in mind that I have fostered the production of a number of books on such subjects, written by an international selection of distinguished and dispassionate scholars. The first of these, *Twentieth Century Iran,* treated an important regional issue in considerable detail. The present volume, in contrast, surveys the global strategic scene in broad terms, attempting to evaluate the significance of developments since the end of the Second World War. Within the overall framework the authors, all of them well-known as experts on particular aspects of strategic matters, have been left free to develop their subject as seemed best to them. The result is, I believe, a valuable and provocative work that will serve both as a survey of a vital aspect of world politics and as a stimulus for debate on many topics.

It is only by a clear understanding of how the present strategic world has evolved that we can hope to master its many dangers and establish a more secure international environment. I am confident that this book makes an important contribution to such understanding.

Hossein Amirsadeghi

Editor's Preface

It is clear that the revolution in military affairs that has occurred since 1945 has involved much more than the mere introduction of nuclear weapons. The use of atomic bombs against Japan undoubtedly constituted an important threshold, but it took the development of thermonuclear weapons and missiles to make an unmistakable qualitative difference in destructive power. Many other technological innovations, as in the field of electronics, have also had far-reaching effects. Even the whole range of developments in military technology, however, would not explain all the fundamental changes on the post-war strategic scene. Radical changes in public attitudes within both the so-called post-industrial societies and the less developed countries have profoundly altered the context of strategy while, in a possibly more transient way, the particular alignments that have characterised the world since 1945 have also influenced the course of military affairs.

Much uncertainty must necessarily surround the long-term consequences of these developments. For over thirty years now, however, both policy and strategic theory have been coming to grips with the immediate implications of the changes and attempting to make some assessment of likely future trends. It therefore seemed worthwhile inviting a number of students of strategy to write, quite independently, an assessment of a particular aspect of strategic thought and practice since 1945, about which he or she has long been concerned. The range of topics is not exhaustive and the perspective is chiefly 'western'. Nevertheless, the volume constitutes, I believe, an unusual combination of broad coverage with a depth that results from long reflection. I hope it will serve both as a useful survey for the newcomer to the study of modern strategic thought, especially for the great number of university and college courses devoted to such matters, and a stimulus to the further speculation of the specialist.

Laurence Martin

1

The Role Of Military Force
In The Nuclear Age

by Laurence Martin

As the world of military affairs has rapidly evolved since 1945, a great deal of scepticism has developed in the West as to whether armed force remains a useful instrument of policy in the nuclear age. Because beliefs both popular and expert about the utility and moral acceptability of force condition the ways in which it is maintained and wielded, the debate about its usefulness is itself an important element in the balance of power. Scepticism does not become effective only when it leads its exponents to a total rejection of military action; in lesser forms it can colour, if only subconsciously, the much wider and more practical debate over the proper level of defence expenditure and preparedness.

The roots of modern scepticism about the utility of armed force seem to originate mainly from developments in three areas: military technology, social policy, and the pattern of international politics. On the military side, the immense increase in the potential destructiveness of warfare in the age of nuclear weapons has naturally bred doubts as to whether armed force can be contained within limits proportional to political purposes. This doubt is not wholly new. The scale of destruction wrought by the application of modern industrial capacity to warfare in the great world conflicts earlier this century greatly reinforced an even older perception that war was a costly, inhumane and unreliable way of pursuing political ends. A powerful and systematic philosophical critique of war has flourished since at least the seventeenth century, and the foundation of the League of Nations and the United Nations, whatever their imperfections, testified to the growing political need to make at least a gesture toward alternative methods of settling disputes. Nuclear weapons, with their combination of crude destructive power and amenability to methods of delivery capable of making the potential catastrophe so sudden as to preclude even the opportunity for diplomacy or second thoughts, have taken earlier twentieth-century misgivings to

1

new depths, expressed in such well-known phrases as President Eisenhower's 'There is no alternative to peace.'[1]

At the same time, as war came to be seen as potentially much more destructive, changes in important attitudes to society also reached a new universality of acceptance. Almost everywhere it has come to be thought that the chief and proper purpose of the state is to foster the economic welfare of its citizens and that this goal is best served by investment, trade, and good economic management. At least as economic goals, such once traditional functions of military policy as the conquest of territory and opening of markets have been generally discounted. Beyond that, the concepts of 'welfarism' and economic equity have extended beyond domestic society and permeated international relations. Thus, among the democracies at least, conquest has come to appear wrong as well as unprofitable. There is a strong preference for regarding both international and domestic politics as processes of incremental change and bargaining rather than as contests of power.

Finally, the structure of international politics since 1945 has made its contribution to the idea that armed force may soon be unnecessary. The dominance of a bipolar Cold War has provided yet another opportunity for optimists to believe—as was their tendency in both World Wars— that, were this one enemy once reduced or this conflict once resolved, an age of harmony would follow. This illusion, for illusion one fears it must be, was encouraged by the pattern of co-operation developing within the Western camp, with all the common political and economic structures that emerged in the 'fifties. The Atlantic world was said to be a 'security community', defined as one within which armed conflict was unthinkable.[2] There was little inclination to temper such optimism with the reflection that the harmony had been shortlived on the scale of history and had been achieved in the face of a common threat, the classic condition for mutual but usually transient solidarity. The more sanguine, prevalent opinion has been that, among the democratic, developed nations at least, we have finally witnessed fruition of the long-cherished hope that the industrialisation of society would breed peaceable men and lead states to see their self-interest in co-operation.[3]

The belief that military action was no longer, if it ever had been, a useful instrument for pursuing national advantage encouraged the hope that military preparations might also become unnecessary for self-defence. For if nations no longer had an incentive to undertake aggressive action, the vicious Hobbesian cycle whereby some arm to defend themselves, only to stimulate the defensive preparations of others which are, in turn, perceived as offensive, might be broken. A belief that war had become unprofitable for self-advancement, unnecessary in self-defence and, at the same time, unprecedentedly dangerous, would constitute a powerful case for neglecting military preparations. It therefore becomes exceedingly important that the democracies in which ideas of this kind are prevalent, though rarely, of course, in such explicit and abstract form, should consider very carefully what the role of armed force actually is in the contemporary world.

Even to establish that armed force no longer served useful purposes would not, of itself, ensure that it was never used. For the world is full of irrational and dysfunctional behaviour. Indeed, those of a pacifistic turn of mind, who are most inclined to describe force as useless, frequently maintain that it has never been a profitable instrument: that it has been endemic only because of a great illusion. Yet they must confess that the illusion has been subscribed to by the majority of statesmen and that war has been continual. Thus, from that perspective, uselessness has not been sufficient to abolish war. That would require a universal perception of uselessness—a very different matter. Consequently, in the present day, we must enquire not only into whether Western behaviour is increasingly suffused with scepticism about the value of military activities, but also into how universally and symmetrically such a notion is entertained world-wide. This is a question with very practical implications, not merely because, on the Hobbesian model, nations may be driven to defensive military activities merely because others entertain the idea that offensive military power is useful, but also because asymmetrical attitudes to force may give it a utility that would otherwise be lacking. Indifference to military preparations and a revulsion from warfare on the part of one nation may actually increase the returns aggressive or threatening conduct may confer on another. Discrepancies of this sort undoubtedly contributed greatly to the outcome of diplomacy during the era of appeasement in the 'thirties and became a conscious object of Hitler's diplomacy. Considerations of this kind are also relevant to the related question of whether the undoubtedly increased inhibitions surrounding many forms of military action in the nuclear age arise inevitably from the very nature of modern weapons and contemporary society, or are merely the product of the specific balance of power that the great powers have managed to maintain in the post-war years.

*   *   *

Any more minute examination of the contemporary utility of military force must begin with the strategic nuclear balance, which is itself the single most important source of the widespread belief that armed forces may be outliving their usefulness. There is little doubt that the ever-present possibility of nuclear destruction on a global scale is the main cause of popular revulsion from the thought of major war. A great deal of public apathy about military questions is prompted by the conviction that war between the greater powers would be a holocaust that no precautions could alleviate and is consequently a prospect so fearsome that war will never be initiated. Nor would many deny that the potential of nuclear war has introduced a new sobriety and caution into the mutual relations of the great powers.

The realisation that international affairs would henceforth have to be conducted and strategic policy designed under new constraints was neither immediate nor universal after the first nuclear weapons were used in 1945. Some perceptive thinkers quickly saw that these were in some respects 'absolute' weapons and identified 'deterrence' as the security policy most appropriate for exploiting them.[4] But most actual military conduct continued for several years on much more traditional lines. Lacking nuclear weapons, the Soviet Union naturally minimised their significance and, although it acquired them as soon as possible, it continues to this day to conceive their role in much more intimate relation to conventional armed forces than has been typical in the West.

In the early nuclear years, however, the North Atlantic powers also approached their security problems in traditional ways, regarding Europe and North-East Asia as the front lines of United States' defence, and setting up alliances of familiar type based on the conceptions of mobilisation and expeditionary forces. More than thirty years after the first nuclear attacks, not a few strategic problems within the Western alliance were still those of reconciling arrangements established in a pre-nuclear frame of reference with the implications of the now unmistakable if ambiguous nuclear revolution.

Once the thermonuclear weapon had been perfected, fissionable material had become relatively plentiful, and nuclear weapons had fallen into the hands of several nations, a rapid evolution of strategic thought took place. This thought was probably most productive and certainly most publicised in the United States, where two major specialised strategic concepts for harnessing nuclear weapons emerged. These were, sequentially, the doctrines of Massive Retaliation and Mutual Assured Destruction (MAD).

The bulk of American strategic thought, and the area in which it achieved most sophistication, was that devoted to the techniques for maintaining an adequate retaliatory force to preserve deterrence against a nuclear attack. The concept of a 'secure second strike' and the technical requirements for preserving such a capacity were early fruits of this thinking.[5] Much less attention was devoted to the question of what other, more positive purposes a strategic nuclear force—that is, one capable of attacking an enemy's heartland—could serve. It was a characteristic of the briefly ascendant doctrine of Massive Retaliation—it is not clear that anyone of significance ever paid allegiance to the whole and literal meaning of the phrase—that its advocates did believe that the capacity to launch large-scale nuclear war could be used as a coercive instrument to ensure the satisfactory outcome of international confrontations over issues far short of national survival. Scepticism about the credibility and hence the efficacy of a massive and undifferentiated threat to influence minor issues stimulated a critique that led in two directions. The first of these was toward a doctrine of limited war for limited issues,[6] the second toward a belief that nuclear weapons, at least in their more powerful forms, were good for nothing but neutralising each other in a framework of mutual deterrence. Here was a specific instance of the belief in the uselessness of weapons for positive purposes that has infected attitudes to military force in general.

The belief that strategic nuclear weapons were of no use except to deter their opposite numbers gained credence at a time when it was generally believed that no defence was possible against the newly deployed intercontinental ballistic missiles. Soon, however, the evolution of techniques for defence against ballistic missiles, even if not yet adequate to provide an effective counter to massive attacks, bred fears that the mutual vulnerability thought necessary for deterrence might be undermined. As a result, those who saw mutual vulnerability as the source of strategic stability between the super-powers, defined as abstention from both nuclear aggression and an active arms race, raised MAD to a principle and made it the preferred object of policy rather than merely the consequence of a particular but perhaps passing stage of technological evolution.[7]

To the fundamentalist advocate of MAD, the function of strategic nuclear weapons becomes entirely negative: the deterrence of attack by the strategic nuclear weapons of others. In practice the United States has been compelled by its extended interests and obligations to allies to maintain the possibility of initiating nuclear action and, consequently, of hoping for some capacity to dominate the escalatory sequence that might follow. Thus, strategic nuclear weapons have continued to play a role, at least in American 'declaratory' military policy, related to lesser issues than the simple deterrence of nuclear attack. Clearly no declarations of restrained intent could render such powerful weapons wholly irrelevant to the diplomacy and political atmosphere of the world in which they existed. But even if strategic nuclear weapons were universally thought to serve no purpose other than the neutralisation of other nuclear forces, their essentially negative role would by no means deprive them of utility.

On the contrary, their mere existence would be—and, indeed, is—the only firm assurance of immunity from attack and the only reliable guarantee against extreme pressure from other, blackmailing, nuclear powers. These possibilities are well recognised in practice, even if not always expressed in such terms, so that the preservation of these largely 'negative' nuclear forces is regarded as the supreme issue of national security policy and the manipulation of the international nuclear balance is considered the dominant diplomatic issue.[8]

Moreover, there is every reason to believe that this is no merely transient phase of history. Despite the once-prevalent endorsements of General and Complete Disarmament as an ultimate goal, despite President Carter's more recent assertion that the abolition of nuclear weapons was his final purpose, the actual historical tendency is to build nuclear weapons ever more firmly into the international system. The Strategic Arms Limitation process, though certainly providing limited constraints on military policy and becoming an important element in strategic calculations, is in fact devoted to perpetuating the role of strategic nuclear weapons. Each participant's confidence in the outcome of agreements rests precisely on the residual deterrent left to it. However frequently misunderstood and misrepresented in public, Strategic Arms Limitation is not an alternative to giving nuclear weapons a major role in international politics, but merely one way of defining that role. In this respect, the Strategic Arms Limitation process parallels the more general shift of hope and attention from efforts to secure disarmament proper to pursuing the limited goal of arms control.[9]

It has also become obvious since the early 'sixties that, even if strategic nuclear weapons are regarded as wholly negative, mutually self-deterring instruments, this does not mean that the details of the balance can be neglected. Early in the 'sixties, when the notion of stability through MAD was first emerging, the appearance of technically advanced missiles such as Polaris and Minuteman encouraged the idea that the strategic arms competition was emerging on to a plateau where, in the absence of any effective defence, mutual deterrence might be permanently assured by quite small arsenals of strategic weapons needing no further perfection.[10] Subsequent years have clearly demonstrated that no such technologically-determined plateau exists. The invention in the mid-sixties of practical methods for defence against ballistic missiles did much to puncture the shortlived complacency, even though the overall performance of the defensive systems could not yet offer substantial immunity from a major, sophisticated attack. Since then, other developments such as multiple warheads and improved accuracies have shown how the dialectic of offence and defence persists even at the strategic nuclear level, so that the balance between one order of battle and that of its antagonist remains a subject for anxious attention. The 1972 Treaty limiting anti-ballistic defences reduced immediate anxiety about the destabilising effects of such possibilities, but continued research and development keep alive the ultimate spectre of one party to mutual vulnerability purchasing itself immunity. Later scares about such devices as particle beams and lasers testified to the sensitivity of the issue and to the possibility that the time-scale for its actuation might not be very long.

Thus strategic stability, in the dual sense of confidence that there would be no nuclear aggression and of sluggishness in the arms race, cannot be taken for granted. Instead, it is the object of anxious study, active research and, from time to time, the vigorous deployment of new strategic systems. The zeal with which the super-powers take these precautions, with the lesser nuclear powers doing their best to follow, is powerful testimony to the belief that the often seemingly remote and irrelevant strategic nuclear forces are really fundamental to the preservation of national interests and survival.

While it is therefore clear that the strategic nuclear forces play vital roles for their owners and require careful attention even for the minimal purposes of preserving an adequate deterrent against the ultimate possibility of nuclear threats to the nation's survival, the state of the strategic nuclear forces is in fact related to a much wider range of issues. Whatever the pure theory of MAD may suggest, it is inconceivable that the mere existence of such immensely powerful instruments of destruction would not condition other levels of military affairs and influence the outcome of international conflicts. Early ideas for harnessing this influence, such as Massive Retaliation, may have been discredited, but a debate has continued, with varying intensity, about how strategic nuclear power can be linked to national security interests below the level of mere immunity from nuclear attack.

In the Soviet Union, so far as one can tell, there has never been an inclination to divorce the nuclear balance from the other methods of managing conflict. In the West, especially the United States, the debate that had been briefly shelved in the early 'sixties revived at the end of the decade, when the Soviet Union was generally acknowledged to be reaching rough nuclear parity. The decision to handle this eventuality by resort to SALT made it necessary to justify, more explicitly than ever before, a particular strategic balance between the United States and the Soviet Union and to explain, among other things, what its effect would be on the wider relationship between the two adversaries. The fact that this juncture arrived just as the United States was suffering severe diplomatic setbacks in South-East Asia and the Middle East lent some acerbity to the discussion.

At the heart of the dispute was the question of whether, even within a strategic nuclear balance that ruled out large-scale nuclear attacks as a national policy, degrees of superiority and well-devised strategic doctrine could confer ascendancy on one side in crises and confrontations. At the risk of merely caricaturing what were complex arguments, made all the more elusive by being entwined with passing political manoeuvres, the debate can be summarised in terms of the positions associated with Henry Kissinger as Secretary of State and James Schlesinger as Secretary of Defense.

Kissinger's view was encapsulated in his much-publicised outburst: 'What in the name of God is superiority? What is the significance of it, politically, militarily, operationally? What do you do with it?' Later, he made much the same point in a speech in Phoenix, Arizona, in which he averred that imbalances of military power had historically been of great significance but that this was no longer so between nuclear powers. Not since the Cuban missile crisis of 1962 had asymmetries of nuclear power affected the outcome of any conflict between the Soviet Union and the

United States. According to this view, degrees of nuclear power were meaningless, always provided, of course, that sufficient parity was maintained to deny the enemy a disarming first strike. Specific conflicts must therefore be worked out with the traditional coercive and co-operative instruments of statecraft. The nuclear balance is not irrelevant, in this view, because all diplomacy must henceforth be conducted under the shadow of possible catastrophe. This shadow, it was sometimes suggested, might be 'linked' to particular disputes. But this apparently did not entail the use of or the threat to use nuclear weapons; rather it implied a warning to the opponent that he, too, had an interest in mutual restraint in nuclear policy and that, by persisting in this or that provocative behaviour, he might weaken the understanding that protects both against accident and instability. This idea parallels the hope, often expressed, that goodwill arising from arms limitation agreements and negotiations would spread to wider issues.[11]

From this perspective it must be admitted that the strategic nuclear forces cannot be expected to contribute much to the management of particular conflicts. In its proper form, as articulated by Kissinger, however, the conception is not based on a naïve expectation of extracting a great deal of co-operative behaviour from adversaries merely by preaching the needs of strategic stability. Instead, the approach requires a willingness to muster all the traditional instruments of power politics below the nuclear level. Thus such set-backs as the United States suffered in Angola are attributed to failure to make the necessary paramilitary efforts rather than to excessive faith in exhortations based on the spirit of SALT and detente. It may be objected that not enough was done to explain this aspect of the philosophy to the public and that the explanation is open to the suspicion of being an *ex post facto* justification for the fortunes of American foreign policy. Admittedly, in the immediate aftermath of Vietnam, the United States went through a period of extreme antipathy to foreign commitments, especially any holding out the prospect of entanglement in guerrilla war. But it remains doubtful whether democratic public opinion can learn to combine the active pursuit of arms control agreements at the strategic level with equally active military efforts, perhaps including actual hostilities, at lesser levels of conflict.

In the contrary view, associated with Schlesinger's advocacy of 'limited strategic options' (LSO), variations in the strategic nuclear balance, even under conditions of essential equivalence so far as mutual annihilation in all-out war is concerned, may affect the outcome of specific confrontations. This might happen in at least two ways. First, perceptions of disparities of force, measured by such crude indices as numbers or size of weapons, might affect the calculations of third parties lacking the ability to undertake sophisticated strategic analysis. Even the nuclear adversaries themselves might not be immune to some sense, in crisis, that the side with bigger forces would come off best in an all-out struggle, even though there might be no very convincing theory as to how this could happen.[12]

According to some esoteric analysis, however, which was put forward in the early 'seventies, there might indeed be ways in which 'superiority', thought meaningless by the advocates of MAD, might be turned to practical military and consequently political advantage. Strategic ingenuity, if married to quantitative or qualitative superiority, might devise ways to use strategic nuclear weapons to prevail in conflict: ways ranging, according to scenario, all the way from essentially symbolic attacks launched in the confidence of overall superiority, to large-scale, phased, disarming strikes, tailored so that the all-out retaliation still within the victim's physical capability always remained his worst option in the face of the attackers' even larger surviving forces.[13]

It is not necessary to argue, of course, that such attacks are likely; it is sufficient merely to believe them practicable, to endow them with political significance. The fear that the Soviet Union's growing strategic forces might endow it with such capabilities was enough to arouse the desire for a countervailing capacity in advocates of LSO. An added and more positive stimulus was provided by the difficulty of reconciling the sense of strategic stalemate, nurtured by SALT and the doctrine of MAD, with the continued dependence of many American allies on the ultimate commitment of the United States to initiate nuclear action if conventional defences failed. The possibility of differentiating between degrees of nuclear war and making possible nuclear attacks on targets which were valuable but not a matter of national survival for the Soviet Union, offered the prospect of a threat that the United States might still plausibly make on behalf of its allies. The ability to do this, however, would depend on an appropriate doctrine and an adequate margin of force above the level of mere deterrence.[14]

By the end of the 'seventies the debate between the advocates of LSO and the proponents of MAD was subsiding in a somewhat inconclusive compromise. The notion of less-than-total strategic nuclear war was at least fairly widely recognised as one possible eventuality, relevant war-plans had apparently been elaborated, and several appropriate adjustments had been made to American strategic forces; but the doctrine was by no means given the emphasis that had seemed likely in the Schlesinger years. To some extent, the outbreak of this doctrinal controversy illustrated the fact that many who had turned to MAD as the basis of stability early in the 'sixties had not thought through and reconciled themselves to the political consequences. Indeed, for much of the McNamara era it had not yet been necessary to do so because, while lip service was paid to the uselessness of superiority above a certain common level of nuclear armament, the United States nevertheless for the moment retained a considerable margin over the Soviet Union.

The controversy could be said to illustrate two differing applications to the nuclear age of the classic injunction that military force should be the instrument of policy. For some, the fear that the potential destructiveness of nuclear weapons might escape control and wreak damage out of proportion to any political aim, suggested that such weapons should be wholly excluded from the methods of international conflict; for others, the principle that weapons should serve political purposes meant that ways must be found, however tortuous, of engaging even these new devices with the tasks of foreign policy. For them, LSO were an effort to obey the frequent injunction of the late General André Beaufre that, if nuclear weapons were to have an ultimately stabilising effect on international conflict, it would be necessary to preserve some salutary instability at the strategic nuclear level.[15]

The urge to evolve a strategy capable of engaging nuclear weapons to specific conflicts has been reinforced by the growing awareness that the Soviet Union, despite the pretensions of Western arms control enthusiasts to educate the allegedly backward Russians, has never recognised a sharp division between nuclear weapons and traditional forces. There is ample evidence that Soviet leaders regard nuclear war as extremely dangerous and some reason to believe that they would prefer a world in which nuclear weapons were held in abeyance while communist forces waged the kind of ideological, subversive and even, if need be, conventional, warfare at which they excel. Nevertheless, Soviet military analysts refuse to admit that, if nuclear war comes, it need be an undifferentiated disaster in which no-one could win. On the contrary, great emphasis is laid on designing Soviet armed forces so that they can prevail at any level of hostilities. Hence the constant insistence on seizing the initiative, if necessary by pre-emption. Hence also the fact that, if the notion of deterrence is to be found in Soviet military thought, it is consistently embedded in a context of 'war-fighting' and of eliminating the enemy's own capability for continued resistance, in contrast to the dominant Western conception of threatening the 'recovery' capacity of the enemy: a doctrine rational only as an attempt to deter hostilities in the first place. It is from this perspective, also, that the significance of the Soviet interest in civil defence must be seen, exaggerated though it may have been in some quarters.

Coupled with the possibility that improvements in long-range weapons, particularly in accuracy, may indeed permit limited, discriminating, 'strategic' attacks, all of these Soviet characteristics have fed the fear among Western proponents of LSO that a future major confrontation between the super-powers might be between one regarding nuclear war as a catastrophe to be avoided at any price, and the other viewing it as a dire hazard that could nevertheless be surmounted. Such an asymmetry, it is argued, would lead to the West being the side to back down, rather as, some believe, asymmetrical anxieties about the dangers of the nuclear balance have led the United States to make disproportionate concessions in the SALT negotiations.[16]

*   *   *   *

Those who bear responsibility for national security must obviously take the possibilities of limited nuclear aggression seriously and take what military precautions seem prudent. But if the super-powers in possession of massive retaliatory forces had only their own immunity from nuclear aggression to consider, they could probably rest easy over a wide range of nuclear balances with their primary opponents. For if models of limited or even larger-scale disarming nuclear attacks have some theoretical plausibility, in the real world the attendant risks would be so great that few governments would have the confidence to make the experiment. Exponents of strategic speculation and designers of force-postures against 'worst case analyses' properly let their imaginations roam; statesmen, on the other hand, have so far shown great caution in face of the vague but powerful sense of danger with which the mere existence of nuclear weapons has suffused the world.

But the super-powers also have much wider conceptions of national security interest than their own mere immunity from attack and have naturally tried to project their military shadow for positive and negative purposes. The efforts to engage strategic nuclear power to some of these purposes have been paralleled by the deployment of a vast range of more traditional armed force. The immense efforts made by most nations to deploy and exploit such conventional forces testify at least to the vigour of the belief, whatever the reality, that the investment continues to pay practical dividends.

By far the greatest array of modern military power, probably the most potent mass of armed force ever deployed in history, is deployed in Europe. It is for this arena that most modern weapons are designed in the first instance, and it may serve as an example of the purposes such efforts are generally believed to serve.

The forces deployed in Europe are designed for a variety of roles. A key-characteristic of the European military scene since 1945 has been Soviet superiority in terms of conventional forces. For many years this preponderance was thought to be offset by the nuclear guarantee of the United States and, if the exact value of that guarantee was hard to determine, the psychological value of its supposed existence was considerable. The Soviet achievement of rough parity has eroded this reassurance and has been accompanied by the vigorous improvement of Soviet conventional forces in all respects. What purpose their forces are intended to serve is inevitably a matter of speculation. They certainly ensure Soviet dominance over Eastern Europe, and thus serve a vital Soviet political and ideological purpose. Equally, they provide the ability to invade Western Europe with a fair prospect of success if need should arise. From the Soviet perspective it may also be important that their large conventional forces and their occupation of Eastern Europe provide protection against a Western attack.

Perhaps of more practical interest in the day-to-day world of affairs, however, is the possible ability of Soviet military power to win political deference over a wide range of issues. If such deference reaches a certain ill-defined level, it is popular to describe it as 'Finlandisation', by analogy with the narrow political line the Finns feel they must walk to earn immunity from invasion. There is some controversy about the extent to which this process has in fact affected the Soviet Union's other Western neighbours and about the nature of the mechanism that is at work if it does.[17] Patently, at a time when the risks of actually employing force are high, there would be great advantages in a method of securing gains merely through its possession. Equally, a general belief that the risks were high might itself be manipulated for such purposes; this, it may be repeated, was a mechanism at work in the 'thirties. Clearly, the process depends on calculations in the mind of its victim—calculations which may be influenced not simply by the mere existence of an overbearing military force but also by explicit threats and manoeuvres.

A whole literature has sprung up recently about this political use of force in the narrow sense of demonstrations.[18] Not all concessions made in the face of overwhelming force are necessarily to be regarded in the negative light of nerveless 'appeasement'. Some may be wise and proper efforts to accommodate conflicting interests: always a major and, indeed, essential part of diplomatic intercourse. The results of such a process depend, however, on the perceptions of the beneficiary; if concessions are regarded as the fruits of military superiority, then they may very well be not only deprived of their intended emollient effect but also encourage the continuation of military pressure.

How far such mechanisms may have been at work in Western Europe is the subject of some controversy. To many, it appears that the Soviet Union has secured a great deal of deference that is inexplicable except in terms of its immense military power. The double standards observed by much Western opinion, for example in Scandinavia, with regard to East-West relations, the expectation that concessions in arms control negotiations will be made by the West, the eagerness to enter into trade and credit agreements with the Soviet Union on terms extremely favourable to the Russians, the unwillingness of some members of NATO to engage in military exercises or dispositions thought provocative to the Soviet Union, can be cited as evidence of anxiety to placate a super-power that, while having the lesser leverage on each specific issue, is a great military power that might rattle its sword. At a much more global level, it is apparent that, while the Soviet Union claims and is generally acknowledged to be one of the two leading world powers, the claim rests almost entirely on status as a military power at a time when communist ideological appeal is at low ebb.[19]

While there may be argument about what practical political benefits Soviet military power may have won in Europe in the post-war years, there are few who dispute that there must be some level of Western military inferiority below which Soviet leverage would become intolerable. NATO forces serve the necessary function of providing a countervailing influence. Exactly how to characterise and to assign priorities within this function, performed in conjunction with the strategic nuclear contribution already discussed, has never been fully agreed. In the event of actual aggression, the forces are intended to provide at worst a pause for negotiation or for deciding what escalatory measures to take and, at best, in the view of optimists, a full defence even without the use of nuclear weapons. The conventional forces also provide the wherewithal to make proportionate responses to lesser military incidents. In political terms, the apparatus of conventional defence involves the United States in European military affairs at all levels and, it is hoped, thereby establishes a convincing earnest of American commitment to European security. Equally, the major part the Europeans can play in the common defensive effort helps to erode what otherwise might be an enervating sense of helplessness at the mercy of the nuclear super-powers. The persistence with which most parties to this coalition and its strategy have rejected purely symbolic postures, and attempted to maintain a plausible capacity to mount at least a substantial local resistance, suggests that, even in periods of detente or mutual deterrence, calculations as to what would actually happen if war occurred condition the political effect of military postures.

Statements that the function of military forces in Europe is primarily 'political' must be received with great caution. The relative remoteness of the contingency of actual warfare does not mean that the latent effect of military forces is independent of calculations, even if subconscious, of their ultimate worth in battle.

Thus, while Western military forces in Europe are thought to fulfil important political purposes, including the preservation of sufficient self-confidence in the face of Soviet power to prevent the erosion of Western European independence of action, they do so by virtue of their expected effectiveness in a future war that, if generally thought unlikely, is nevertheless commonly believed possible. This belief is sufficiently lively to persuade the members of NATO to build tactical nuclear weapons into their strategy in an effort to raise still further the deterrent risks of escalation and to make Britain and France maintain national nuclear forces to ensure a European voice in the process.

The persistence with which the Western powers have sustained such great military efforts, despite the many other demands made on resources within democratic systems, testifies to the persuasiveness of the arguments for believing in the continued utility of military force. There can, however, be no ultimate proof that deterrent forces have served this purpose, for the supposed threat may not exist or may have been fended off by other, ill-understood influences. It is therefore not surprising that there are those who argue that many justifications for these military efforts are illusory, that the Soviet Union would not in fact use its military preponderance to overcome or occupy its neighbours, and that the Western Europeans would not feel obliged to be increasingly deferential to Soviet preferences if the military balance turned decisively against them. There is little in Soviet behaviour within its sphere of influence in Eastern Europe to reinforce such optimism but there is no way wholly to refute it.[20]

The most plausible form of the argument against the need for active military preparations for deterrence and self-defence is the belief that the Soviet Union's own best interests lie in leaving its neighbours undisturbed and in profiting from the resultant trade and technological exchanges. In other words, it is asserted that the prevalent economic priority pervades even the totalitarian world and will therefore produce co-operative behaviour. In a narrower sense, much the same philosophy underlies the view of some strategic analysts that, were war to come, the Soviet Union would moderate its conduct of the battle so as to preserve the 'asset value' of Western Europe.[21] Faith in the defensive efficiency of economic assets has even been generalised into the belief that great powers can become 'civilianised'. The prototype of this is said to be Japan, and it is suggested that the European Economic Community might tread the same path.

In the case of Japan itself, leaving on one side the fact that its military efforts are far from negligible in absolute terms, any supposed vindication of civilianised security policy must be qualified by the reflection that it has been achieved entirely within a security framework extended by the United States. The anxiety apparent in Japan as the United States disengaged from South-East Asia, and enunciated such constricted conceptions of national security as the Nixon Doctrine, suggested that the Japanese were well aware of what the absence of militarised protection might mean. Numerous Japanese voices have been raised to try to persuade the United States that, because increased Japanese military efforts might be politically counterproductive both regionally and in relation to the Soviet Union and China, Japan's contribution to the common defence should continue to be limited and primarily economic, while the United States continues to extend the military guarantee.[22] Thus the case of civilianised Japan cannot be argued against the utility of military force. It is merely further testimony to the historically well-established pattern whereby, in favourable circumstances, some countries can shelter cheaply under military protection furnished by others. Western Europe, with its contiguity to Soviet land power, its dangerous attractiveness to the European satellites, and its long participation in an active common defence, could scarcely hope to emulate even the reality of the Japanese security system, let alone the spurious conception of a civilianised security.

More generally, it would seem that excessive faith in the efficiency of non-military means to counter or substitute for military capabilities represents a common misinterpretation of international affairs. It is true, of course, that many, indeed the great majority of, international transactions take place without coercion and certainly without the use of force. Equally, it is true that other forms of coercion exist besides armed force and that these can be efficacious even against states with superior military power. It does not at all follow, however, that economic and other instruments of foreign policy are a universal substitute for force or that force cannot often trump all other means.[23] Even to demonstrate that force may not achieve the purposes the wielder desires, does not prove that the victim will not suffer for his lack of defensive capability. Military force cannot, it is true, serve all purposes, and the fact that some of the most pressing contemporary security problems such as, for example, the assurance of energy supplies, do not appear readily tractable to military solutions, doubtless encourages the belief that force is becoming irrelevant. In fact it is, as it always has been, merely less than all-sufficing. War is a relatively rare event for most nations, but is none the less important for that.

On examination there is, therefore, little in the post-war experience of the developed nations to suggest that military means have ceased to be a vital instrument of policy. This does not mean, of course, that military power continues or will continue to perform exactly the same roles as in the past or to do so in the same way. There have in fact been no major armed clashes between the major powers of the developed world since 1945. This in itself makes for considerable uncertainty as to what changes in public attitudes and state behaviour would occur if even a single serious outbreak of warfare took place. For the moment, however, it seems that while, as we have seen, armed forces continue to play a vital part in the security policies of the developed nations, that task will chiefly be discharged through the latent influence of 'force in being'. This raises certain problems. One is the difficulty of sustaining public support over the long term for expensive institutions that rarely if ever perform the ultimate function for which they are ostensibly designed. Another is the more narrowly technical question of how to design forces the role of which is mainly deterrence and the indirect support of diplomacy.

For most of the post-war era, although the doctrine and practice of deterrence steadily crystallised, both of the armed camps in the Cold War built up forces very similar to those that would have been suitable for fighting the World War that had just ended. Nuclear weapons were added to this familiar model, the strategic ones as an extension of the previous experience with long-range bombing, and the so-called tactical nuclear weapons as an addition to firepower on the battle field. Military organisation remained virtually unchanged so far as the 'teeth-arms' were concerned.

In the post-war era, the Soviet Union retained large forces for all levels of conflict as befitted its predominantly 'war-fighting' philosophy. It has continued this pattern to the present day, creating the Strategic Rocket Forces to fill a role formerly neglected by Anglo-American standards, and steadily filling out, especially in the 'seventies, any gaps that existed in its all-round capacity for offensive warfare. The Western powers have generally set themselves a similar goal of overall defence at all levels. Because fully adequate forces for this have never been provided, the reality has been the effort to create sufficient defensive potential at each line to discourage attack by promising enough resistance at each level to raise the spectre of escalation to the next.

From time to time there have indeed been suggestions of shifting definitively from defence to pure deterrence. The idea that NATO forces might merely create a 'tripwire' for massive retaliation was one such notion. More recently some of the advocates of relying chiefly on the threat of immediate recourse to tactical nuclear weapons—strategies associated with such phrases as 'mini-nuke' and 'radiation barrier'—have stressed the deterrent rather than the defensive merits of such a posture.

Most of these formulae have been conscious efforts to short-circuit the full military investment necessary to mount a convincing defence across the board and, as such, they have failed to win official endorsement in most Western countries. The one exception is perhaps France, where there has been a persistent if not always clearly articulated perception of the point that the deterrent effect of military forces cannot easily be divorced from their ultimate war fighting value. In recent years, however, there seems to have been more appreciation of the value of consciously fostering the deterrent and crisis-management capability of armed forces, not as an alternative, but as an adjunct to their fundamental utility in full-scale war. Thus it may be that, as it becomes more accepted that the actual uses of armed force under the inhibiting shadow of the nuclear balance are increasingly likely to be latent, oblique, limited, and directed more to influencing political situations than to seeking a verdict in battle, these functions will be reflected in the design of armed forces themselves.

On this principle it seems to be becoming recognised that armed forces justify themselves in large part by their role in transmitting diplomatic signals, inspiring confidence in allies, discouraging foes, influencing crises and signifying degrees of commitment—the last a particularly important purpose when much of the framework of security rests ultimately on destructive nuclear capabilities that, being so disproportionate to specific issues, depend for their effect very much on what degree of vital interest the possessors are thought to have in a conflict. The design of strategy to serve political purposes even at some cost to military efficiency is no new phenomenon. Deployment of the Sixth Fleet in the confined waters of the

Mediterranean may be one example. On a grander scale, the dedication of NATO forces to a forward defence, sacrificing many of the benefits of flexibility, is another. The principle may extend to the design of weapons. While the Western preference for staying power over numbers in weapons, as, for example, in the configuration of Western as compared to Soviet surface ships, or the traditional pattern of the Western to the Soviet division, rests mainly on theories of efficiency in combat, it is increasingly recognised that a price is paid in common perceptions of power and, where flexibility rather than total capability of single units is of value, perhaps even in strategic utility. Consequently it is not surprising to find voices raised to advocate a higher value being placed on the symbolic worth of units and on the case for building more, but less capable, forces to influence perceptions.[24] This is consistent with other ways of suiting armed forces better to the roles of demonstration and the flexible response to emergencies that, while requiring a military response, are such that it may be more important that the action be swift, conspicuous, decisive, or demonstrative of allied solidarity than that it should be powerful in terms of aptitude for sustained combat.

*   *   *

It thus becomes clear that, despite what to some seems superficially to be a state of inhibited irrelevance, armed force actually provides the essential underpinning for the international political system between states. Moreover, despite some persistent hopes to the contrary, the introduction of nuclear weapons has not made the military balance any easier to maintain or more suited for benign neglect. Instead, it must be and is the object of more anxious attention and more lavish expenditure than ever before in peacetime. This phenomenon appears not to be the result of wilful and wicked human aberrations; it flows logically from the nature of modern military technology.

Nevertheless, actual direct warfare between the developed states has scarcely gone beyond the level of border forays and this has bred an expectation of continued armed peace rather than open hostilities on a large scale. The absence of warfare has fed the belief that if it came it would be hard to control, and this has led in turn to doubts as to whether armed action serves useful national purposes.

Few such doubts and inhibitions have infected the less developed countries of the so-called Third World. Here, a multitude of newly sovereign states have acquired an unprecedented array of armaments. What has been particularly noteworthy, however, is the high incidence of actual warfare among the countries of the Third World. Some of these outbreaks have been on a large scale by any standards and other, lesser episodes of violence have also occurred, some notorious but many scarcely noted in the world at large.

It might be premature to draw the obvious conclusion that in the Third

World military force and warfare retain all their old utilities as political instruments. Obviously many state and non-state actors have used force, and have had considerable success in attaining their political objectives. The frequency of violence both revolutionary and between succession states, and its latter-day spread to Africa, provide strong arguments for believing that it will increasingly be war as usual amongst Third World states, as they settle their domestic problems of authority and gain the leisure and prosperity to devote themselves to external conflict. Against this it can be argued that many of the wars have been for the readjustment of territorial and other legacies of the colonial era, and are therefore a transitory phenomenon. Those who believe the effects of industrialisation on society have been a source of spreading peacefulness in the developed world can argue that similar processes will set in elsewhere. While countries of the Third World are free from the inhibitory fears of rapid and devastating escalation, felt by the nuclear powers and their close allies, they do labour under other inhibitory influences such as the frequent incidence of super-power interference. This intervention varies in motive: sometimes activated by the desire to damp down local conflict for fear that it might spread, and at other times a simple pursuit of self-interest even, if necessary, by aggravating local disputes. But in either case the Third World countries run the danger of losing control of the outcome and seeing it determined by the interests of others rather than by their own.

Clearly the ideology of welfare that has enhanced political and ethical inhibitions about force in the advanced societies is at least paid lip service in the Third World. These states share the advanced countries' need to cloak their military actions in defensive rhetoric, and there are occasions, as in some of the acts of the Organisation of African Unity, when it seems that a true sense of solidarity, propriety, and common danger has indeed had an ameliorative effect. There are also signs, as in the Persian Gulf, of the emergence of regional systems with local great powers to manipulate a conflict-management system. Such systems are not, of course, evidence of the declining utility of armed force but, as the high levels of armament acquired by potential regional great powers indicate, merely particular formulae for exploiting the capabilities of armed force.

We are thus not entirely without grounds for speculating that the role of armed force in the Third World may come to resemble that in the developed world, becoming an instrument wielded more by threat and implication than by actual use in warfare. It must be admitted, however, that this is merely a possibility that a hopeful eye might discern in the emerging political situation. The record so far suggests that frequent warfare will be the reality for some time to come. While this has often taken the form of insurgencies and guerrilla actions, there have also been a large number of conflicts exhibiting the full shape of twentieth-century conventional warfare with all the latest technological refinements. By the end of the 'seventies the arsenals of the Third World were capable of supporting wars of truly impressive proportions.

The Third World has also been the chief arena for the hostilities conducted ·by the developed countries since 1945. This activity has been an almost exclusively Western one, the chief events being a number of wars of decolonisation fought by the Europeans and two immense wars of containment fought by the United States in Asia. The motives for these activities were mixed, and certainly the specific nature of each war must be attributed in large part to local and particular circumstances.[25] In so far as there was a common theme to these military efforts, it arose from two parallel and interrelated motives. The first was the belief that Western well-being, both economic and political, required a 'compatible' world: one in which the West enjoyed wide access for trading purposes and in which as many countries as possible lived either under democracy or under systems holding out some promise of progress in that direction. The second motive arose from the hegemonic conflict with the Soviet Union and, on a different scale, with China. This created the presumption that any extension of communist influence would both erode the compatibility desired by the West and further strengthen the communist powers. The two motives thus became entwined and almost impossible to disentangle in much of the rhetoric of containment. Local issues also became synthesised by the theory of a 'domino effect', by which one defeat would lead to another, both in a political and a strategic sense. Inevitably, once a specific problem reached the stage of armed conflict, the more negative, physical conceptions of containment tended to overshadow the more positive themes of access and compatibility.

By the time the Vietnam war had ended, Western enthusiasm for this kind of activity had greatly diminished. The wars of decolonisation had frequently been expensive and unpopular. The West did not have a great deal to show for them, although it cannot be proven, of course, that the outcome might not have been worse if the effort had not been made. Some operations, such as the two major British engagements in Malaysia, were generally reckoned successes. But the major issues of decolonisation had expired by the end of the 1960s and more recent experiences, particularly that of the United States in Vietnam, have been chastening. The costs have been very high and the benefits increasingly questioned.

On the cost side, the development of theories and techniques of insurgency and guerrilla warfare had meant that even a substantial military power in conventional terms can be made to pay a very high price for victory. It seems probable that no recipe for victory exists where the opponent is an ideologically energetic insurgent movement able to assume the mantle of nationalism or the Western 'client' is weak, venal or incompetent. Technology has put powerful destructive capabilities into small packages capable of being handled with modest training by relatively few troops. It may well be true that, in Vietnam, the United States made serious errors in the ways in which it tried to apply its technological and quantitative superiority. There may have been a simplistic identification of sophistication in weaponry with size, weight and complexity. The effort that went into mounting a ponderous air war might have been much more productive if invested in sensors, reconnaissance and mobility. Nevertheless, it does appear that on balance there has been a technological shift against a distant would-be-intervening power, in favour of a local power wishing to offer resistance. Cheap, easily serviced and packaged weapons offer a formidable threat against the expensive organisational apparatus and logistic chain required for the projection of a modern military force.[26] Where the intervening power is a democracy, high costs in men and materials resonate through public opinion to impose high political costs. It is generally agreed that, while the insurgent forces fared pretty well on the battlefield in Vietnam, their really decisive victories were won within the American political system.

The source of these victories lay not merely in the high costs imposed by the Communists, but also in changed American valuations of the goals for which intervention was being conducted. At the time of Korea, opinion in America and in most of the West, encouraged by the staunchness of the South Korean regime and the overtness of the aggression, seems to have accepted that serious issues were at stake. Of these the most obvious was the prevention of successful aggression against South Korea, and the most fundamental a desire to prevent such a success becoming, on the generally accepted model of Munich, an encouragement for a later series of aggressions. The relatively traditional nature of the fighting, and the consequently successful application of American military skills, doubtless made it easier to interpret the war in familiar terms, and if there was public impatience, it was more with the cautious approach of the American government than with the purposes of the war itself. And, of course, the war lasted only three years.[27]

However, by the time of the struggle in Vietnam, which involved American forces for at least twice as long, the wars of European decolonisation were largely lost, and both American and European confidence in the purposes and techniques of containment had worn thin. Not only had military force become much more difficult to apply in Afro-Asian arenas, but the West's own bad experiences in colonial wars, the split between Russia and China, and the general volatility of nationalist movements, led many to believe that the intractability of the Third World that had frustrated the West would also automatically cauterise communist incursions.[28] During the 'sixties, preserving Western access to a compatible world had lost some of its appeal as a motive for resisting communist aggression and upholding friendly regimes. There remained a natural reluctance to see the sphere of democracy contract, but experience of post-colonial Afro-Asian independence had not fostered excessive optimism about the maintenance of parliamentary systems. At the same time, eagerness to preserve access to markets and raw materials had been weakened by the realisation that the growth of trade was most pronounced between the developed countries themselves and by the belief that what the Third World had to offer, it could not afford to withhold. This was the period of believing that 'the Arabs can't drink the oil'. Somewhat similar reasoning could be extended even to the Communist bloc by the hope that it would pay a price for Western technology. Access therefore seemed more likely to be won by the economic dynamism of the West than by its military prowess.

Complacency of this sort was shaken very sharply by the oil price rises and embargoes of 1973. This episode showed at least one very serious vulnerability on the part of many western countries and demonstrated the capability of an oligopolistic group of nations to exercise economic coercion. But while the oil crisis of 1973 did something to shake public optimism about the irrelevance of military force to Western interests in the Third World, the reversal of opinion was only partial. Oil is generally believed to be a unique case. There is apparently no other commodity both so vital to the West and so much under the control of a few states. Those states can probably muster united action over only a very small range of issues and those, with the possible exception of the American interest in the integrity of Israel, are not vital to the West. Western efforts to apply economic pressure on the Soviet Union over such issues as civil rights demonstrated the severe limits of economic pressure as a coercive instrument where the issues are important to the sufferer. Oil, it is true, was shown to be a weapon that could be wielded with some force and this condition is likely to exist for some years to come. Nonetheless, there was very little support for the notion of adopting a direct military answer to the problem; that is, to follow up the suggestion of an invasion of the Gulf to secure oil supplies. The latter threat may have served, and been chiefly intended to serve, the purpose of reinforcing caution on the part of the oil powers, but there was little support for the idea that an actual invasion would be a wise or successful operation.[29]

Thus, as the 'seventies drew to a close, faith that Western economic power could be used as a substitute for armed force had been shaken in both East-West relations and in dealings with the Third World. There was, however, no reason to derive the conclusion that armed force could preserve economic interests. Promoting Western interests of any kind in the Third World by recourse to military action was certainly one respect in which the utility of armed force seemed to have declined precipitously and permanently. The British debate over the retreat from 'East of Suez' and the enunciation of the 'Nixon Doctrine' raised abstention from military intervention into a principle.[30]

Just as this revulsion of feeling seemed irreversible, however, some second thoughts were engendered by a rapid increase in the Soviet inclination to use military forces as an instrument for projecting power. As a professed revolutionary state, the Soviet Union has always taken a close interest in conflict wherever it occurred, but neither its capability nor its propensity to do anything by way of military intervention had ever compared to that of the West. In the 'sixties and 'seventies, however, the global logistic reach of the Soviet Union, by both sea and air, increased greatly. The most overt and dramatic feature of this expansion has been the modernisation of the Soviet Navy and its much extended pattern of deployment. This extension was accompanied by an elaborate rationale, chiefly articulated by Admiral Gorshkov, in which particular stress was laid on the role of naval force in projecting and protecting 'state interests'. Along with this novel development have gone major investments in airlift and the active acquisition of a very variegated array of military facilities, such as overflight rights, and refuelling and replenishment installations. These, in turn, have been associated with military assistance, training programmes and a network of mutual security agreements. It is impossible to disentangle the complex interplay of these Soviet military activities, either as causes or effects, from the other arms of Soviet foreign policy, such as trade, economic assistance, propaganda and subversion. On the military side, however, the net result has been a very significant growth in Soviet capability for armed action, at least on a small scale, almost anywhere on earth.[31]

What these developments portend has naturally been an absorbing subject for speculation. The general grandeur and prestige of the Soviet Union is clearly intended to derive considerable added strength from the military presence and potential such wide-ranging capabilities support. In fundamental significance, perhaps the establishment of the Soviet Union as a permanent factor in the Middle East is the primary early fruit of the lengthening Soviet reach. Merely as a neighbour, however, the Soviet Union could never be wholly ignored in the Middle East. More novel, and certainly for many observers more portentous, was the employment of Soviet military power in Africa and the few but possibly ominous instances where the Soviet Union's own armed forces were directly involved. The latter phenomenon could be seen in the aircover provided by Soviet pilots in Egypt and the Yemen, in the airlift of Cubans to Angola, and in the screening role of the Soviet Navy in more than one West African imbroglio. The arrival of the Cubans also constituted an important strategic innovation; combined with Soviet logistics and arms supplies to local forces, they clearly constituted an instrument that could achieve remarkable results in the virtual military vacuum of Africa.

The catalytic effect of these Soviet military forays has been large; they contribute substantially to the conviction that armed force remains a potent instrument of political action in the Third World. It is less easy to evaluate these events in terms of Soviet interest. In the first place, it is not clear whether the Angolan, Ethiopian and other African adventures are the harbingers of a major shift in Soviet strategy, tending toward larger military operations as a major tool of high policy, or are merely a marginal spin-off from a rising tide of Soviet military power designed and acquired for the more central purposes of national security. Nor is the purpose of each particular intervention easy to identify. Is each part of a coherent expansionist policy, or merely an *ad hoc* adaptation to a specific contingency?

Assistance to wars of national liberation escaped even the period of Khrushchev's deepest overt scepticism about traditional military power. The Middle East, South-East Asia and parts of Africa have witnessed the emergence of indirect Soviet military intervention—by way of supplies, training and advice—on an heroic scale. In contrast, the instances of direct intervention by Soviet forces have been minuscule by former Western standards, with an intermediate place occupied by the proxy operations. The novelty of the direct operations has perhaps tended to produce an exaggerated estimate from Western analysis. As yet, indeed, the amount of sustained 'projected force' the Soviet Union could wield at a distance is severely limited and would appear all the more so in the face of competent resistance or Western interdiction. To a certain extent, the decline in the West of a sense of global, bipolar conflict, characteristic of the Cold War, has reduced the risks intervention entails for the Soviet Union. Nevertheless, there is a strong impression that the world has witnessed a change of style. If Soviet-sponsored campaigns in Angola and the Horn of Africa prompted what might have appeared an excessive amount of attention, it may have been because, while Western defeats in colonial wars or the American defeat in Vietnam could be depicted as the negative rewards of Western error, the later Soviet successes in Africa seemed to be the positive achievements of a new and autonomous Soviet initiative.

There is no reason to anticipate that the scale of specific Soviet or Soviet-sponsored military operations in the Third World will necessarily become large, aping the expeditionary forces beloved by the Western military establishments. Very small contributions by the Soviet military forces themselves have been blended with military assistance, training, proxies—Cubans, East Germans, etc.—and the endemic covert and subversive operations. In the same spirit, Soviet 'bases' consist of a wide variety of facilities and rights, frequently duplicated and overlapping. The more comprehensive and formally established bases, once such a feature of Western deployment, would be difficult to reconcile rhetorically with communist ideology and are in any case probably unattainable in today's world. Setbacks and explosions occur, as they have for the West, but the effect is minimised by the informality and evasive nature of the Soviet relationships, and the rebuffs are apparently absorbed without, as yet at least, a revulsion from the overall policy—a stoicism made easier by the absence of a critical domestic political society or intrusive mass media. The circumstances being so different, there is no justification for assuming that because military intervention and the sponsorship of client states turned out badly for the West on several occasions, they must necessarily prove failures for the Soviet Union. Nor, of course, is there any ground for believing that, even if Soviet adventures should prove unprofitable, they might not do great harm to Western interests.

The overall picture is thus of a shift in Soviet policy that is variegated, cautious, frequently oblique, but none the less important for that. To some extent the picture is confused by what appear to be two connected but probably only coincidental innovations on the global military scene. The first is a series of changes in the ways military force can be made effective by great powers. These changes arise from the overshadowing presence of nuclear deterrence, the dissemination of new weapons to a much wider group of national and sub-national groups, altered public attitudes, and a variety of other influences tending to put a premium on indirect and ambiguous action. The second innovation is the emergence of the Soviet Union as a world power, one by political style well adapted to the indirect approach—an approach also ideally suited to minimise the significance of remaining Soviet logistical inferiority. From the Soviet perspective, the balance sheet of gains in the Middle East, Africa and South-East Asia must look extremely favourable, even taking account of occasional not insubstantial setbacks, as in Egypt. The judicious use of military power, in a variety of oblique and limited ways, has made the Soviet Union a factor in strategic calculations which the West could previously have made with reference only to local, indigenous, capabilities.

The indirect and even covert role of Soviet military force poses particular problems for a Western response. At the end of the 'seventies, the new Soviet activism was injecting some cautionary notes into the chorus of scepticism about the value of military 'power projection'. The painfully learned lesson that a mixture of indigenous revolution and the intrusive meddling of communist great powers produces a quagmire in which counter-intervention can easily sink is not readily forgotten, however, and there is consequently considerable weight in the argument that it is the wiser course to wait for local turbulence to set its own limits to communist success. Meanwhile, some argue, Western economic and political influence could be mobilised to hasten the process of containment. The objections to this policy are that it may underestimate communist determination and ruthlessness, that it takes time, and that economic instruments are very difficult to apply to particular political purposes. Nor is it clear that a coalition of democracies can orchestrate a coherent policy of economic pressure any better than collaborative military efforts.

An alternative to the discredited strategy of undisguised military counter-intervention is the covert support of local resistance. As a response to public distaste for overseas military commitments, and sometimes to ease the political embarrassment of 'host' governments, covert or deceptively-presented operations have been tried in such areas as the Congo, Cuba, Laos, Cambodia, and Angola. The results were not encouraging. Pretence is not easy to maintain, and public concern about the democratic control of foreign policy ensures that, when covert action is discovered, it is commonly subjected to even graver censure than overt operations. In the United States, in particular, such legislative actions as the War Powers Act or the investigations of the C.I.A. have seriously circumscribed the Executive's freedom of action and have raised the potential political costs of failure even where legal loopholes remain. [32] If governments in Europe have been subject to less severe accountability, it is in part because their overseas military activities have also been fewer in recent years. The greatest exception to this has been the sustained, and for many years relatively obscure, campaigns waged in Africa by small French forces.

In designing a Western military response to spontaneous, communist-inspired, or any other variety of military activity thought harmful to Western interests, there are paradoxes to be faced with regard to the scale and timing of action. Large-scale military operations arouse correspondingly large anxieties within democratic public opinion and may magnify the disapproval of third parties. Moreover, many of the situations encountered are not amenable to the mere application of brute force. On the other hand, the alternative process of blending small direct military actions with such other instruments as military assistance, economic aid, and the other available tools is likely to be slow, giving ample opportunity for criticism to reach larger proportions before any countervailing success can be reported. Many Third World situations are, indeed, unlikely ever to reach permanent solutions. Merely staving off failure must be reckoned a success, but whether public opinion will recognise this is another question.

For all these reasons, public opposition in democracies may henceforth put a permanent curb on military action and may therefore make force virtually unusable in many situations. Major events, whether perhaps some frightening Soviet victory or a heartening Western success, might change this by compelling public recognition that force still prevails. Even so, misgivings in the democracies and the intractable nature of the issues typically arising in the Third World suggest that military action in the future is increasingly likely to be executed by small, professional, highly specialised and responsive forces carefully composed for particular situations. It is true that, wherever a hostile super-power is involved, a counter-intervention may require ultimate linkage to a deterrent against nuclear blackmail. But, when added to domestic attitudes and the nature of the issues likely to be encountered, this overshadowing fear of escalation makes it all the more probable that tactics and political will are more likely to be decisive than purely quantitative considerations of military power.

This does not mean that military capability is irrelevant to success. On the contrary, clear-cut advantage in the local arena is an important, probably the decisive, source of potential success and therefore of practicability in broader political and diplomatic terms. Ever since the Suez debacle, it has been obvious that it is vital to possess forces well suited both to local circumstances and the wider political climate. What constitutes suitability will vary very much with the occasion. If speed is of the essence, either to achieve local success through surprise or to defuse domestic criticism, then operations may have to be quick and massive. If cost and public concern about cost is paramount, then a slow and incremental approach may be wiser. Since it is almost the essence of Third World contingencies that they do not lend themselves to prediction in detail—though the possible areas of trouble may be roughly discernible—flexibility of options may be the best asset with which military forces can provide a political leadership.

There is much recent and emerging military technology to secure such flexibility, and it is probably in this way rather than by the pursuit of cruder notions of superiority in mass or fire power that the technological sophistication of the West can best be harnessed to the problem. Intelligence, surveillance, reconnaissance, mobility, and the capability for discriminate hitting power are qualities likely to be at a premium. Given the political inhibitions that attend the decision to act in such cases, not the least virtue of such military qualities would be to minimise dependence on prior notice of an impending operation, thus reducing both the strategic warning given to opponents and rivals, and the pressure for premature commitment.[33]

The Western alliance being a coalition, it is clear that the political content of military intervention includes the orchestration of interallied co-operation or at least mutual tolerance in such matters. During the post-war years, events in the Third World have frequently found the Western allies in disarray. American distaste for European colonial wars troubled the earlier years and is, indeed, enshrined in the strict geographical limits written into the North Atlantic Treaty. Later, American entanglement in South-East Asia produced analogous misgivings in Europe. Such divergencies are inevitable, given disparities in national interest and diplomatic style. The price is, however, considerable, not merely in loss of the benefits of practical co-operation, but in the realms of both domestic and foreign opinion. Collaboration and consequent mutual endorsement can frequently minimise political costs, though it may also on occasion be advantageous to let a single actor enjoy a tacit licence.[34]

For many years United States actions in South-East Asia partook of this nature, sometimes publicly criticised by others who privately were not sorry to see someone else shoulder the burdens of containment. Ultimately, of course, unease about events in Vietnam became overwhelming, but, to the last, Western European governments were much less hostile to United States policy than were vociferous sections of the American public. In the aftermath of Vietnam there was great uncertainty, not merely as to whether the United States would ever again undertake military interventions but also about what role if any the Western Europeans might reassume. These questions doubtless explain the otherwise apparently disproportionate attention paid, on the one hand, to the inhibitions restraining United States policy in Angola during the Cuban intervention, and, on the other, to the French role in bolstering the Mobutu regime in Zaire. Attempts to interpret the Federal German police raid on the hijacked aircraft at Mogadishu as the forerunner of an interventionist German military policy testified more to the hopes of the interpreters than the intentions of the Federal Republic. But efforts to redefine SACLANT's responsibilities to cover the Southern Atlantic and other proposals to enable NATO to deal as an alliance with threats arising outside the Treaty area were more serious testimony to the belief that the days of armed conflict in the Third World might not yet be completely over for the developed countries. It remained to be seen whether the greater vulnerability of Western Europe and Japan to many possible upheavals in the Third World by reason of proximity or dependence on trade would revise the trend whereby the major burdens have been carried by a United States thrust forward more by its role as a super-power than any specific national interests.

The inhibitions that worked against direct reinvolvement by the United States and its allies in Third World conflicts have led in recent years to some inclination to encourage the emergence of regional great powers, in the hope that they can police local quarrels and thereby discourage Soviet or Chinese intrusion, not so much by mounting direct opposition as by quelling local disturbances that would otherwise offer opportunities for external meddling. Several potential emergent powers showed some willingness to accept such a role, most notably Iran. This formula, of course, constituted yet another testimony to the extent to which international order continued to be organised along lines determined by military power and potential.

Partly because of the strength of popular opposition to military power in some sectors of democratic society, great-power policy towards the establishment of regional security systems was complicated by hostility to the supply of arms and other military assistance. Such doubts have been reinforced by uncertainty about the future disposition of emergent regional great powers toward the West and by difference of opinion as to precisely how regional balances work. Not all attempts to manipulate them prove stabilising. Nevertheless it became increasingly clear that, in a world where military power remained dominant and in the Third World was frequently exercised in actual combat, it would be quite unrealistic for the Western powers to try both to disengage themselves and to condemn the efforts of local powers to fill the vacuum by acquiring sizeable armed forces of their own. Thus, arms sales and even policies toward nuclear proliferation cannot be disentangled from the military relations of the developed and less developed world. Not that the military effort mounted by regional powers was a mere consequence of great power policies; clearly the richer and more technologically capable of regional powers would not lightly sacrifice the influence and autonomy that military power can purchase and which was now within their grasp.

                          *   *   *

Even this cursory contemplation of the international scene since 1945 reveals quite clearly that military power and armed force remain fundamental instruments of policy. This rather simple observation is worth making only because of the perverse and pervasive tendency within the democracies that, against overwhelming evidence, persists in treating military activity as an aberration. Widespread public distaste for military affairs, compounded no doubt by increasing personal disinclination from military service in affluent societies, has itself become a major incentive for governments to prefer oblique and indirect strategies of conflict management. Such subtleties have, in turn, reinforced the illusion that military power can safely be neglected.

The motif of indirection is least conspicuous in the centre of the military spectrum, in the conventional wars of the Third World and the extensive preparations of the great military coalitions. Elsewhere, the emphasis is on the latent or the devious. At the pole of strategic nuclear power, the main principle is deterrence, and even the doctrines for ultimate use of nuclear weapons have recently shifted toward limited application: toward the symbolic and constrained, toward warfare to be conducted under rules so subtle that many fear they may not be practicable. At the other extreme, that of sub-conventional war, of the manipulation of proxies, the supply of arms and training, and the mounting of demonstrations, the emphasis again is on an indirect approach. Even in the European context, in the central confrontation of our day, there is movement toward redesigning forces to suit more closely their functions in crisis-management than merely a trial of brute strength.

Thus, while armed force has certainly not lost its usefulness, it is evolving in the way it functions. There is a shift toward the threat rather than the deed, the shadow rather than the substance. This does not mean, however, that military forces do not still have to be adequate and appropriate to their purposes. The shadow must be a relevant one. It proved impossible for the United States to use the threat of becoming less co-operative in strategic arms negotiations as a substitute for direct local opposition to Soviet adventures in Africa. Efforts to use economic leverage also failed. In the short run the direct application of force is a trump card; there is no immediate answer but defence or surrender. There are many particular purposes, such as freeing a hostage, thwarting an attack, repossessing a ship, for which no other tool is so quick or so precise.

There are admittedly many novel inhibitions against the use of force. This is, an argument not for the uselessness of force but for skill in its application. If the age of inhibited, latent, indirect force continues, as seems likely, armed forces will need to widen the options of their masters by being finely tuned to their increasingly complex political role. Timeliness and controllability have become cardinal virtues. The alternative is not the abnegation of military power but a choice between crude outbursts of violence or submission to those who adapt more successfully to the shifting strategic scene.

2

The Not So Hidden Hand

by Louis-François Duchêne

Economic Factors in the World Balance since 1945

In an age dominated by material change, few need to be convinced of the importance of economic factors in world security. It is quite another thing, however, to establish the links, because economic influences are so often contextual and indirect. Many of the most pregnant economic influences are those that affect political purpose and morale as part of a total social and cultural process. For instance, attitudes to military affairs in the West and the Soviet Union are mingled at every level with socio-economic ones. Economic power itself is not a mere statistical achievement; it involves collective attitudes, acquired by whole communities over long periods and for reasons which initially may have had little to do with their ultimate economic consequences. Technological innovation and material growth spring from political and social sources and feed back into them. In appearance material, they are in fact associated with social outlooks, relationships, institutions and trajectories of individual and collective will that are not. By the same token, economic growth generates, magnifies and changes social forces which, in their turn, further shape and condition the environment in which policies and strategies are born. To speak of economics is often to bring society as a whole on stage.

Economic forces have acquired unprecedented importance in modern times because the industrial revolution shifted the emphasis from competing for control over resources, largely territorial, taken as more or less given, to generating those resources oneself by expanding markets and inventing machines. Before the industrial revolution, economic superiority was not necessarily the yardstick of power. The nomads who conquered the Roman, Persian and Chinese empires were manifestly not the economic equals, let alone superiors, of their prey. The industrial

revolution changed all that. Between 1700 and 1815, Britain drew ahead
of France, in traditional terms a far larger nation, because of a long
commercial, financial and at last industrial lead. In 1840, Britain was the
world's first power because it alone produced nearly one-third of the
world's manufactures. History from 1870 to 1945 is largely a study in the
economic and political challenge to that lead by Germany. The
emergence since 1945 of the United States and the Soviet Union has been
based on the new-found ability of twentieth-century technology and
management to mobilise vast areas in the service of the state. The United
States for a brief period immediately after the war produced virtually half
the manufactures of the world (see table 1). Its relative decline since is
associated with the fall of that proportion to a still substantial quarter. *A
fortiori*, the political scene during this period has been virtually
monopolised by the industrial northern hemisphere as a whole. This
situation has begun to change in the 1970s because industry has spread to
a number of poorer countries, while others, controlling vital resources
like oil, cannot be dictated to, partly of course because of schisms
between the industrial powers themselves. In the circumstances, the
general obsession since the war with economic success as the purveyor
not only of release from ancestral poverty but also of state power is
understandable. Rapid growth and the shifting material balance has
probably been, with nuclear weapons, one of the two central strategic
factors of the period.

This was foreshadowed by the nature of the allied victory in 1945.
Politically, the world war ended with the total defeat of pre-war fascism.
Fascism was the product of failure to control the slump between the wars
working on the tradition of militaristic nationalism which had already led
to a statistically probable accident in 1914 and re-emerged in the 1930s,
embittered by economic, social and political grievances, to still more
virulent violence. In this sense, the ruin of fascism was the final defeat of
the compromise between nascent industrial mass society and the clerical,
territorial and military hierarchies of the earlier agrarian world.
Accordingly, the end of the war produced more than a new struggle for
power between the victors: it rejected the militarism for which the
defeated regimes had stood. Whatever the actual power of the military in
post-war societies, no post-war political culture in an industrial society
advocates militarised values. All claim to subscribe to ideals of political
freedom or economic equality derived from the American, French or
Russian revolutions. The hegemony of the super-powers is quite different
from the European world empire which disappeared so rapidly in the
wake of two lost wars in not being overtly territorial. The Soviet Union
claims that socialism has solved its 'nationalities' problem. Although it
remains in eastern Europe the most traditional of hegemonists, it works
through local communist parties in the name of the working class. United
States dominance has been accompanied, in western Europe and Japan at

least, by determined efforts, in a New Deal style, to help increase prosperity there and so damp down social conflict and political opposition. The developing countries accuse the West of economic neo-colonialism because, in a period of 'economic miracles', western Europe's and Japan's loss of territorial empire appeared an unexpected irrelevance while the material subordination of the poor remained.

This relative 'civilianisation' of world politics has been sealed, however conditionally, by the apocalyptic vision of mass nuclear catastrophe released over Hiroshima. This has been the culmination of a trend since 1815, during which wars between major powers have become less frequent but increasingly destructive. The industrialisation of war has steadily raised the level of casualties and shifted the balance from soldiers to civilians (see table 2). Popular abhorrence of war was a political force before the war in countries like Britain and France. The casualties of the Second World War seem to have extended this attitude much more widely among industrial societies. Though military factors still play a central role, not least through the residual threat of reversion to nuclear war, there has been a shift towards the civilian bands of the political spectrum, or at least to lower levels of violence—either in less powerful countries or by less powerful protagonists such as urban guerrillas.

Such a shift tends to lay a greater stress on the economic components of power. Economic stakes play an increasing role in the political charade of war that inter-state rivalry becomes. The Cold War broke out in its virulent phase as a direct consequence of the West German currency reform in 1948 which the Soviet Union, rightly, saw as the decisive act integrating West Germany in the West and withdrawing it from Soviet influence. The attempt to revive western Europe's power after the war was carried out through integration in the European Economic Community. When Jacques Soustelle tried to persuade his sceptical compatriots that a French Algeria was vital to their future, he went prospecting for oil in the Sahara, and found it. The crisis of 1956, which marked the end of old-style British and French imperial power, took place over Nasser's nationalisation of the Suez Canal, seen as a threat to oil supplies. The watershed between the post-war period and the new international dispensation of the 1970s was probably OPEC's successful assertion of power with the oil embargo of October 1973. Strong economic but not nuclear military states like Germany and Japan have acquired a political influence which would probably not have been accorded them when war was still the *ultima ratio* of nations.

Beyond that, economic factors have shaped the whole way in which political struggle since the war has been defined. The defeat of the fascists left the post-war stage to the reformist and revolutionary wings of the pre-war system, represented by New Deal Americans on one side and Stalin's Soviet Union on the other. These promptly fell out and became the establishment and radical opposition of the new order. They nevertheless shared a number of values which gave its special character to the post-war dispensation. One was the conviction, reinforced by the pre-war slump, that though wealth might not be sufficient to institute democracy, equality and the happiness of Man, breaking the bonds of ancestral poverty was the urgent pre-condition of all three. Another was that there was no foreseeable ceiling on material growth except one set by men themselves. A third principle followed from the other two, that failure to diffuse wealth was not a fate but (like the pre-war slump) a crime against democracy and equality. In the socialist and in many developing countries, growth was more a symbol of the collective control of the national destiny than of the individual's self-fulfilment in a western sense. Nevertheless, even these power drives appealed to a broad belief in liberation and justice through economic progress. For Khrushchev, overtaking the United States, promised for 1970, and Sputnik, launched in 1957, were the earnest of the superiority of socialism. For the United States, landing the first man on the moon in 1969 was the symbol of continuing leadership. For the poor countries, rapid development seemed the only hope of escape from the vicious circle of high birthrates, low production and economic and, therefore, political dependency. There was one world at least in this common assumption.

The expansiveness of economic policies and popular attitudes almost everywhere resulted from 1945 to 1973 in an unprecedentedly steep, widespread and long-drawn-out boom (see tables 3A and B). Annual world product increased nearly five-fold and trade about eight-fold while population somewhat less than doubled. This has exerted, and continues to exert, complex effects on the world balance. It has also given much of its political tone to the period, an odd mixture of surface anxieties of cold war haunted by nuclear catastrophe and, even in the poorest countries, of the (often angry and frustrated) underlying confidence of a second, later and greater Victorian expansion.

The Three Worlds

Naturally, because of the different situations of the three worlds, economic factors have played very different parts in their respective strategies. The rich reformists essentially represented a cartel of the powers who in pre-war politics constituted the whole field of tension and now represent merely one corner of it. It collected together the old establishment, enlarged to include the old challengers, Germany, Italy and Japan, and was inevitably placed in a conservative strategic posture, however novel its actual policies might be. Conservatism obviously pushed the West to assume that it was possible to overcome the conflicts which threatened its traditionally privileged position; and this happened to fit in with its intellectual traditions from the early industrial revolution.

The 18th-century philosophic radicalism which underlay both liberal political democracy and classical market economics assumed a natural identity of interest (characterised in Adam Smith by the division of labour) and an artificial identity of interest to be encompassed by government, say in education, when the market could not embrace long-term social goals. In either case, it proposed that wealth could be diffused by the increasing international division of labour and that administration could overcome obstacles to the common good. This was essentially the spirit of American-led western policy after the war: economics was not a zero-sum game, the interest of everyone could profit by the general growth and prosperity. This approach infused the Keynesian ethos of post-war western policies of growth and full employment; the establishment, under American auspices, of the numerous international economic organisations raining incomprehensible initials on the world; and, most spectacularly perhaps, Marshall Aid, and development assistance in general.

This conception of policy had at least two major political results. The first was that the discovery, at least in appearance, of the formula for continuous economic growth reduced the importance of controlling territory in international politics. The European empires disappeared like melting snow after the war but were easy to forget when the frontier of opportunity lay elsewhere. To take an admittedly extreme case, it is hard in 1979 to credit that on the eve of the creation of the European Economic Community in 1956, 31 per cent of French exports went to the then French Union and only 26 per cent to France's neighbours in the impending Common Market. In 1975, the proportions were respectively 5 per cent and 50 per cent; exports to the French Union had doubled in dollar terms while those to the European Community had multiplied by 22. Post-war growth in trade took place primarily between industrial economies selling manufactures to each other and less (unlike in the 19th century) between industrial economies and primary producers, the relative value of whose exports gradually fell in the 1950s and 1960s.

The second consequence of American post-war economic policy, at least in the industrial world, was to inject some of the principles of domestic good government very forcefully into balance of power politics. Of course, the aim of Marshall Aid was to 'contain' the Soviet Union, which duly called it 'dollar imperialism', first in forbidding Poland and Czechoslovakia to respond to the offer and later in all Cold War propaganda. Indeed much US aid provided straight support to embattled conservative 'front-line' allies against communism, like Taiwan, South Korea, Jordan, Vietnam, Laos and Cambodia. The revisionist historians have even suggested that American post-war policy was directed to weakening Britain and so hastening the post-war consolidation of American primacy. But when it looked as if the American world position would be undermined by the ruin of western Europe and Japan, the

United States responded, as the New Deal had done at home, by providing credits to refloat the allied economies. So long as Soviet power was 'contained', American purposes could be served by serving the interests of others. Even more surprising than Marshall Aid, on traditional assumptions, was American support for west European integration. The Americans took a calculated risk that the gain to them from a uniting western Europe would outweigh the long-term dangers of nurturing a potential (but remote) economic and political competitor. That this was power politics should not conceal the extent to which it was also new. It showed an awareness of societal processes which was a first sign of the increasing post-war mingling of domestic and international politics. In the same spirit, probably the greatest achievement of the post-war policies of the Western diffusionists was the establishment of the beginnings of a collective management of the international economy.

The Second, or Soviet-led, World has been essentially a reaction to the balance of power established in favour of the old establishment by the first industrial revolution. It is not the first reaction, but it has been much the most radical one. Whereas the first challengers, Germany and Japan, tried to displace the old elite while largely accepting their system (with important reservations), the Soviet Union from 1917 onwards deliberately broke all contact in order to set up an alternative system of its own. This has had two roots, one ideological, the other in the last resort geographic. Ideologically, Leninism is essentially geared to seizing power from a position of initial weakness, in that revolutionaries start out as an opposition minority in the way that the Soviet Union itself originally did in the world. The rationale is that capitalism exploits labour, in a self-reinforcing mechanism to which the only riposte is a calculated political destruction of the forces rooted in private property. Since capitalism is international, this implies not only the destruction of the enemy within the gates but also the isolation of the revolutionary fortress from the territory held by the enemy outside. However, such a policy, conceivable in large countries like the Soviet Union or China, would have been far harder to initiate if the revolution had broken out, as Marx would have expected, in an advanced industrial society heavily dependent for prosperity on foreign trade. The only socialist country to move towards a modified market economy, Yugoslavia, has become more and more influenced by capitalist features. The smaller countries of eastern Europe, with a much greater dependence on exports than the Soviet Union, face considerable difficulties inside the system. These create potential 'contradictions' in the socialist bloc substantially greater than those between the more evenly balanced states of western Europe and the United States of America.

Economics seem to be directed to two major ends in Soviet power policy. The first is to build up industrial societies quickly from primitive beginnings. There is little doubt of the Soviet success in achieving this. It

has been rightly argued that these results might have been achieved with
less social cost in other ways, that Russia was already the world's fifth
industrial producer in 1913, that Japan has grown still faster, and so on;
the fact remains that in a short while eastern Europe has become a
substantially industrialised area and that the proportion of world
manufactures coming from the centrally planned economies has risen
from 15 per cent to nearly 30 per cent between 1950 and 1976 (see tables
1, 3 and 4). The second object has been to build up Soviet economic
power as a source of political magnetism and prestige. Socialism, being as
superior to capitalism as capitalism earlier was to feudalism, must rapidly
produce an altogether higher order of scientific, technological, economic
and social performance. However, since the political stress is on keeping
the healthy socialist society well away from the capitalist infection, and on
central state planning in each socialist country, the real role of economic
process in international policies has in many ways been reduced to this
demonstration effect. Soviet aid, for instance, is quite minuscule (see
table 5), with the exception of the economic support to a few key allies
like Cuba, or military aid to revolutionaries, as in Ethiopia. Thus, though
Soviet growth rates seem to have been higher than those of the West,
economic policy, in the form of a shaping influence on the international
economic process, has so far played a much smaller role in Soviet than in
Western political strategy.

In a sense, much of the importance of economic strategies for the
industrial states has been due to nuclear stalemate. They seem already to
have entered, in Alastair Buchan's seminal phrase, an era of 'change
without war'. Growth has confirmed the organisation of the northern
hemisphere in two camps whose mutual opposition tends to draw all
other potential conflicts between allies on either side into its single
magnetic field. This is not the case among the poor countries who
represent two-thirds of the world's population and whose conflicts seem
ubiquitous. It is tempting to argue that these are due to the appalling
social impact of modern standards, products and expectations on
unprepared societies. This may be so. It is nonetheless striking that Latin
America, which emancipated itself from Spain and Portugal 150 years
ago, has had only one war in the past generation (the week-long
Honduras-Salvador flurry of 1969), while most of the many other wars
have involved succession problems left by the ebb of empire. What is
certain—and more important—is that populist conflicts prove terrifyingly
tenacious. Around Israel, in Lebanon, in southern Africa, in Vietnam,
the fighting flares up again and again over decades. The experience of the
post-war period suggests that while mass societies may reject the military
when they feel secure, they tend to become correspondingly intransigent
under threat. In either case, policies to control or outgrow conflict are
made more difficult.

However, the overwhelming problem for the poor countries has remained development. This has not been quite the failure that is sometimes painted. Rates of growth of the developing countries have been higher since 1950 than in developed market economies and in a few growth per head has been high. Between 1963 and 1976 Brazil and South Korea grew by 5.3 per cent per annum and 8.4 per cent per annum per head (see table 9). Unfortunately, these are exceptions. Normally, high population growth has reduced rates of growth per head in most countries to modest levels, below 3 per cent per annum (see Table 3B), starting from very low initial standards of living. The developing market economies still produce under 10 per cent of world output of manufactures (see Table 1B). In these circumstances, it has not been enough for the poor countries to throw off the political yoke of empire. The second and decisive factor of dependence has been economic inferiority.

The poor have consistently attempted, in the non-aligned movement and elsewhere, to make their distinctive voice heard above the din of the competing industrial groupings. The basic issue of development has none the less remained posed mainly in terms of the two alternative routes offered by the industrial states. There has been a constant tension between the strategies of gradualist diffusion and the sharp revolutionary break. A minority of countries, often the poorest, have chosen revolution: China in 1949, Cuba and South Yemen in the 1960s, then in a rush since 1970 the three states of Indo-China, Afghanistan and at least three southern and eastern African countries. The majority, however, have so far chosen continuity: what Germany and Japan once achieved can be repeated by right and similar combinations of protection at home and aggressive selling abroad. Yet, initially the rhetoric suggested revolution which, given the enormity of the problems, might have seemed the normal course. Many reasons have been given for this surprising outcome. It may simply be that the process of self-affirmation from a position of weakness has naturally generated a kind of populist nationalism not too sensitive in the last resort to outside political influences. East Asia, including communist China, the Indian subcontinent, Islam and Latin America, have all in different ways shown themselves somewhat impervious to imported solutions, both before revolution and after. The contrast with a fragile Africa suggests that this may have something to do with the strength of the pre-existing political culture, the state tradition and the hold on society of indigenous elites. The failure of Cuba to influence Latin America in the 1960s, compared with its success in Africa in the 1970s, suggests that the depth of the local political structure may be the key. Certainly, the post-war ideologies both of the West, with its emphasis on 'interdependence', and of the East, with its stress on international class war, have been confounded, in rich and poor parts of the world alike, by the stubborn and shaping strength of nationalism. This has become one of the dominant facts of the later evolution of the post-war system from the early bi-polar structure in which the super-powers filled the vacuum left by the collapse of Europe and its world empire to a crowded 'multi-polar' stage today. This can now be said, for the first time, to constitute a truly 'global' system filled with actors at every level of effectiveness and influence.

Growth and the Balance

The rapid growth of the world economy since the war has on the whole favoured policies stressing the diffusion of power and prosperity. This may seem obvious, for the West has had the enormous advantage of superior wealth and past associations with most countries in the world. It was not so obvious in 1945. The folk memory was of the spectacular inter-war failures of the capitalist system; pre-war, and indeed war-time, Soviet performance shone brightly by comparison. It was not before the middle 1950s that fears in the West itself of a new international depression began to fade. In that light, nationalisation seemed a guarantee of the social control of industry; centralised planning seemed far more dynamic and stable in the pursuit of growth than the market; and even in the rich countries, socialism, certainly in western Europe, offered a promise not only of greater justice, equality and compassion but also, for those very reasons, of greater efficiency as well. These arguments weighed all the more strongly with poor countries as they emerged from colonial constraints. If empire was a mask for capitalist profit-making by the imperial metropolis, the only way out of thrall was rigorous self-help on the lines pioneered at such cost but with such success by the Soviet Union. In the new nations, forced industrialisation through huge Kombinats in heavy industry seemed at first the only way to break out of poverty. Nationalisation, the redistribution of incomes, import substitution in manufactures, seemed the only way forward to regimes as far apart, mentally and on the map, as Nehru's India and Perón's Argentina. If perhaps the Soviet Union was not a model for very poor countries, Maoist China with its peasant communes, its lack of machines, its sudden, disciplined freedom from flies and floods, offered an example of even more egalitarian enlightenment making do with a minimum of resources and techniques. The contrast with British and American oil politics, with the Dutch and French in Indonesia, Indo-China or Algeria, with American support for traditional dictatorships in Taiwan, Korea or Jordan, shone in the mind of every radical. Moreover, the Soviet Union was always available with support for any leader, like Nasser, ready to challenge the West. Political interests, old resentments and the promise of a better formula for development all tended to place the burden of proof on the West, not the struggling and heroic socialists who had shown in the Soviet Union how poverty and Hitler could be overcome. For a long while it seemed, and was accepted, that Soviet growth rates were, and were likely to remain, far higher than those of the West, and that incomes were much more comparable (see Table 6). Despite American power, the West was in many ways on the political defensive in the early days of Cold War. McCarthyism in the United States was largely a reaction to the novel and frightening sense of finding oneself for the first time mentally under siege.

The United States none the less had enormous military and economic superiority and, under stress, used its opportunities in more novel and imaginative ways than Stalin. That the Western economic-political sphere was rapidly consolidated was partly due to Stalin's political mistakes, such as encouragement of the North Korean invasion of South Korea and the revelation, with the East German riots of 1953 and the Hungarian and Polish crises of 1956, that all was not well in the workers' paradise. However, it was at least as much due to the economic buoyancy of western policies under United States leadership prepared to provide credits to allies, keep an open market available for their exports to north America, and allow them to protect themselves and discriminate (in the 1950s) against the dollar and American goods. The initial expectations of western performance were more than fulfilled by the Western European and Japanese economic 'miracles', the very name of which denotes surprise, that began to affect political consciousness in the middle 1950s. There followed an economic and social revolution by which virtually the whole population of western societies reached, for the first time, at least modest standards of middle-class consumption. In the rush for the mass consumer society, there was greater social quiescence, for twenty years, than at any time since the mid-Victorian hey-day of a century before. The political effect was undoubtedly a consolidation of the western world and a revival of confidence in the system. In particular, there was a sense of success in the linked emergence of common forms of western economic management and of European integration, a feeling of having found a new, internationalist approach to world problems. This eliminated one-half of the post-war equation by which capitalism was widely felt to be on the eve of collapse whilst socialism was riding in on the wave of the future.

The other half of the equation also began to change as the political and economic evolution in the East demonstrated some of the inevitable differences between promise and performance. This became most evident when, after Stalin's death, Malenkov and then Khrushchev inaugurated a policy of 'peaceful co-existence', meaning political competition by all means short of war. 'Goulash' communism, the claim that socialism would soon outstrip capitalism by its superior peaceful performance, was a large part of Khrushchev's optimistic and basically pacific strategy. He had none the less chosen dangerous grounds for competition. For one thing, it meant a retreat from the thesis that wars of national liberation should be pursued to the point of risking nuclear conflict to overthrow capitalism, the 'paper tiger'. This was one of the first issues round which the Sino-Soviet quarrel ostensibly crystallised in the mid-1950s. For another, the socialist countries themselves began to be aware of serious shortcomings in their own development. These are not easily to be found in the statistics, since growth in socialist countries has remained substantially higher than the average in the West, even in the weakest area, agriculture. In qualitative terms, however, the picture has been rather different. As socialist economies rose in the 1950s above their low initial levels of post-war production, which favoured centralised planning, they began to encounter obstacles. 'Consumer demand, for so long ignored became more important . . . Yet the system was not designed to respond to demand . . . It was built to respond to orders from above, and for the achievement of large-scale investment projects and expanding the volume of production.'[1] The regime could not become highly responsive to demand because this would have turned it into some kind of market economy, like heterodox Yugoslavia or, worse, Hungary in 1956 or Czechoslovakia in 1968, where economic de-centralisation accelerated into political rebellion. Yet, without some devolution, the system remained stubbornly inefficient and productivity low. The socialist economies have slowly acquired the image of being economically second-rate. Worse, the system involves political privileges of access to goods in short supply even more galling to the unprivileged citizen than rationing by the purse in capitalism. Civilian technology lags behind the West, consumer goods are of poor quality, shortages, inefficiencies, queues and over-manning abound. Despite the West's inequalities, and in the 1970s inflation and unemployment, its products and technological superiority have firmly remained the yardstick of performance. Recipients of Soviet goods, even radical regimes like Iraq, have often felt that the equipment received is simply not good enough.

Since the Soviet Union itself had thrown out the challenge to capitalism, such comparisons inevitably have political effects. Khrushchev once attacked the individually-owned motor car as the symbol of bourgeois selfishness and claimed the Soviet Union would stick to collective transport. Ideology is hardly reinforced when the Soviet Union then invites Fiat to erect a plant as part of a programme to produce 2 million cars a year: enough to destroy claims to social originality, not enough to suggest superior performance. Similarly, the net result of Sputnik was to spur the Americans not only to establish a long lead in nuclear missiles in the early 1960s but also to land the first man on the moon in 1969. Soviet claims for socialism have been so much based on 'scientific' superiority in technology and production that such reverses are bound to dent its political prestige.

In practice, these setbacks might have had less impact had it not been for a more general inappropriateness of the Soviet model for the poor. After all, capitalist growth in itself, though considerable since the war, can, it may be argued, increase rather than reduce conflicts within poor societies. The masses in the less developed countries have had their appetites and demands whetted by growth, but only a privileged minority in the towns and countryside have greatly or even moderately profited by it. Inequalities have grown, not lessened. The industrial powers' government aid has fallen, as a percentage of rising wealth, to low levels as the urgency of cold war fell off (see Table 5). The rich countries have been induced to free the entry of manufactures by developing countries into their markets, but have hedged those concessions around with reservations, which recession looks like increasing. They have done a little to stabilise receipts from raw material exports and sometimes cancelled or re-scheduled debts. All this creates the beginning of a climate of obligation, but progress has been slow and limited. In these circumstances, one might have expected the evolutionary route to have less success, and the revolutionary route more, than they have so far had.

One reason for this has undoubtedly been that in many countries growth has sufficiently extended the elite to reinforce the incumbent regimes. Urban guerrilla operations in Latin America have merely brought the military more firmly into power. The military run the vast majority of poor countries as the only fairly disciplined administration available. This might not have sufficed, however, if Soviet, or semi-Soviet, prescriptions for import substitution, nationalisation and re-distribution of incomes had proved more successful. Radicals have tended to give two explanations for this failure. One has been that the 'national bourgeoisies' and land-owning classes have no intention of carrying out ruthless reforms which undermine their own power. The countries which have carried out a real land reform can be counted on one hand. The other has been that the capitalist system has seen to it that these policies could not work. The United States has indeed shown, for instance, in Chile in 1975, that in tense domestic crises in poor countries, subversion is not a monopoly of communists. But these would not be sufficient explanations if underlying forces were working more powerfully the other way. The fact is that Soviet conditions are very different from those of most developing countries. The Soviet Union, with the world's largest territory and reserves of raw materials and with one of the world's lowest densities of population, is by choice and situation also the most self-sufficient economy in the world. Since it has emphasised autarchy in its own planning (a deliberate part of the strategy of sealing itself off from capitalist influence) it largely also cut off what market it had to offer to developing countries.

In fact, small countries, whether they are market or centrally planned economies, cannot pass a certain level of development without building up exports, and to do so have to compete on world markets. Even though they usually continue policies of import substitution the pressures propel them towards a market economy unless they are politically restrained like the east European states (see Table 11).[2] Accordingly, radical but pragmatic regimes, like the Algerian or Yugoslav (and even Hungarian and Polish), display a marked bent for trading with economic partners like France, Germany and the United States. Though interdependence frequently leads to contentious relations, these appearances are superficial and deceptive. Relations, contentious or not, produce a closer link than the lack of them and even lead in the end to cooperation. Post-war experience has shown repeatedly that cooperation tends to succeed confrontations which both sides realise might be destructive. Western-OPEC relations have shown this since 1973 just as SALT has done between the super-powers. Moreover, there is a cultural analogue to the economic contrasts between the open and closed societies. The United States has not only enjoyed the prestige of being the world's unchallenged technological leader, it has also educated a very large number of graduates (and not just military ones) from less developed countries. As a result, the nationalism of technocrats in new countries, even when anti-American, often proposes policies ultimately based on American precepts. This has been a much more potent factor in the (possibly temporary) reversal of fortunes between the super-powers in the Middle East in the 1970s, despite the enormous handicap for the United States of backing Israel, than might have seemed conceivable when the Soviet Union began to take up the Arab cause in 1955. Finally, with the years, the supposed contrasts between socialism and capitalism in promoting growth in less developed countries as well as industrial ones have, like so much else in the initial Manicheism of the post-war East-West struggle, become somewhat blurred. In the 1960s, countries like Taiwan or South Korea, long regarded as the reactionary poor relations of mainland China or North Korea, have very rapidly begun to pull ahead. In these circumstances, the trade unionism of the Third World in dealing with the West and its conservatism at home look less paradoxical than at first sight.

Economics and the Strategic Balance

Though the superiority of the West in economic interchange has greatly influenced the strategic background, it has had only a very indirect impact on the military balance as such. The unique dominance of state over society in the Soviet Union and the power of social forces over governments in western-style democracies have played a key role in partly disconnecting economic and military factors. This was not the case, of course, immediately after the war, when the contrast between American wealth and Soviet poverty was extreme. The United States then, and throughout the 1950s, had unique means to project strategic power around the world and used them. Even then the Soviet Union, with its special capacity to bend the resources of society to top state priorities, minimised the differences. In 1949 it was only four years behind the United States in exploding a fission device and in 1953 two years behind with the hydrogen bomb. It maintained such large forces in central Europe that by accident or design, and despite the re-entry of American troops in Germany in 1951, it became recognised that in the last resort the Soviet Union held Europe 'hostage'. Similarly, after the Cuban humiliation of 1962, the Kremlin set in train a long-term military programme which has built up the Soviet armed forces in every dimension. By the late 1970s, they have reached rough parity with the United States in virtually every domain. Even today, no computations suggest the Soviet economy surpasses 60 per cent of the American. The implication is that the Soviet defence effort is relatively far larger. Though admittedly the figure comes from that interested party, the CIA, it is plausible that 11-13 per cent of Soviet gross national product goes into defence against 6 per cent for the United States. Some critics of the CIA argue that its estimates are actually too low and that the Soviet figure should be between 13 and 15 per cent of gross national product. This should be a great strain on the Soviet economy and is likely to become still more so as it slows down. Will this result in the exhaustion of the Soviet military effort? The precedents at least argue against it. In the mid-1960s, there was a school of thought in the United States which argued that American economic superiority was so great that it should be possible to exhaust the Soviet Union in a speeded-up arms race. However, this seemed to make little sense, since the United States did not have the ability to prevent the Soviet Union acquiring an assured second-strike retaliation capacity. In the event, it is the Soviet Union which has caught up, not the United States which has surged ahead.

The fact is that western societies, with the partial exception of America, have been less ready to stress the military factor, a trait which reflects the higher power in western democracies of civilian lobbies of all kinds. American and British demobilisation after the war was steep and rapid, in contrast to the maintenance of Soviet forces under arms. NATO force goals have never been quite met. There has been constant pressure to reduce forces, one source of which has undoubtedly been economic. Rising living standards bear hard on labour-intensive professions like the armed forces. Manpower costs rise to the point (about 50 per cent or 55 per cent of the budget) where, within existing financial limits, it becomes impossible to provide enough equipment and operational training to keep the forces battle-ready. The budget has then to be increased or manpower cut down. Surprisingly often, the budgets are increased: on average, and with the exception of the United States in the 1970s, defence expenditures in real terms of the NATO countries seem to have risen slightly. On other occasions, though, manpower is cut down – and in these cases never reverts to former levels. In this way, British forces have fallen from 455,000 personnel in 1961 to 330,000 in 1977.[3] A militarism was already noticeable in the war weariness of Europe after the war, in contrast to the United States where the confrontation with the Soviet Union attracted immense patriotic backing at home. From this point of view the United States seemed relatively old-fashioned. However, the Cold War psychological investment in American foreign policy was at least partly broken by defeat in Vietnam. The result has been the veto currently placed by Congress on Presidential intervention in foreign parts outside NATO, and the rapid expansion of Soviet intervention in Africa, south and east, since the collapse of the Portuguese empire and Ethiopian monarchy. This could mark a substantial shift in the super-power balance. In some ways one could even say that the Soviet Union is (perhaps temporarily) the only traditional great power left in the world.

These developments take one beyond economics into social change, but the two can hardly be separated. There was indeed in the later 1960s a striking contrast between the failure of the United States in Vietnam and the Soviet success, at least tactical, in suppressing heresy in Czechoslovakia. This suggests reflections about the relative strength and weaknesses of the all-powerful Soviet State and of western parliamentary democracies, governed by a much more flexible but also less focused socio-economic process.

In the 19th century, European-style societies were turned by the French revolution into populist states intensely aware of nationhood. Nevertheless these states naturally inherited attitudes from their previous agrarian and hierarchical existence, particularly when Bismarck in Prussia managed to marry nationalism with conservatism. The combination of traditional paternalism and a form of militarism still uneasily installed at the top with nationalism as a primitive form of democratic and egalitarian feeling at the bottom, went a long way to explain the mobilised imperialism of the late 19th century. Outside Europe, the populist state encountered little resistance. The areas the Europeans reduced to colonial or semi-colonial status were, in European terms, notoriously 'under-administered'. It was not just Europe's superior weapons and economic weight that loaded the dice against traditional societies. So did their own habit of regarding all but local authorities as a kind of distant and capricious fate, akin to the weather which looms large in the peasant consciousness. The imbalance between the newly mobilised European-style nation and the endless varieties of old-style societies in which most of the people hardly participated, between industrialism and a range from stone-age pastoralism to the higher agrarian society, was so great that European empires were almost a form of nature's abhorrence of a vacuum. In the later 19th century, Britain held India with an army of 65,000 Europeans out-numbered by 75,000 Indian Sepoys.

The situation has now changed at both ends of the spectrum. The mass consumer societies of the West today have reached a point where they display symptoms, though in ways a Marxist would hardly recognise, of a withering away of the state. The state is more all-embracing than ever; but in stretching out to cover more and more of society it reflects both the growing multiplicity of organised group interests which have to be placated and the general climate favouring varied individual perceptions of interest, and so it is hampered in its authority. General de Gaulle, though to foreigners the acme of charisma, proved helpless in the face of every social pressure he confronted (the miners' strike of 1963, the farmers in 1965, the students and workers in 1968, the shopkeepers of 1969). Much the same happened to the would-be totalitarian regimes in Hungary and Czechoslovakia which collapsed from within in 1956 and 1968. Primitive national loyalties are giving way to more critical and variegated public attitudes rooted in individual conceptions of human relations. One can hardly doubt, for instance, that between 1914 and 1978, amilitarism has made immense strides throughout the industrial world, related to the decline in the numbers of a *petite bourgeoisie* having only primary education. So has the belief that all peoples have a right to self-determination which played such a part in persuading the imperial powers themselves that decolonisation could not, because ultimately it should not, be resisted. The anti-colonialism of Roosevelt was a good example of this basic western outlook. National arrogance and fear of lost power held up the *Zeitgeist*, but they could not in the end gainsay it. In short, in western societies, the process of individualisation has reached a point where it is hard once again, as in the 18th century, for the state to mobilise its citizens, not because of scarcities or 'under-administration', but because of the standards of individual fulfilment growing in the logic of the culture. In the West, the idea of progress has reached a post-patriotic stage when the state is expected to serve the individual, not the individual the state as in the early populist societies. The reluctance of western Europe to undertake military policies since the war and the reaction, though relatively belated, of American society to intervention in poor countries overseas, are both rooted in this basic development of advanced industrial societies.

Change, however, has also been transforming the rest of the world, but not in the same way. Many of the once-colonised peoples have been moving out of their various forms of pre-industrial parochialism into the stage which many of the European states experienced at the dawn of their own industrial revolution. It is difficult not to see in the revolutions of many of the developing countries from China and Yugoslavia to Algeria and Biafra and even perhaps Ethiopia since the war, examples of that proto-populism, often highly authoritarian, which goes under the name of nation-building. Many, perhaps most, poorer nations, under the impact of industrial civilisation, are beginning to develop a collective self-determination at the very time the richer ones are tending to move beyond that stage to one of more individual citizen self-determination.

Whereas in the 19th century the most powerful nations were early populist states imposing on pre-industrial ones, today the richer states are in some ways post-patriotic, while the new ones are early populist. With such changes at both ends of the spectrum, it is not surprising that power relations in the world are profoundly altered.

Where society is still unmobilised, the imposition of the will of a post-patriotic greater power remains easy, as for the United States marines in the Dominican Republic in 1965. When, however, it faces a highly mobilised early populist society, like Vietnam or Algeria, the situation becomes radically different. If a defeat of this kind is possible, the question arises of what happens when a populist great power intervenes against a smaller and more advanced culture, with at least some features of the post-patriotic (anyway highly urban) societies. It is striking that the Soviet invasion of Czechoslovakia in 1968 very effectively snuffed out resistance. The same was largely true during the Nazi war-time occupation in all but the rural or backward countries, Poland, Norway and Yugoslavia. Modern urban societies, dependent on co-operation to survive and used to the creature comforts provided them by the productive system, are vulnerable to successful military intervention. It may well be that, contrary to appearances, it is not relatively poor countries like Vietnam which are vulnerable to occupation, but advanced societies like those in western and even eastern Europe. Even the Yugoslav emphasis on total defence, derived from the success of the war-time partisans in a country which was 80 per cent rural, and mountainous at that, may become anachronistic as the population moves (though more slowly than in other parts of Europe) into the towns.

Too much should not be made of a single instance, but a basic question does arise from the success of the Soviet Union in acquiring major industrial power with few signs of domestic political liberalisation. There have after all, been other examples of industrial success without liberalisation, in Germany and Japan before 1945. If the Western assumption that other states are essentially on a similar trajectory of more diffused democracy, political power and ultimately individualism, is incorrect and parochial, it may herald a Western decline some already claim to detect. If it is broadly correct, the co-existence of different stages of democratic development may pose critical problems at particular junctures but the pressure will in the long run be towards a certain community of culture and outlook around the world, increasingly civilian.

In the immediate prospect, the major power-issue remains the growth of Soviet military force. This could result in both strengths and weaknesses. One clear strength is the ability to project power, to take advantage of political upheaval in the weakest societies, mainly those of Africa, and to promote revolutionary regimes. Soviet influence, after marking time for a long while between the end of the war and the post-Vietnam period, has advanced rapidly in some of the weakest and poorest states since 1973. Moreover, there is no record as yet of any state, once the communists take power, reverting to another regime. That this is not inconceivable is obvious from the recurring upheavals in eastern Europe, but these attempts have been quashed by the Soviet Union and the only cases where diversity, in foreign policy terms, has arisen in communist states are when they fall out with one another. These cases are quite frequent. They include China, Yugoslavia, Albania, and even Rumania, all of which in varying degrees have fallen out with the Soviet Union, Vietnam which has fallen out with China, Vietnam and Kampuchea which have fallen out with each other, and Albania which has fallen out with everyone in turn. This has done much to change Western estimates of a communist world danger no longer seen as monolithic.

The loss of ideological initiative which is represented for Moscow by the split in the world communist movement, the growth of Eurocommunism, and the Soviet Union's almost total loss of political attraction for western Europe, is a very serious setback. Further, the Soviet Union has by its necessary reliance on state power tended to alienate all the other major powers, not only in north America, but in east Asia and western Europe as well. From this point of view, the *rapprochement* between communist China and Japan, though slow, cautious and still limited, could be a development of momentous importance for the future balance. Latent opposition even extends to eastern Europe where Soviet hegemony has been maintained not by a common civilisation and democratic legitimacy but by control over the local communist regimes which in most cases are almost certainly unpopular. All this has put the Soviet Union, in stark contrast to the immediate post-war period, on the ideological and political defensive. It suffers from a potential isolation which is a major weakness and, given its great military power, could even at the extreme pose dangers for world peace.

Diffusion of Power

The dominant ultimate effect of the long boom has been the diffusion of power. This has taken place in many dimensions: from the United States to the Soviet Union in the military rivalry of the super-powers; from the super-powers to other industrial countries in the northern hemisphere; domestically, within western societies, from state hierarchies to all sorts of lobbies, of which the most important, at least in western Europe, are the trade unions; and even from the industrial world as a whole to a top range of developing states which are beginning to become significant producers and exporters of manufactures.

At first, this tended to confirm and stabilise the power system born out of the Second World War, in as much as diffusion reinforced most regimes domestically and so inhibited change in the political frontiers between the competing world systems. No socialist society changed its government, though several tried; the western countries experienced quite exceptional social peace; and among the poor, the revolutions which quite frequently occurred were normally nationalist. Between the Chinese Revolution of 1949 and the victory of the Vietminh in 1975, the only countries to become communist and profoundly to change their relationship to the systems were Cuba in 1959 and the People's Democracy of the Yemen in 1967. When President Nixon, in 1970, enunciated his Guam Doctrine, based on the existence of at least partially self-regulating regional power balances, he was only acknowledging one of the plain truths of post-war development. Economics was not the only factor in this. Economic factors entered very little into the Sino-Soviet quarrel and only partially affected East-West detente, but in the case of the reviving influence of western Europe and Japan and the emergence of the oil exporting states they were manifestly of major importance.

The effect, towards the end of the long boom, say around 1970, was not a confirmed and accepted world balance but one with a number of tacitly convergent perceptions. The upsurge of Soviet, and apparent retreat of American, military power was giving anxiety not only to western Europe but to Japan and China. On the other hand, detente seemed relatively strong in its role of nuclear stalemate. At the 24th Congress of the Communist Party of the Soviet Union in 1971, Brezhnev gave priority to overcoming domestic obstacles against growth and to obtaining western credits for that purpose. Many regimes in the Third World, where growth was higher than in the 1950s, were showing signs of consolidation. Off-shore East Asia was building up a record of exceptional economic growth; in Latin America, the radical offensive of the 1960s in the wake of Cuban revolution was petering out in a rash of military regimes; and in Islam, the Nasserite policy of bringing in the new world of the Soviet Union to redress the balance of the old with the West, was running out of steam as the influence of rich conservative oil regimes like that of Saudi Arabia grew. The expulsion of 20,000 Russian service personnel from Egypt in 1972 gave dramatic force to this shift. All this added up to a multiplication of perspectives and preoccupations, drawing attention away from the earlier exclusive obsession with cold war and, in the Third World, with Bandoeng-style attempts at non-alignment. This was not a stable situation, but it did provide a balance rooted in many varied developments on the one hand, and on the other in a common recognition of a certain number of forces, none of which were accepted, nor even expected, in 1945: nuclear stalemate, continuing high, global economic growth worldwide, and the ideologically unwelcome but enduring power of nationalism in all three worlds, of West, of East and of the poor.

It took Western recession and the oil crisis of 1973 (which magnified but did not engender it) to underline the extent to which a quarter century of rapid growth and the diffusion of power had created new problems and balances which changed the foundations of policy-making.

The long boom, to which each society had responded in its own way and at its own pace, had gradually created gaps between both industrial and developing countries which made mutual adjustments cumulatively more difficult to achieve. Moreover, the demands on primary resources and fuels placed by the huge expansion of the world economy had begun to reverse the advantage of manufacturing societies over primary producers which had existed ever since the industrial revolution. Economic forces which damped down conflict at the outset of the long boom had by the 1970s, simply because of their own economic and social extensions, begun to be sources of friction in themselves.

One of the most crucial changes has taken place in the domestic power relationships in the western industrial societies, the motor force of the post-war world economy. The combined double-figure inflation, recession and high unemployment that affected almost all western societies in the 1970s were a sign of pressures which gradually brought to an end the domestic peace of the previous two decades. Inflation clearly had roots in the new-found mass social security and higher levels of education brought about by growth. Having less poverty to fear than its ancestors, the new generation was more demanding, more impatient of inequalities and hierarchies, more insistent on individual self-determination. Significantly, 1968, a year of insurrection to some extent all round the non-communist world, but mainly in the industrial West was first and foremost an anarchist revolt in the universities which broke with the previous, rather technocratic stress on economics. Ultimately, the change in consciousness brought about by 1968 was the injection, as a politically relevant force, of the view that economics alone is no more the salvation of Man than the old liberal panacea of political freedom proved to be by itself in the 19th century. Here, as André Malraux noted, was a real *crise de civilisation*.

On the immediate scene, however, the rising tide of working-class demands for a redistribution of incomes was more important still. Radicalism in the factories contrasted with a merely moderate shift to the left at general elections. Nevertheless, a steady growth in public spending on social welfare in the 1960s was followed from 1969 onwards by increasingly inflationary wage increases, strikes, and at the extreme violence, particularly in Italy and (without the violence) Britain.[4] This basically political inflation was heightened by Vietnam, the enormous boom in demand for raw materials and foods in 1973/4 (due to agricultural failures in the Soviet Union), and finally by the sudden almost five-fold increase in oil prices in the winter of 1973/4 (see table 7). By 1975 it was clear that the long boom was definitely over, killed in the last resort by socio-economic tensions within and between countries. Western Europe was in some ways the epicentre of this crisis, because it was there that the contrast between neighbours reached a peak, notably as between West Germany on the one hand and Britain and Italy on the other, the first having 5 per cent average annual inflation in 1975 and 1976 and the other two 19 per cent and 16 per cent respectively. It is astonishing that the European Community, considered for two decades as the frame of political and economic strength in western Europe, did not fall apart. That this did not occur was largely due to the elasticity provided by floating exchange rates and the dependence on international markets of each of the member states, which meant they did not dare risk formally closing trade frontiers. Such policies were proposed, notably but not only on the left, in Britain, France and Italy in order to promote a redistribution of incomes but were not taken up.

A second consequence of the diffusion of power was to wear down the capacity of the United States to lead the western economy. In the 1960s, when the big American corporations were attracted to invest heavily in western Europe by high rates of growth and profit, dramatised by the new common market, this did not seem so. It was widely assumed that the industrial extension of the American empire was about to begin. Jean-Jacques Servan-Schreiber, in a famous book, *Le Défi américain*, spoke of American companies in Europe as potentially the world's third industrial power, a theme taken up in different styles by de Gaulle and by Harold Wilson, who even spoke of 'industrial helotry'. The contrast with Japan, which with great pertinacity prevented the American corporations from taking part in the much greater boom on the Japanese market, suggested that western Europe was becoming an American economic satellite. United States firms dominated the high technology sectors, many of them deriving from federal defence and space programmes. Yet, over the years, these fears have waned. The number of non-American companies among the top hundred increased between 1959 and 1972 from 25 to 42;[5] the Japanese have successfully knocked the Americans out of a number of important markets, such as colour television, and they now propose to challenge IBM itself in computers; and in 1971, Germany displaced the United States as the world's leading exporter of manufactures. Indeed, the relative shift in economic power from the United States to West Germany and Japan has had political effects, particularly in Europe where France and Germany in the late 1970s have edged closer to each other to affirm European Community policies implicitly in competition with the United States. More generally, when, in 1971, President Nixon abruptly curtailed the convertibility of the overvalued dollar into gold, the United States in effect renounced its economic leadership of the capitalist world. He gave warning that the United States would henceforth act not as the sole patron of the system, but as one nation, albeit an uniquely large one, inside it. Unfortunately, collective leadership has proved infinitely more difficult than monarchy. Germany and Japan, the next two strongest economies, bent upon exports rather than propping up the system as a whole, and America, concerned about the whole but (for instance on energy) often from a national point of view, failed to agree on common priorities. The common management of the international market economy, in many ways the proudest boast of western policymakers after the war, has been placed under increasing strain, and protectionist forces are gaining ground in almost all countries.

Given these strains it might have been assumed that the Soviet block should have been able to seize the western crisis as a 'historic opportunity for socialism'. Eastern Europe has no acknowledged unemployment (though some concealed), less inflation (some of it imported from the West), steady growth rates (though slowing down) and no particular sense of obligation to (nor demand from) the developing world. Yet it has not proved easy to turn these advantages to political account. The socialist economies, in the 1970s, were beginning to move out of the phase of extensive growth (when shifting peasants into factories sufficed) into an intensive one (when yields must rise in the factories themselves), and the Soviet Union faces in the 1980s very steep declines in the prospective growth of the labour force.[6] Productivity does not seem to be growing faster than the sum of inputs of labour and capital, as would be normal in the West. Accordingly, growth has slowed down. The Tenth Five Year Plan (1976–80) provides for growth of only 4.8% p.a. in utilised national income and the actual increase in 1977 seems to have been only 3.5%.[7] This is happening at a time when demands on the productive machine are steadily rising—from defence, from agriculture (still the weakest sector) from rising consumer demand, from the rapidly increasing costs of obtaining raw materials and fuels and transporting them from Siberia, and from the need in some countries (notably Poland) to satisfy a contentious public by sprinting out of socio-economic trouble through faster growth. The result has been high recent imports of technology and investment on credit from the West and the piling up of debts to the point where they now represent, on average, about one and a half years of Comecon exports to the West. Surprisingly, then, the would-be contrast between capitalist and socialist performance has remained almost as muted in western recession as in boom. The difference has not been enough to take the limelight away from the embarrassing political challenge to the Tsarist face of socialism by Soviet dissidents and, in western Europe, by Eurocommunism. No development underlines the subtle changes in the balance in the past thirty years more than the rather defensive effort of western communist parties to make electoral progress by establishing their *bona fides* as good democrats at a time when the OECD regions have 17 million unemployed and a rate of growth oscillating around 3% p.a which implies further unemployment.

Resource Politics

The most spectacular innovation of the 1970s has probably been the discovery of growing political limits to the availability of resources. The watershed was the increase in oil prices forced by Libya at the end of 1970, though the major shock came in 1973 with the oil embargo organised by OPEC during and after the Yom Kippur War (see table 7). This was the first time economic sanctions had produced major political effects in a crisis. In many ways it marked the end of the imperial era far more than did Europe's earlier political retreat from empire, because it affected the West at the core of its strength, in the industrial economy.

The oil crisis underlined not only the vulnerability but also the divisions of the West. It was essentially made possible by the extremely rapid increase in American imports from the Middle East after 1970, which turned America from the source of supply of last resort for its allies into a major and still growing competitor for the Middle East supplies they cannot do without. On the other hand, oil has so far proved politically less potent than many imagined at the time. There are several reasons for this. One is that the industrial consumers have devised a system of stocks and rationing that discourages all but a complete embargo. Much more important, though, the OPEC regimes themselves, intent on development and desiring not to encourage revolution as a threat to their own tenure, are not anxious to kill the goose that lays the golden egg. They have not even reacted strongly to the devaluation of the dollar which, together with inflation in the countries they buy from, has substantially reduced their real earnings. Unfortunately, too, oil and the wealth procured from it are not a sufficient answer to the problems of OPEC development planners. Though oil provides abundant capital, it distorts the home economy, raises the value of the currency, increases wages, overprices exports and otherwise impedes the industrialisation needed for when the oil runs out. The thirst for western goods and technical assistance remains enormous. Further, the enormous dollar surpluses accumulated by the OPEC countries, far from destroying the international financial system as originally feared, have, if anything, strengthened it by helping to keep the developing countries solvent and growing at a time of industrial recession among the rich. Finally, it will be difficult for producers of other raw materials to follow the example of OPEC. This is partly because recession, encouraged by high oil prices, helps to damp down demand. It is also because no other product except grains, in the hands of the United States, depends at the margin so completely on one producer as does oil on Saudi Arabia.

The problems of resource-limits lie elsewhere, but they are none the easier for that. The first is that the shock to the industrial economies produced by the rise in energy prices has tended to sort out the sheep from the goats even more ruthlessly than the normal process of competition. Germany, for instance, now has a surplus in its balance of payments with the Middle East, while weaker European exporters are in deficit. The premium placed on adjustment further weakens the weak and makes their contribution to the process of general adjustment that much more problematic for the future.

The second is that OPEC has encouraged a widespread process, begun long before, of assertion of authority by the nations with raw material reserves. National priorities of long-term conservation, of maximisation of prices and of processing on the spot, have become more potent and those of short-term production to meet demand in consuming countries less so. As a result, investment by the international mining companies is slowing down even more than it already had, under similar but weaker political pressures, in the 1960s.

Third, control over raw materials cuts sharply across existing power configurations. 'Not only western Europe and Japan but almost all of the east European countries and about 70 per cent of all developing countries have only very limited reserves and minerals'.[8] Raw material reserves tend to favour the big battalions, countries like the super-powers Canada, Australia and South Africa, with China, Brazil and India to some extent as runners-up. Small countries, with some lucky exceptions (like Jamaica for bauxite), are far less well endowed. In particular, southern Africa and the Soviet Union between them almost monopolise some minerals like cobalt, chromium and platinum, which are important in metals production and for which it is difficult in the short term to find substitutes. Moreover, big countries also tend to be the best placed to exploit new resource areas, like the seabed, not least because their large land areas usually but not always (Japan is an exception) give them the largest off-shore maritime zones (see table 8).

If American energy policies remain as self-centred as they have been, western Europe and Japan may, by the mid-1980s, regard United States policy, or the lack of it, as a serious threat. There is no economic reason, only political ones, why a traditionalist regime like Saudi Arabia should furnish the West with the oil it needs in order to grow. If a ceiling is reached where Saudi production no longer rises, or the regime changes so that the old political caution no longer applies, the implications of competition between the United States and its allies could be most serious. Such potential incompatibilities raise major issues cutting across the familiar picture of a united 'First World'.

Equivalent, though different, issues arise from the contrast between the Soviet Union, as the world's greatest reservoir of fuels and raw materials, and eastern Europe. This helps Moscow to sustain its control of the region, but to the extent that the USSR cannot fulfil its potential production, the east European countries will have to appear on the world market as new importers, notably of Middle East oil. This has implications for East-West politics. The only discernible pattern (except that of random opportunity) in recent Soviet involvement in southern Africa, the Horn and Afghanistan is that all the countries concerned are either raw material producers or possible bases for political activity against regimes which are themselves producers of raw materials, such as the oil exporters of the Gulf. If a series of radical coups could be accomplished in these areas, would the world balance shift? Almost certainly to some extent, though it would probably be necessary to risk extreme reactions from the West and to turn the Soviet Union into a major market for raw material exports. If Soviet policies of self-sufficiency continue, the commercial currents towards the West will tend to re-assert themselves, as in the cases of Algeria, Iraq and even potentially Angola. From this point of view, the West has an interest in helping the Soviet bloc to maintain its self-sufficiency by helping (up to a point) to develop Siberia. It is one of the complex factors that enter into the question of what Western policy should be for technological investments and exports to the Soviet Union.

Last but far from least is the plight of the many developing countries which have few, or no, raw materials. There is little doubt that the process of growth is tending to leave a long tail of such countries, many of which threaten to become the international welfare problem of the future. This faces the new rich as well as the old, and it is notable that the OPEC countries devote a much higher percentage of their gross national product to aid than the West, and still more, than the East (see table 8). OPEC aid, however, is mainly confined to the Islamic world, which poses a problem for the majority of other countries.

Proliferation

In a way, however, the most profound challenge is probably that of proliferation. This is usually defined in the narrow terms of the arms trade, or of nuclear-waste materials spreading round the world. In essence, it is a much broader phenomenon by which the industrial revolution and all the capacities that go with it spread to an ever-widening group of countries. This means that it will become harder for the industrial countries to legislate for mankind primarily in the light of their own interests. Industrialisation has been going forward rapidly in a minority of ten to fifteen countries with a combined population of about 300 million people representing perhaps a fifth of the non-communist developing world. Others are also growing: the World Bank now identifies 54 'middle income' countries out of the United Nations' 151. This group could be a political pivot in future. If they break their way successfully into the circle of the more prosperous industrial countries, like Japan before them, the problem of world poverty will be that much more tractable. But precisely because they are direct competitors of the old industrial countries, they pose the greatest challenge to settled domestic interests in these countries which are increasingly seeking to enjoy the fruits of past growth. The industrialising developing countries supplied only some 3 per cent of the consumer markets of the OECD regions in 1976, but in a protectionist climate even that has proved too much for the importing countries' capacity, or willingness, to adjust in the more heavily affected sectors like textiles, clothing, footwear, steel and ships.

One good sign may be that the growth of the developing world today seems less dependent on prosperity in the OECD area than was previously assumed. About a third of the markets of the newcomers are in Third World areas, including OPEC. Some of the newcomers have had rates of growth since 1973 twice, or three times those of the OECD area (table 9). The World Bank states there will be little difficulty in continuing to finance the growth of such countries in the near future, though private bankers are not so sanguine.[9] Nevertheless, OECD markets remain vital to the virtuous (or vicious) circles of the world economy. Expectations of developing countries are still basically expansive. The danger is that refusal by OECD economies to adjust may frustrate these hopes and cumulatively produce more repressive political conditions. In that case, confrontation between rich and poor, the dog that has failed to bite during the boom years, might still be aroused.

This puts a new complexion on the proliferation of means of destruction round the world. The oil crisis and the rise of OPEC have at least to some extent, in the Middle East, turned the arms trade from what was once a sellers' market into a buyers' one. Arms suppliers have woken up late to the dangers. The discussions between the super-powers which have now opened on restraints on conventional arms trade come at a time when the number of countries producing their own major armaments has already become significant.[10] Arms of all types—combat aircraft and battle tanks at one end of the spectrum, and precision-guided munitions, often light enough for a single operator, at the other—are steadily spreading. The latter potentially reverse the trend since the Middle Ages for the power of governments over means of violence to grow out of proportion to that of non-governmental groups, and have obvious implications for guerrilla warfare. Such issues are also posed at the blurred confines of civil and military activity, particularly over nuclear reactor programmes. The control of nuclear proliferation has been complicated by the view of the Germans and French (but not apparently the Japanese) that reactor sales may be a way to keep the lead in the export race in the late twentieth century. This, and the desire to diversify uranium supplies, because the United States has become an increasingly erratic source, seem to have conditioned the deal by which Germany provided reprocessing facilities to Brazil, a country which makes no secret of its determination to become a nuclear military power. As a result of such divisions between industrial states and of the spread of capacity to new ones, control by the few is fast becoming an anachronism. If arms control, in the wider sense, is to prevail, it will have to be as part of a political process of collectively accepted self-controls by both the 'haves' of today and the aspirants to possession tomorrow. By diffusing power around the world, economic growth has increased the need to devise more effective ways of collective international management but has almost certainly also made this much more difficult to achieve.

In some ways the risks may be less great at the level of states than at that of societies and international terrorism. New opportunities—aircraft to hijack, world cities to bomb, television to communicate the shock; possibly new intensities of resentment that come in poor countries with the awareness of some power to affect the richer ones combined with the continuing frustrations of development; even the impotence of would-be revolutionaries confronted, in rich countries, by the bureaucratic conservatism of accepted mass democracy: all feed international guerrilla activity. Such grievances aggregate round more traditional ones like those of the Palestinians or the Irish Republican Army. The fear that industrial society depends on ever more numerous, small and vulnerable strategic points which multiply the targets for increasingly lethal weapons, feeds the traditional nightmare of the rich that saboteurs may yet bring Babylon down in flames.

The paradox is that, on the whole, international terrorism so far has been confined to relatively limited techniques, such as hijacking, kidnapping and individual assassinations. The reason may be political: in spite of theories that the reactionary society must be terrorised into waking up to its concealed fascist nature, urban guerrillas basically need to appeal to mass opinion, or a sufficient section of it, and cannot do so by indiscriminate outrage. On the other hand, if limited methods fail, there will be incentives to raise the stakes to technically more difficult but also more coercive measures. The fear of this lies behind opposition to the spread of nuclear reactors, especially breeder-reactors, on the grounds that storage and transportation may be too vulnerable to sabotage. There is no guarantee that such dangers will not increase anyway. If the industrial powers fail to adjust to change and spoil the prospects of the more effective developing countries, there is at least a risk that the dangers will increase still further. The capacity, or lack of it, of the established industrial world to co-opt economies that basically seek to integrate into the club, and not to throw them into the arms of forces seeking confrontation, could be the key to the future balance.

Conclusions

As the world approaches the 1980s, then, there are as many basic questions awaiting the test of events as there were in 1945. They are not the same questions, but they are equally earth-shaking in their potential. To what extent may the different phases in the socio-economic cycle through which different cultures are patently passing affect the capacity of societies to adjust to each other's purposes and performance? How constricting will the political and even perhaps to some extent material limits to growth prove to be? How will resource-politics redistribute power around the world? How far will proliferation, the symptom of a crowded world that has to learn to live with tighter proximities, be controlled and, if it is not, to what extent may social Darwinism again rear its ugly head? How, in such a context, can a relatively open world-society be maintained and how far will the political and social strains of reaching compromises produce a more oppressive political climate within and between societies?

Before the war, the French poet, Paul Valéry, threw out a famous phrase to the effect that *'l'ère d'un monde fini commence'*. The post-war political scene with its virtually universal political struggle between two systems of economic, social and political progress, certainly displayed symptoms of this completed, though far from unified, quality. The economic scene, though, was still one of headlong expansion, greater in performance than ever before and well-nigh unlimited in pretensions. The combined effect of the cultural changes since 1968 and of doubts about the level of growth that can be maintained in future, in perhaps both Western and Soviet blocs which have dominated the post-war scene, is to call this freewheeling attitude in question. In these circumstances, economics, instead of providing the rising tide which conceals many of the reefs, may give them more prominence again. The odds are that, in future, economic factors will be not more important than in 1945–73 but more noticeable. People notice they depend on breathing only when it becomes difficult. In practical terms, three major questions seem to be posed about the interaction of economics and the world balance.

The first is whether the West, the centre of the post-war dispensation for the capitalist two-thirds of the world, will have the elasticity to adjust to the diffusion of industry to new countries. The rate of that diffusion should not be exaggerated, but the more it develops, the more any further advances will be felt if adjustment lags. It is inevitable that, as economic progress, at least in the western culture, gives more and more power of affecting decisions to broad strata of society, the more adjustment to third parties will depend on domestic lobbies whose historic experience has been one of seeking to assert rights against privilege rather than of conceding to others in poorer but distant countries privileges they are far from feeling they possess. One of the dynamics of democracy is to give the many the sense that they represent rectitude against privilege. Domestic political systems are geared entirely to redressing the balance within nations. There are few international organisations, still less a widespread international legitimacy, around which conflict can be arbitrated. This is a basic difference between the national social problems of the nineteenth century and the international social problems of today. Adjustment is made more difficult by the speed of economic change which means that uncontrolled shifts in trade can, and already have, rapidly knocked out whole sectors of production in rich countries. It follows that if industrialisation is to spread, one of the key problems will be to order the rich societies domestically in ways—perhaps entailing shorter working hours in return for slower rates of income growth—which make it possible to reconcile the domestic redistribution of costs and benefits with the international one. If not, there is a serious danger that the risk of confrontation between the old and new under-privileged may indeed lead the international political system into greater contentiousness and increasingly repressive ways.

The second question is whether new circuits can develop in the world economy reducing, though almost certainly not eliminating, the need for greater adjustment between the 'First' and 'Third' Worlds. There are signs of this already in the redistribution of finance and markets from OPEC towards the more vigorous developing countries as a result of the 'recycling' of petrodollars. Industrialising countries now sell more to the Middle East, to others of their kind, to eastern Europe and possibly even to Japan or at least east Asia. The offshore east Asians, or rather those belonging to the Sinic culture, have shown a consistent tendency to higher growth than any other cultures in the world. The single exception has been the middle kingdom itself, communist China, which is now embarking on ambitious development plans. With or without mainland China, there are signs that the balance of the world economy is likely to shift somewhat from the Atlantic to the Pacific. If China in its turn were to expand its economy, even by rates reminiscent of the Soviet bloc in the last generation rather than of east Asia, this tendency would be powerfully reinforced. From this point of view, a closer relationship between China and Japan, which seems only natural, could have a major impact on the economy and the polity of the world. In general, it could only be healthy; too exclusive a dependence of the developing world on the United States and Europe could become a political liability for rich and poor alike in the next generation. The problems of such a shift could nonetheless be great.

The third question is how economics is going to affect the East-West rivalry which, along with high growth, has been the most prominent shaping factor of the post-war generation. The signs of a slowing down in both the West and East may affect the Soviet Union most because its economy, large though it has become, is still basically only semi-developed. Will this enforce a slowdown in the steady growth of Soviet military power since the early 1960s, at a time when NATO seems to be reacting to the arms challenge more than in the past decade? Will the steady recourse to western technology have a cumulative effect in making Soviet growth rates, even moderate ones, come to depend on the Western connection, and if so achieve the aims Kissinger proposed for detente, the creation of mutual links that cumulatively restrict conflict? Or will Western help merely make it easier for the Soviet Union not to choose between priorities and serve the further expansion of its military-political potential? One of the major issues for the 'First' World is the attitude to take to economic cooperation with the Soviet Union, and the arguments for and against are not at all simple. It is quite possible the West may serve several interests in helping the USSR develop Siberia; and, so far, warily, this has been the trend (policy is too systematic a word). A major debate is required on this issue.

There is a parallel issue concerning possible revolutions in the 'Third' World. Quarrels between communist states and the reliance of even radical regimes on economic connections with the West have tended to take some of the fever out of Western attitudes to Marxist or pseudo-Marxist revolutions in poor countries. The Middle East and energy, however, are not necessarily to be dealt with in such a self-possessed manner. This might be true whether the Soviet Union were closely involved with change there or not. Energy is probably the great variable in the balance between East and West while the slowdown in the Soviet economy, even though one could argue it might lead to increased internal turbulence and therefore also increased external aggressiveness, seems more likely to reduce the current expansion of Soviet power. Over the political dynamism of the Soviet Union there is certainly a major economic question-mark, and it looks like growing.

All these uncertainties—the flexibility of the Western response to industrial challenges, the ability of new economic circuits to help the development of the poor, and Soviet expansion and the long-drawn-out energy crisis—are in some sense subsumed in a single larger one: is the spread of the number of countries making similar demands on the ecological system of the planet such as to create a scramble for resources which degrades the political system? Is the pre-1914 world of social Darwinism and territorial competition likely to emerge in a new form as more countries make demands on the system? New calculations of the distribution of income in the world made by Kravis and others at the University of Pennsylvania suggest that in 'real' terms, the differences between the richest and poorest are smaller than used to be thought when these were measured solely in money (see table 10). The average income of the poorest countries in Asia and Africa is about one-eighth that of the western industrialised economies. This still means very large increases in world output between now and the turn of the century to close any substantial part of the gap. Will this be materially or politically possible, and what power shifts will it entail? Given the demands made even by slightly falling rates of growth of population in the poor countries, there must either be very substantial increases in demands on the ecological system or (if growth slows down) minimal and even perhaps negative increases in income per head in the next generation. The effects of this on the political order cannot be predicted, but the possibility of a more contentious international system, and of a quite high level of political disorder, cannot be ruled out. Even if nuclear war is excluded, this does not exclude lower-level violence, including possible nuclear blackmail by non-governmental groups, in a contentious global system threatened by latent civil war and violent anarchy.

The most creative political innovations of the post-war period have nearly all concerned the birth of rules and institutions for the common management of confrontation. This has been true of aid; of full employment policies to stop the beggar-my-neighbour deflation of the 1930s and sustain growth; of SALT to control the nuclear arms balance between the super-powers; of the dialogue between the industrial states and OPEC; and of a large number of international mechanisms, more or less effective, to handle the international context of national problems. It is in many ways the most encouraging development since the war, and essentially an innovation of that period. There has not really been anything like its domestication of international politics before. Still, it remains only a very limited beginning. Because of the 'King's Peace' of nuclear stalemate in the midst of great social upheaval and latent violence, the world seems condemned to a kind of contentious confederalism, conditional as all confederal links are (the Swiss confederates fought five wars with each other in five centuries before becoming a federation in 1848). Confederalism is a transitional stage when powers recognise the limits of their individual capacity to take decisions but still feel that the central contract, and its administrative powers, have at best a highly conditional legitimacy. This is clearly the predicament of the world today.

A series of basic problems were tackled in the last generation and, partly by luck, partly by American hegemony, in a period of high growth, a limited compromise was reached. Rapidly, however, the problems to be tackled are growing beyond the competence of this system and it is necessary constantly to extend it. The system cannot extend itself; extension depends on the compromises the societies are ready to reach with one another. Now that it looks as if economic growth will be less universally buoyant, they may be more difficult to conclude. Yet the problems look like being such that the price of failure may on occasions become very high indeed. This price may be seen very often as strategic; but the failure will also, very often, be economic and an aspect of a shifting material balance between the societies of the world. In these circumstances, the capacity to devise international agreements, meaning frequently, perhaps normally, the creation of new international rules and possibly institutions, is likely to be crucial to the evolution of the world in the next generation. In this sense, the 1970s have opened a new era as firmly as the end of the Second World War itself; and the challenge is at least as great.

Statistical Appendix

Table 1
World Industrial Output
(percentage shares)

A

Country	1888	1947	1950
U.S.A.	32.1	47.7	38.6
U.K.	18.3	8.6	8.4
Germany/W. Germany	12.9	n.a.	5.4
France	10.7	3.7	3.6
Russia/Soviet Union	8.0	2.1	4.1
Japan	n.a.	1.3	2.0

Woytinsky, *World Population and Production*, Twentieth Century Fund, New York (1953), pp 1000-1003.
n.a. = not available.

B

Country/Group	1950	1976
U.S.A.	41.0	25.1
Other developed Market economies	37.5	37.7
Centrally Planned economies	15.5	29.2
Developing Market economies	6.0	8.0

E. J. Horn, 'Trade Related Structural Adjustment Pressures in W. Europe', Institut für Weltwirtschaft, Kiel (1978) unpublished paper.

Table 2
Killed in World Wars I & II
(in '000s)

Country	Military WW1	WW2	Civilian WW1	WW2
France	1,320	167		400
Other W. Europe				
(incl. Italy)	1,492	487		480
Germany	2,000	3,760		3,090
E. & S.E. Europe				
(incl. Austria)	2,265	1,560		6,854
USSR	1,700	10,000		15,000
China	—	2,200		20,000
Japan	n.a.	1,507		672
Other Countries				
(incl. U.S.A.				
& Turkey)	557	434		91
	9,328	20,115	15,000*	46,587

The totals are, of course, spurious, being the addition of some figures precisely known and others which are mere orders of magnitude (eg. the USSR and China). The orders of magnitude alone can be retained.

Sources:
Europe, WW2 and Military in WW1, C. Clark, *Population Growth and Land Use*, Macmillan 1967 p.121; for China, Japan and Other Countries, Quincy Wright, *Study of War* 2 edtn, Chicago 1965, p.1542; for Civilian Casualties in WW1 see note below.

*Note on Civilian Casualties in WW1
'Very few civilians were killed as the direct result of military activities—some sources put the loss as low as 100,000. However, 'abnormal' civilian mortality in the war and immediate post-war period was about 5 million (outside Russia). A good deal of this was due to disease . . . In Russia . . . losses in the revolution were very high because of civil war, disease and famine . . . losses from 1914–23 were 10 million dead on top of the 1.7 million soldiers killed from 1914 to 1917. Total 'abnormal' loss of life was therefore about 25 million from 1914 to 1923, of which about 12 million deaths were directly due to war.'

Angus Maddison, *Economic Policy and Performance in Europe 1913–1970* in *The Fontana Economic History of Europe* ed. Carlo M. Cipolla, Vol. 5(2) p.447.

Table 3
World Growth Rates
(percentage rates per annum)

A

Output per man p.a. in Selected Industrial Countries		
Country	*1870–1960*	*1950–1965*
U.S.A.	1.8	2.0
Sweden	2.0	3.2
Germany	1.6	4.9
France	1.5	4.2
Italy	1.3	4.3
U.K.	1.3	2.2

John Knapp, 'Would Britain profit from the EEC?' *Round Table,* April, 1967, pp 166–176.

B

Type of Economy	1950–60		1960–70		1970–76	
	GDP	GDP per cap.	GDP	GDP per cap.	GDP	GDP per cap.
Developed Market Economies	4.1	2.8	5.1	4.2	3.0	2.1
Developing Market Economies	4.7	2.4	5.2	2.7	5.3	2.8
Centrally Planned Economies (CMEA)	9.3	7.8	6.7	5.8	6.3	5.4

Unctad Handbooks of International and Trade Statistics, 1972 and Supplement 1977.

Table 4
Soviet Growth Rates

For technical reasons, there are wide differences in estimates of Soviet growth rates: compare Table 4A with Table 3B. For some of the difficulties see Alec Nove, *An Economic History of the USSR,* pp. 381–388, 'A Note on growth rates'; and Paul Cockle, 'Analysing Soviet Defence Spending: the Debate in Perspective' in *Survival,* Sept/Oct 1978 pp. 209–19 published by the International Institute for Strategic Studies (IISS) London.

A
Annual Average Compound Rates of Growth
of Total Output

Region	1950/60	1960/70
Western Europe	4.4	5.2
Eastern Europe (CMEA)	5.6	4.9

B
Soviet Industrial Production Index

Year	USSR Official	Powell-Moorsteen
1937	100	100
1945	120	77
1950	227	156
1961	747	407
1969	1440	n.a.

Angus Maddison, *Economic Policy and Performance in Europe 1913–70*, Vol 5 (2) p.478; and B.R. Mitchell, Statistical Appendix, Vol 6 (2) p.694 of *Fontana Economic History of Europe*, (ed) Carlo M. Cipolla.

Table 5
Official Aid Disbursements in 1976
(as a percentage of GDP)

	percentage	GDP
OECD Countries	0.33	
of which USA		0.26
EEC		0.43
Japan		0.20
OPEC Countries	2.09	
Socialist Countries	0.03	

OECD Observer, July 1978

Table 6
Income Distribution

According to Peter Wiles, *Distribution of Income: East & West* (North Holland/American Elsevier) 1974, Table VIII p.48, from which the figures below are extracted, the differences in the distribution of income (gross of income tax) between Britain (but not America) and countries of the CMEA seem smaller than is often assumed. The method of comparison is to divide the level of income of the 5th percentile of people from the top of the income ladder (level 95) by that of the 5th percentile of people from the bottom (level 5). Statistical uncertainties and special cases make it impossible to take levels 99 and 1, which would probably show greater differences between East and West.

Country	P95/P5
U.S. 1968	13.3
USSR 1966	6.0
U.K. 1969	5.9
C.S.R. 1965	4.5
Hungary 1967	4.2
Bulgaria 1963–5	3.84

Table 7
Crude Oil Posted Prices 1970–4 ($)

Date	Arabia Light (34°)	Libyan (40°)
Jan 1970	1.800	2.170
— 1971	1.800	2.550
— 1972	2.479	3.673
— 1973	2.591	3.777
Oct 1973	5.119	8.925
Jan 1974	11.651	15.768

Strategic Survey 1973 (IISS) p.35.

Table 8
Area gained by Selected Countries Under
the Maritime Economic Zone
to 200 Nautical Miles

Country	Sq Nautical Miles ('000s)
U.S.A.	2,222
Canada	1,370
Japan	1,126
EEC	704
Norway	591

Sherwood E. Frezon, 'Summary of Oil and Gas Statistics for Onshore and Offshore Areas of 151 Countries', U.S. Department of the Interior, *Geological Survey Professional Paper No. 885* (Washington, Government Printing Office, 1974) p.156; *Triangle Papers 9*, 'A New Regime for the Oceans,' Oda, Johnston, Holst, Hollick and Hardy, Trilateral Commission, 1976.

Table 9
Output Growth Per Capita Per Annum
in Some Industrialising Countries
and OECD

Country	1963–73	1973–6
Hong Kong	6.8	5.2
S. Korea	8.0	9.0
Singapore	8.3	3.7
Taiwan	7.4	3.2
Brazil	5.3	5.3
Turkey	3.4	6.0
OECD areas	3.8	0.8

Table 10
Disparities in World Market Economies Per Capita GDP
in 1970 in percentage shares
(World Market Economies=100)

Type of Economy or Region	Popu-lation	Per Capita GDP		
		Nominal	'Real'	As % Asia 'Real'
Developed Market Economies	30.6	279	242	864
Developing Market Economies	69.4	21	38	136
of which: Africa	13.6	17	30	107
Asia	44.6	14	28	100
L. America	11.2	57	86	307

'Real' i.e. at purchasing power parities as against exchange rates ('nominal'). Kravis, Heston & Summers, 'Real GDP per capita for more than 100 Countries', *Economic Journal*, July 1978, pp.215–41.

Table 11
Shares of Selected Regions in World Exports
(1955–75, percentage shares)

Regions	1955	1965	1975
Developed Market Economies	64.7	68.8	66.1
Developing Market Economies:			
OPEC	25.4	x 5.7	13.0
non-OPEC		13.2	11.0
Centrally Planned Economies	10.0	11.7	9.9

E. J. Horn, 'Trade Related Structural Adjustment Pressures in W. Europe', unpublished paper, Institut für Weltwirtschaft, Kiel, 1978.

3

Strategic Intelligence:
Problems and Remedies

by Klaus Knorr

Introduction

Intelligence is one of the most critical elements of statecraft directed
toward the outside world; it permeates the making of all foreign policy
that is not regarded as routine and unproblematic; and although it is also
relevant and important to estimating international opportunities for
cooperation, intelligence has been cultivated most attentively in matters
of threat-perception because gross misestimates in this area place at risk
the very survival of states. Although intelligence is concerned with other
than military threats (e.g. economic), the plan of this volume demands
concentration on military threats. Both overestimates and underestimates
of external threats can produce calamitous consequences. Underestimates can produce disaster and, even if they do not, can make
war more probable and costly. Overestimates can lead to excessive
military build-up that is economically wasteful and, by causing anxiety,
additional military preparations and animosity abroad, can make
international conflict and the outbreak of hostilities more probable.

In the following, we will (1) conceptualize the objectives of
international threat-perception; (2) indicate the historical record of
intelligence activities; (3) present a particular case of strategic surprise in
order to introduce an analysis of the fundamental problems besetting acts
of threat-perception; and (4) discuss possible improvements of statecraft
in this area of concern.*

Strategic intelligence attempts to estimate acute and potential threats.†
Acute or actual threats are those that suggest conflict to be imminent.
Potential threats are attributed to states that have developed or are

---

*I wish to thank Robert Axelrod, Thomas G. Belden, Richard Betts and Paul Pillar for helpful comments
on an earlier draft.
†Essentially the same analysis applies to states intent on the aggressive use of force.

developing the capability to proceed to actual threats and attack, and whose peaceful intentions in the future cannot be taken for granted. Although potential threats are regarded as more hypothetical than actual threats, they are not necessarily a matter of the longer run and therefore not safely of lesser concern. As many historical examples remind us, a potential threat can turn acute suddenly and unexpectedly. If Weimar Germany was at worst a potential threat to its neighbours in 1930, Hitler's accession to power and rapid military expansion under his rule made this threat acute in a very few years. The developing split between the Soviet Union and Communist China abruptly raised serious security problems in Peking.

The objective of intelligence is not only to estimate whether or not a threat exists, but also to assess its precise nature, e.g. the likely places and modes as well as the timing of attack.[1] Since many attacks in the past succeeded quickly because the victor achieved strategic surprise, the prevention of surprise by means of intelligence estimates that give timely and proper warning is a central objective of threat-perception. The correct estimate of an actual threat facilitates the design of proper responses, whether by alerting and mobilizing forces of defence and attempting to reinforce deterrence, or by encouraging a course of accommodation. The correct estimate of potential threats is a basis for providing adequate forces for deterrence and defence in the hope that the potential threat will not become acute while, on the other hand, avoiding provocative responses that are apt—by way of self-fulfilling prophecy—to increase the threat. In either case, threat-perception is oriented toward the capabilities and intentions of actual or potential opponents. Both can change over time, and intentions can change more quickly than capabilities. These dynamics make conjecture about future developments a part of the estimative process. Indeed, because it takes a great deal of time to bolster forces for deterrence and defence by developing and producing new weapons systems, conjectures about the capabilities of actual or potential opponents, including arms, military budgets and even national economic output, range far into the future. Defence budgets depend on such long-range estimates.

Even good intelligence estimates—clear, timely and valid—cannot, of course, ensure good policy; and when estimates are not good in any or all of these terms, it is sometimes difficult to distinguish between failures of threat-perception and of policy-response.* But without proper intelligence estimates, states—unless they are lucky—can at best hope to improvise and muddle through in the face of surprise. This is risky and costly, and only basically very strong and resilient countries can afford it.

---

*For example, the huge losses suffered by the Soviet army in 1941 resulted from both the German achievement of strategic surprise and Stalin's insistence on a linear defence of the Soviet boundary, permitting no strategic withdrawal, even though the Germans had previously executed dashing *Blitzkrieg* in Poland and France.

Reasonably accurate threat-perception is clearly a precondition of any effective posture for survival in the larger sense and the longer run.

It is precisely because international threat-perception plays so critical a role in international affairs that it is imperative to assess its quality as a matter of statecraft. Unfortunately, this is difficult to do. Relatively few recent estimates, and those for the most part American, are in the public domain; and the historical record of threat-perception when estimates were made by leaders and governments without elaborate intelligence services has not so far been examined systematically.

Moreover, any useful appraisal of the ex-post-facto success of past estimates depends on one's criteria for judgment and a suitable classification of cases. In the area of strategic intelligence, these problems can be illumined by comparing estimates of the capabilities of states with estimates of their intentions in matters touching on peace and war. Capability estimates are usually about continuous things raising questions of more or less (e.g. GNP, military budget, numbers of divisions), and can be more or less right or wrong. On the other hand, estimates regarding critical intentions of governments concern also questions of either/or and then are either right or wrong (although the attribution of degrees of probability mitigates this dichotomous character). Moreover, capabilities that move on a continuum are more conjecturable (that is, more predictable with some degree of confidence) than are estimates of critical intentions and decisions, because many components of capability are observable and countable* and not only do not usually change much from year to year, but are incapable of abrupt and substantial change,† whereas the intentions of governments and their expression in observable behaviour can change very abruptly and with great consequence. Of course, capability-estimates that overestimate or underestimate foreign capabilities considerably and persistently can have great *cumulative* consequence. The fact that critical government intentions can change abruptly does not mean that they change with great frequency. The intelligence service of country A may estimate year after year that a military attack on its ally X by state Y is highly improbable, prove correct in nine years and incorrect in the tenth. But the consequence of the one failure may be enormous.

Crude success-failure ratios tell us little about the quality of intelligence estimates. While the obstacles to a statistical evaluation of strategic intelligence seem to be insuperable, there is an alternative approach to assessing the quality of statecraft in this area. This is to start with very consequential past events and to examine the record of threat-perception preceding them case by case. Such study suggests that the quality of

*Observability and countability are reduced to the extent that states are engaged in qualitative rather than quantitative arms competition.
†Certain capability changes that can be sudden and substantial as a result of mobilization and new deployment express a sudden change in intentions.

intelligence has been extremely and surprisingly poor.* Although this is not widely known as a general phenomenon, misperceptions have apparently played a significant, and often crucial, role in the precipitation of wars and during war as well, whatever period of time or part of the world one turns to. However, this approach naturally tells us a great deal only about *under*estimates of external threats. It is more diffficult to use historical search in the pursuit of *over*estimates. Nothing dramatic is apt to happen if a state overestimates a threat and increases its military forces as a result. For example, there is some evidence that the Soviet leaders overestimated threats from the United States and a reconstituted Germany during the late 1940s and early 1950s, but the consequences of this misperception, if it was real, are hard to trace among all the factors that actuated Soviet behaviour. Even if, following excessive military preparations in reaction to an overestimate, a notable event, perhaps even war, does ensue, it is historically difficult to attribute it to the failure of the strategic estimate. The subsequent event may then seem to confirm the original estimate even if, by inducing excessive military responses, it contributed to its genesis. The historical approach is even less productive when it comes to identifying cases of *correct* strategic estimates. If such perceptions led to an improved posture of deterrence and no actual threat materialized, we do not usually know whether or to what extent this absence of crisis or war was determined by the adequate response to a good estimate or by other factors. It seems to this author nevertheless reasonable to deduce from historical experience that the record of international threat-perception in the vital strategic area is disconcertingly poor.

In the following section, we will refer to some cases which contribute to the strong impression that the record of international threat-perception is far from good, and which will serve us in analysing the difficulties encountered in the estimating process. Some of these difficulties are inherent in the nature of the job while others of an aggravating character result from situational conditions that may or may not be present in particular instances. The analysis will concentrate first on estimates of intentions and then, more briefly, on estimates of capabilities.

Prior to the Yom Kippur War of 1973, Israeli intelligence—which enjoyed an enviable reputation on account of past efficiency—had given a guarantee to the Government that there would be ample advance warning of any Arab attack, and the Government had accepted this guarantee.† On this basis, Israel maintained only thin forces along the

---

*For an extensive discussion of historical cases, see Klaus Knorr, 'Threat Perception', in Klaus Knorr (ed.), *Historical Dimensions of National Security Problems*, Lawrence, Ka., University Press of Kansas, 1976, pp.78-119.
†For a detailed analysis of this case of surprise see Shlaim, pp.348-380. Other similarly instructive and well-researched case studies are Roberta Wohlstetter's book on Pearl Harbor and Barton Whaley's on the German attack on the Soviet Union (see the Appendix for the bibliographic references).

Suez Canal and on the Golan Heights, planning to mobilize its highly trained reserves only if an attack seemed imminent. Yet, on Oct. 6, the Egyptian and Syrian forces struck and achieved strategic surprise, invading territory controlled by Israel. Once the Israeli Defence Forces were mobilized, they counter-attacked vigorously. But while they succeeded in throwing the enemy back, they suffered very sizeable casualties in the process. American intelligence, which had kept a close watch on the situation, also had failed to predict an Arab attack (even though such a prediction was made at a lower bureaucratic level).

Although the intelligence failure deeply shocked Israel, it must be emphasized that this kind of error is common in the annals of intelligence. Some recent examples may be cited to support this important point. Strategic surprise was suffered by the Soviet Union when Germany attacked in 1941, by the United States in the same year when the Japanese attacked Pearl Harbor, by the United States again in 1950 when North Korea invaded South Korea and subsequently when China intervened in the Korean War, by India in 1962 when Chinese forces crossed the boundary between the two states, and by Syria and Egypt when the Israelis attacked in 1967. British leaders had underrated Hitler's threat before World War II. Hitler himself was surprised when the British in 1939 honoured their commitment to go to war if Germany attacked Poland. Following World War II, the United States was surprised by the outbreak of several severe crises precipitated by the Soviet Union (over Berlin in 1948, 1958–59, 1961, and over the Cuban missiles in 1962). It was also surprised by the Arab oil embargo in 1973, by the landing of Turkish troops on Cyprus in 1974, by the Soviet-Cuban intervention in the Angolan civil war in 1975, and by the Soviet-Cuban intervention in the Ethiopian-Somalian conflict in 1978. While we know little about recent Soviet intelligence errors, it is plausible that the Soviet government was surprised by the strong American reaction to the emplacement of nuclear missiles on Cuba in 1962. Gross underestimates of the opponent's strength have also occurred often. Thus, the Soviet Union was surprised by the staunch Finnish resistance in the Winter War of 1939–40, the French were surprised by the mode of the German attack in 1940, the United States government erred repeatedly in underestimating the strength of North Vietnam when it had intervened in support of the Saigon regime, and the Indians grossly underrated Chinese military strength in the Himalayas before 1962. Although European governments were alert to the possibility of war in 1914, they had been advised by experts that, as a result of advanced international economic interdependence, a war between industrial nations could not be sustained for more than a few weeks or months, and therefore acted with extremely unrealistic expectations about the requirements and destructiveness of war.

The surprise experienced by Israel in 1973 was evidently not exceptional. How can we account for it and many other cases? Which factors make threat-perception apparently so difficult a task? Although the available empirical and analytical literature is quite small, and much of it of very recent origin, published only after 1973,* there is now enough of a theory of intelligence to enlighten us about the inherent impediments to the making of good estimates.

If an estimate is made at all, it is either lack of information or its misinterpretation that must account for faulty threat-perception. Intelligence officers often do attribute failure to lack of information. A lag between foreign events and the supply of relevant information can be a serious handicap even in this age of rapid communications. It is also trivially true that foreign governments do not supply all the information that intelligence officers like to have. Indeed, they often try to maintain secrecy and to issue disinformation. But then, threat-perception is a matter of 'estimates' that would not be needed if all the pertinent information were unambiguously on hand. One estimates when one does not know. For this purpose one needs only enough information that, if correctly interpreted, permits a good estimate to be made.

Misperception and surprise do not usually result from lack of relevant information. It was all there to be used in the Israeli case and, in fact, a subordinate Israeli intelligence officer put it together correctly and predicted an impending Arab attack on Oct. 1 and again on Oct. 3. But his superiors rejected his estimate and, as late as Oct. 5, held that the chance of an Arab attack was of 'low probability' or 'even lower than low'.

In every case one studies, it is easy to see in retrospect that the relevant information for making a correct estimate was available. But as Roberta Wohlstetter[2] put it, these 'facts'—which she calls 'signals'—are embedded in a great deal of 'noise', that is, material irrelevant to a correct estimate. Moreover, as Barton Whaley has emphasized,[3] there is often also 'disinformation', that is, misleading information introduced by the opponent for purposes of deception. The Egyptians resorted to this in 1973, for example by spreading rumours about the unreadiness of their forces. Hitler used deception in 1941 in order to confuse the Soviets. The problem of separating the correct information from the rest—which is so easy in retrospect, with the benefit of hindsight—is inherent in the fundamental ambiguity of the total information that is being received. 'Facts' do not speak for themselves. All that can be derived from ambiguous information are inferences, and no one inference can ever be compelling because any ambiguous behaviour can be explained by more than one motivational pattern. The Israeli and American intelligence services were, of course, aware before Oct. 6, 1973 of the massive deployment of Egyptian and Syrian troops. But both decided that the deployments indicated no more than elaborate military manoeuvres.

*See the Appendix for a selective listing of the literature.

That inference did fit the 'facts'. The Arab countries had staged such manoeuvres before and touched off an Israeli reaction that, in retrospect, was deemed unnecessary because no attack ensued. As Hitler amassed German troops on the Soviet boundary in 1941, five different hypotheses were entertained by knowledgeable European officials, and Stalin's conclusion that the Germans would not attack fitted the information as well as any other inference.[4] After all, a military threat can be a bluff and military movements that look menacing can be preparatory to making demands rather than starting hostilities.

The provision of correct estimates in such situations is complicated further by the possibility that the 'opponent' is undecided on subsequent steps while making threatening moves. He may be acting on the basis of multiple options and proceed to attack only in certain contingencies, such as that the other side fails to take proper counter-measures. Thus, when the Japanese fleet was steaming toward Hawaii in 1941, its admiral was under contingency orders to attack only if the U.S. fleet was at anchor in Pearl Harbor and if he could achieve surprise.[5] The fact that the opponent's intentions are unsettled or contingent must be taken into account by intelligence officers but does not preclude an estimate that issues appropriate warning. The intentions of foreign actors are necessarily estimated in terms of probabilities. Yet the ambiguity of observed behaviour constitutes a profound problem inherent in threat-perception.

In drawing inferences from available information that is usually fragmentary and ambiguous, intelligence officers use certain assumptions about the behavioural pattern of the potential enemy. These assumptions or preconceptions guide them in distinguishing between signals and noise and in arriving at a conclusion. Intelligence bureaucracies formulate these assumptions, usually with care, on the basis of his past behaviour; and individual leaders are similarly guided by preconceptions or images about what the potential opponent 'is like'.* Stalin's error in 1941 resulted from the observation that, in most past cases, Hitler's aggression was preceded by a period of intense crisis during which he made inordinate demands. This had not happened in 1941 and it was therefore assumed that no real threat of war existed. Stalin also assumed that the warnings about an imminent German attack he received from the governments of Britain and the United States were faked because he believed that these governments were trying to bring about war between Germany and the Soviet Union. The chief assumption of the Israelis in 1973 was that Arab

---

*A classic example of the sophisticated development of underlying assumptions—indeed two alternative hypotheses regarding the German threat to the United Kingdom are carefully delineated—is Sir Eyre Crowe's 'Memorandum on the Present State of British Relations with France and Germany' of Jan. 1, 1907. This essay in threat-perception is very much worth re-reading both for its analytical perspicacity and the presence of some preconceptions that come easily to the representative of a premier power and are questionable in retrospect. There is also the larger but surely unanswerable question of whether this influential document, by affecting British policy, contributed to the outbreak of World War I. See Kenneth Bourne, *The Foreign Policy of Victorian England, 1830-1902* (Oxford, Clarendon Press, 1970), pp. 481-493.

leaders, because they knew that their forces were inferior to those of Israel, would not go to war, unless they expected Israel to launch a strike; and since Israel was maintaining only very small forces on its perimeter, the Arab governments were given no cause for fearing a surprise attack by Israel. A subsidiary Israeli assumption, based on past experience, was that the Arab countries were incapable of planning a joint attack without these plans leaking to Israeli intelligence. In 1941, American leaders did not believe that the Japanese would commence war against the United States because they assumed that their Japanese counterparts must have known that the United States had a military potential vastly superior to that of Japan. On the other hand, Japanese leaders decided to attack the United States because they assumed that a war in the Pacific with the United States was sooner or later inevitable and preferred to fight at a time and under circumstances of their own choosing. In 1962, the CIA disbelieved, despite much evidence to the contrary, that the Soviets were installing nuclear missiles in Cuba because past Soviet military behaviour had been doctrinally disinclined toward embarking on adventurist courses of action and because it was assumed that Soviet leaders would regard any missile deployment threatening targets in the United States as an adventurist move. United States intelligence was surprised by the Turkish military intervention in the civil strife in Cyprus because the Turks had threatened to do so, and assembled forces in nearby ports, on the occasion of previous crises over Cyprus, but had never executed the threat. It was therefore assumed that the Turks were bluffing once again.

It is inevitable that conceptions or assumptions structure international threat-perception because all human perception can approach reality only selectively. They are indispensable to defining situations. It must also be understood that the assumptions that guide expectations are usually not stupid. They are often carefully reasoned. What is clearly wrong, however, in view of the many times that they have led perception astray, is the degree of trust they commonly command. The simple fact is that human actors can produce unexpected behaviour for any number of reasons. Hitler wanted to achieve strategic surprise by means of deception and hence broke the behavioural pattern he had preferred in the past. The Japanese leaders thought that they had no choice because they assumed that war with the United States was inevitable and that they had a better chance to win then than later. The Arab leaders resorted to war mainly in order to set the diplomatic world in motion, and especially to induce the great powers to exert themselves, toward breaking the impasse vis-à-vis Israel. For that purpose they did not need to win the war they started; a reasonably good military showing would suffice. In Turkey, competitive domestic politics in 1974 made it difficult for the government not to act with great determination in solving the Cyprus problem. In short, actors frequently choose or are compelled to do the unexpected.

On the one hand, an actor may want to benefit from surprising an opponent and, in order to deceive, break with well-established practices. Indeed, he may save this capacity for causing surprise until the stakes of conflict are high. This is one reason why confidence in one's ability to predict some foreign government's behaviour, built up while the stakes of conflict were low, may mislead us when conflicts over high stakes arise.[6] On the other hand, a foreign actor may be induced or compelled by any number of things to do the unexpected. Government objectives may be altered as a result of new domestic pressure, changes in relative capabilities, the individual influence of personalities, failures of intelligence, deviations from rationality, and other variable conditions. In the life of governments as elsewhere, things happen by accident as well as design. It is even riskier to base prediction not on the careful study of a particular actor's past behaviour but on general 'lessons of history' that tie the behaviour of kinds of actors to kinds of stimuli, the lesson, for example, that appeasement encourages aggression. There are no easy and reliable lessons to be learned from history.*

Although the future, within some framework of particulars, can be *estimated,* it cannot, of course, be *known.* To estimate is to guess in order to reduce uncertainty dictated by lack of knowledge. The assumptions and preconceptions about reality that structure the guesswork can be more or less rigorously deduced from past behaviour. But—as the historical record discloses and for the reasons we mentioned—even the most sophisticated assumptions can lead threat-perception astray. To depend wholly on any one preconception or set of assumptions is to court surprise. This risk is magnified by the tendency that the selection of an assumption about the real world becomes an act of cognitive closure that easily leads the perceiver to be close-minded and to ignore or explain away discrepant information. It must therefore be accepted that although good estimates can reduce uncertainty about the future, even the best cannot be depended on to remove it.

The inherently difficult problems of international threat-perception we have so far discussed are not the only obstacles to the formulation of realistic estimates. There is an entire further dimension of factors that tend to cause mistakes. It is apparent from many historical instances that the perceiver, far from being unbiased, often approaches his task under the influence, usually unwittingly, of *predispositions* that affect his choice of assumptions and his receptivity to incoming information, and thus are apt to distort his estimates. Several kinds of intervening predispositions have been observed to operate.

*The temptation is to conclude from some memorable past experience that X will follow if A or A and B happen, e.g. that aggression will be encouraged by appeasement. But close inspection is apt to reveal that the earlier causal pattern was complicated by the operation of other variable conditions and, therefore, that the accepted lesson is a simplification likely to cause erroneous expectations when projected into the future. It is the very complexity of unfolding events that, after all, accounts for the conflicting explanations of historians and the endless rewriting of history. For an interesting study of the problem, see Ernest R. May, *'Lessons' of the Past, The Use and Misuse of History in American Foreign Policy* (New York, Oxford University Press, 1973).

First, emotions can condition the act of threat-perception. For instance, it is easy to overestimate potential threats from an actor who is hated. Racial animosity expressed in such slogans as 'The Yellow Peril' were a factor in American threat-perceptions vis-à-vis Japan after the Russo-Japanese War. Complacency and basic anxiety are attitudes that can impinge on threat-perception. Complacency was a factor in Israel following her brilliant victory over the Arabs in 1967. It tends to encourage underestimates of external threats. Anxiety tends to do the opposite.

Second, misperceptions can be generated by strong ideological commitments when rigid general beliefs about the nature of the outside world govern the selection of guiding assumptions. These are then based less, or not at all, on objective empirical analysis than automatically deduced from prior beliefs. An adherent to Leninist ideology will readily assume that capitalist countries constitute the mortal enemy of communist societies. When the Cold War posture had become rigid in the United States, it was not hard for Americans to overestimate the threat emanating from monolithic world communism even after Yugoslavia and Albania had separated themselves from Moscow's tutelage and control and the Soviet-Chinese split had deepened.

Third, bureaucratic behaviour, including bureaucratic politics, in intelligence agencies, foreign offices, and among the military, can act as a distorting predisposition. In addition to the factor to be taken up shortly, it tends to be functional in such organizations to protect assumptions once they have been accepted. Powerful incentives induce individual members to conform and not to challenge such guiding preconceptions. Bureaucratic inertia thus perpetuates expectations about foreign actors that fitted the real world earlier on but have ceased to do so because of relevant changes in the environment.

Fourth, there is wishfulness, which historical study suggests to be the predisposition most frequently at work. Psychologists tell us that to predict what one wants to happen is an insistent human tendency. On the one hand, people who wish to cut defence expenditure because they want to reduce taxes or increase welfare outlays come easily to the belief that external threats are low even when these estimates are not based on any qualifications for engaging in threat-perception. On the other hand, people who profit one way or another from rising defence spending, including the military, tend to overestimate foreign threats. I am not speaking here of the deliberate misrepresentation of threats but of sub-conscious leanings. The British appeasers of Germany in the 1930s inclined toward underestimating the Hitler menace in part because they found the prospect of a major war abominable. They wanted peace. In disbelieving all intelligence information foretelling a German attack, and there was plenty of it, Stalin may have been influenced by his recognition that the Soviet Union needed time for strengthening its armed forces, greatly weakened by the preceding purge of the officer corps, before taking on the German army. Of particular importance is that leaders and foreign-policy officials tend to like intelligence estimates that permit them to pursue favourite policies. Once a particular foreign policy is found desirable on other grounds, it becomes painful to accept evidence of foreign threats in conflict with that policy. It is then more rewarding to ignore unwelcome signals or to interpret them in ways that allow them to be assimilated to governing assumptions.* This predilection is so ubiquitous according to historical experience that it has led to the belief that intelligence production must be separated from the formulation of policy.

Two reasons account for the frequency with which these intervening dispositions operate, and for the remarkable staying-power they display. One results from the purely intellectual problems of threat-perception, in particular the fact that relevant information is usually ambiguous and hence susceptible to multiple explanations. No one inference can be proved in advance to be correct. The implied choice of interpretation gives intervening predispositions great ease of entry. The other reason is precisely that the actor is unaware of their intervention.

Foreign threats can obviously also be misrepresented deliberately. Historical cases are not rare in which a ruler or ruling group tried to bolster waning domestic authority by diverting public attention to external threats and profiting from the sense of solidarity that is often triggered in the face of a foreign menace. More generally, individuals and groups that expect to gain from national response to a threatening environment may assert the presence of such threats not as a result of sub-conscious urges but as a deliberate act of exaggeration. For the same sort of reason, threat-perception can be manipulated also in the opposite direction. In this area, however, we are in the realm of supposition because firm evidence of deliberate misrepresentation is naturally hard to find. But few will deny the plausibility of the hypothesis.

In addition to these *structural* problems of international threat-perception, there can also be *situational* conditions that may aggravate the difficulty of the operation. As is generally observed in the literature, this aggravation tends to occur at times of profound and fast-moving international crises when time-constraints and stress can reduce analytical effort and distort perceptions. Yet it needs to be asked whether crises cannot also produce positive effects by facilitating the correction of preceding perceptions. To the extent that a serious international crisis comes as a surprise or moves in surprising ways, it discredits intelligence estimates previously made and casts doubt on the conceptual assumptions on which these estimates were premised. At the same time, the conduct of other governments in the crisis supplies new information about their possible intentions. As a result, crises offer an opportunity for learning

*This tendency is reinforced where governments are hemmed in by inflexible public preferences.

and this is an advantage even if the learning may have to be done very quickly. Indeed, the need for speed often means that top leaders rather than intelligence bureaucracies will do the learning in the first place. Whether the harmful or helpful effects of crisis prevail is evidently an empirical question.

Estimates of the capabilities of states are an integral part of international threat-perception. Whenever the existing peaceful conduct of countries cannot be regarded as permanent, the estimate of potential military threats rests largely on the estimate of capabilities. When a state is regarded as presenting an actual threat, capability-estimates attempt to assess the precise dimensions of the threat.

One sometimes hears it said that—because it is difficult to estimate the intentions of foreign governments, and risky to rely on such estimates— prudence is served best by an estimate of capabilities and the assumption that foreign actors are apt to do to us the worst they are capable of doing. Critics of this prescription point out that worst-case assumptions automatically overestimate external threats and that action based on them provokes foreign insecurity, arms races and confrontations, and thus ends up by making the world more threatening and dangerous.

It may well be that military services (but not necessarily military intelligence) routinely design contingency war-plans on the basis of worst-case assumptions; and, in the light of our preceding analysis, such practice is not necessarily unsound. However, this analysis and the historical case studies on which it rests also suggest that the prescription is not widely followed in national intelligence efforts. We are unable to say whether underestimates of threats have been more or less common than overestimates. But the large number of recorded cases of strategic surprise indicates that worst-case assumptions were often unimaginative or not considered seriously enough. In some instances, e.g. Stalin's in 1941, best-case assumptions seem to have prevailed. To *consider* worst outcomes, or for that matter best ones, is not of course the same as fashioning policy solely on estimates based on either extreme assumption.

To think that foreign capabilities are estimated easily is an illusion, and the claim that capability-estimates are substantially more reliable than estimates of foreign intentions is highly debatable. To be sure, there are items in capability-analysis that can be directly observed, and counted or measured within narrow limits, such as changes in defence budgets, number of armoured divisions, fighter aircraft, and certain weapons characteristics. However, while these sorts of things are important, they represent only a fraction of overall capabilities. Capability-estimates are ultimately needed in order to decide what, if anything, can and should be done in order to deter external threats when the need for deterrence cannot be ruled out, and to defend if deterrence was needed but failed. In the final analysis, therefore, capability-estimates refer to the test of war, which is the only true test of capabilities.

As the history of warfare demonstrates abundantly, the outcome of war depends not only on quantitative things known beforehand but on a host of qualitative factors, such as troop-training and morale, military leadership, strategy and tactics, military intelligence and communications, the performance of arms under wartime conditions, the behaviour of allies, the ability of belligerent governments and publics to absorb casualties, and so forth. And these qualitative things are difficult to estimate. Moreover, all the elements that determine the military capability of a potential opponent in wartime are significant only relative to the capabilities of one's own side. The implied requirement to estimate one's own capabilities comparatively, including the many qualitative components, opens another dimension on which realistic appraisal is hard to achieve. Is there not a strong inclination, reflecting fairly obvious reasons, to overestimate the capabilities of one's own side, and especially the qualitative aspects for which evidence is ambiguous?*

We conclude, then, that—taking the entire range of ingredients into account—the estimate of military and related capabilities is necessarily based on information that, as a whole, is fragmentary, obsolescent and, above all, ambiguous. The properties of this information are not very different from those that are relevant to the estimate of foreign intentions, and the problems of threat-perception discussed in the preceding analysis apply also to capability-estimates. Again, how the information is interpreted depends crucially on assumptions and preconceptions, as is made clear by the following four examples of mistaken capability-estimates.

The concept of the famous French Maginot Line of fortification (including the missing link to the sea in the north-west) originated in strategic studies undertaken in the early 1920s. The concept—on which French planning for deterring and defeating German aggression came to rest increasingly—assumed that military technology continued to favour the defence over the offence, as it had during World War I. This assumption was not revised when improved tanks and aircraft, and tactical innovations that capitalized on these improvements, made it obsolete in the 1930s. German capabilities were grossly underrated as a result. In 1940, the Germans achieved surprise and, though using fewer troops and tanks than the French, quickly crushed resistance by making an end-run around the Line.[7] Even though some French officers (including Charles de Gaulle) had themselves been thinking about the Blitzkrieg tactics developed by the German army, and even though these tactics had been used against Poland in 1939, the official French strategy

---

*Military planners not rarely overestimate certain components of foreign forces (e.g. numbers of men, numbers and types of arms) in order to appeal for more funds from their governments. They are less likely to say that their troops suffer from bad training and morale, and that their leadership, strategy and tactics are inept.

could be defended on the grounds that the superiority of Blitzkrieg against staunch defences was doubtful or improbable. New information was ambiguous enough in its implications to protect old assumptions that led to defective estimates of foreign capability.

During World War II, the Americans and the British adopted strategies of air bombardment that were based on serious overestimates of German vulnerability.[8] The American bombing offensive, which emphasized precision-bombing of key capital structures in the war economy, was prompted by the mistaken assumption that the German economy was stretched to capacity. That Germany's productive capacity should be overtaxed after several years of destructive warfare was no doubt a reasonable hypothesis. But it turned out that the German economy had actually plenty of slack. The British air offensive against German cities was guided by, among other factors, mistaken expectations about the brittleness of German civilian morale. This underestimate of German capability, in turn, was derived from assumptions, later shown to be unrealistic, about what German bombers would do to British civilian morale. And this overestimate was derived by British planners from dubiously selected information relating civilian casualties to the weight of bombs dropped on London by German zeppelins in World War I. These estimates, incidentally, affected the behaviour of the British government toward Germany during the late 1930s.[9]

The Soviet economy and Soviet defence spending have been important subjects of American estimates. In 1976, the CIA suddenly revised its previous estimates for 1970–1975 that apparently had underestimated the Soviet defence budget by half and the growth of that budget by about two-thirds. The underestimates had resulted from assumptions about the content and structure of the Soviet defence budget and the proper pricing of Soviet efforts that were suddenly recognized as incorrect.[10] It was not new information but a conceptual challenge that caused a long-employed assumption to be reviewed. As Albert Wohlstetter has demonstrated in a number of studies, American intelligence consistently overestimated Soviet deployment of inter-continental bombers and ICBMs from the 1950s to 1961, only to underestimate Soviet ICBM deployment after 1961 with equal consistence. The faulty estimates in both periods ultimately rested on the expectation that Soviet strategic thinking was like American strategic thought.[11] Assumptions that reflect such mirror-imaging are a frequent source of misperception.

Subconscious predispositions intervene in the choice and use of guiding assumptions as readily in estimates of capabilities as they do in the perception of foreign intentions. To refer to the examples of capability-estimates just presented, the change in American estimates of Soviet strategic nuclear forces suggests the familiar learning process that overreacts to past error. It has also been intimated that the later *under*estimates resulted in part from an institutional desire to live down a reputation for producing *over*estimates.[12] The data from which British overestimates of air bombardment were derived would not have remained unchallenged for as long as they did if they had not been kept highly classified.

Wishfulness, which is probably the chief culprit in distorting international threat-perception, was evidently at work in producing and protecting the estimates of the German threat that justified the Maginot idea of deterrence and defence. In the future, the French wanted to avoid the frightful losses of manpower suffered in World War I. They hoped that, unable to break through the defences of its opponent, Germany would be beaten through economic strangulation.[13] This hope to win without a long grinding war on land also inspired American and British planners whose estimates exaggerated Germany's vulnerability to attack from the air.

We are now ready to turn to the question of how statecraft dealing with international threat-perception should be organized and guided in order to cope with the problems described in the foregoing.

Lack of public information makes it impossible to discuss the ways in which intelligence agencies have upgraded their capabilities in recent decades. Even the large amount of detail that has been published in the United States is fragmentary from this point of view. Nor is the extent to which these changes in the American system are representative of world-wide developments a matter of public record. Yet the question with reference to the United States may be instructive. Following World War II, the United States vastly expanded intelligence personnel and budgets, a development which—as in other parts of government—was accompanied by progressive bureaucratization. Personnel serving the estimating function became professionalised and were gradually more than before recruited from persons with training in the social sciences. Over time, social science knowledge was tapped to a growing extent. The period also witnessed a spectacular improvement in technologies (e.g. intelligence satellites, electronic eavesdropping, computers) that were relevant to the acquisition and processing of information. Finally, these services experimented frequently with institutional innovations where estimative deficiencies were recognized.

The average estimative product improved greatly as a joint result of these developments. The intelligence effort clearly benefited from the progress of certain lines of study (e.g. economics, Soviet and other area studies) made at the institutions of higher learning. Over time, there was probably a respectable learning curve. Yet the frequent experience of surprise on the part of the United States casts doubt on any substantial improvement in the intelligence product of concern in this paper. If this is true, some of the identified changes (e.g. more numerous personnel, bureaucratization) may have entailed counter-productive as well as beneficial effects. This seems to have happened, for example, with the resort to sophisticated technologies. They permitted a vast multiplication in the procurement, processing and storing of data. However, the kinds of data susceptible to this process do not touch other kinds that are highly germane to estimating the capabilities and intentions of foreign actors. Moreover, the very mass of data tends to swamp, especially in fast-moving crises, the top echelon at which intelligence judgements are made, and the processing of data is necessarily reduced in quality by the need to rely on large numbers of lower-grade operators and on a programming of computers by standard and necessarily reductionist instructions. Such mechanical procedure prevents the leap of intuitive perception that permits a sophisticated mind to discover significant patterns in raw information. Indeed, there may well be a danger that such human capabilities become less cultivated and may atrophy from disuse, when reliance on technological devices is in the ascendancy.

But if warning of strategic surprise has seen little, if any, improvement, the primary reason resides probably in the intrinsic difficulties of threat-perception we have described, in a lagging appreciation of these difficulties and, hence, in attempts to cope with them. The full severity of the problems has not been realized until quite recently. The analytical literature is mostly new; and the conclusions it suggest have only begun to be heeded by intelligence services.

We have been at pains to demonstrate that bad intelligence performance—one is almost inclined to say unlucky intelligence performance—does not usually result from stupidity or lack of effort. Indeed, it seems facile to blame intelligence services for having done a poor job of prediction in particular cases. They probably did the best they could in want of a trustworthy crystal ball. Nor do the intrinsic difficulties encourage hopes of radical improvement. What can be expected at best is a moderate improvement of average performance. Relevant statecraft, therefore, concerns not only the production of intelligence but also the question of what can be prudently expected from it, the matter of intelligence consumption and, ultimately, adaptation to the fact that the intelligence product can never rise securely above suspicion.

Two conclusions that are sometimes drawn from the recognition that the obstacles to perfect threat-perception are insuperable, should be firmly rejected. First, to eliminate or seriously downgrade formal intelligence efforts could make matters only worse, for no policies can be designed without some sort of assumptions about the future. To do away with professional intelligence officers would be to replace them by amateurs who are up against the same problems with less awareness and aptitude. Second, it would be wrong to conclude that, predicting the intentions of foreign actors being a hopeless task, one had better focus entirely on estimating their capabilities and assume that their intentions will be the worst imaginable. To imagine the worst is by no means easy and surprises could not be avoided if one tried. As demonstrated above, to estimate capabilities is not very much easier than estimating intentions. And to act on worst-case assumptions about foreign intentions might well increase rather than reduce national insecurity.

Coping with the problem of surprise must be instructed by a proper theory of threat-perception and intelligence which, derived from experience, identifies and clarifies the components of the problem. Two lines of remedial effort suggest themselves. One is to broaden and deepen existing theory, the other is to exploit fully the appreciable body of theory already developed.

Among approaches to enlarging theory on our subject, the following questions seem to merit research: (1) Which characteristics of foreign actors provide them with a motive for developing a strategy of surprise? For example, an actor who can win only in a short conflict has a special interest in gaining a quick decision. (2) Which of our characteristics give foreign actors an opportunity and incentive to plan on surprise? For instance, low level of mobilization, unbalanced force structures and cumbersome decision-making in an alliance may do so. (3) What can a foreign actor do to build up a capacity for springing surprise? For example, developing forces capable of quick action without tell-tale mobilization, tiring us out by repeated mobilization and deployment moves, fostering effective secrecy in government councils, presenting us with a behaviour profile that reduces our watchfulness may be things that foster the requisite capacity. (4) How is a foreign actor apt to utilize his capacity for surprise? Will he husband and conceal it carefully until the stakes of conflict are sufficiently high?

In the meantime, already existing theory suggests approaches that have not been sufficiently utilized in upgrading intelligence production and consumption.

Measures to ensure the improvement of intelligence production can be institutional and doctrinal. Institutional remedies are essentially a matter of practices which, if adopted, will entail certain administrative requirements. The key problem in threat-perception is clearly the quality of the assumptions that are brought to the information and guide the selective perceptions of intelligence officers. Several remedial practices seem worth emphasizing. (1) It is obviously important that these assumptions be made explicit and that they be continuously reviewed in the light of the new information. The danger is that, if these things are done, they will be done routinely and without keen alertness to the likely obsolescence of all preconceptions.

(2) As a further check on the fitness of preconceptions, it would seem useful that an explicit attempt be made to identify and evaluate various motivational patterns that could explain the observed behaviour of foreign actors, and various assumptions that, when applied to information about foreign capabilities, would produce different

estimative conclusions. Because no estimate can do more than reduce uncertainty and every estimate can be wrong and, if believed in, cause subsequent surprise, it would seem sound practise to present every probabilistic estimate on matters of great consequence within the framework of accompanying worst-case and best-case interpretation of the same information. Again, the danger is that the two limiting interpretations would be made unappealing and turned into caricatures.

(3) To achieve something of the same purpose, it has also been suggested that intelligence services should practise multiple advocacy or appoint a devil's advocate within their organizations. But it is doubtful that such a person or group can be given enough autonomy of operation, and bureaucratic incentives and influence, to do the job effectively.* The danger is that this advocacy will become routinized and ineffective.

(4) Another approach to this problem—and one already practised—is not to set up one bureaucracy that enjoys a monopoly of intelligence production. A degree of competition is some safeguard against the hardening of assumptions. One drawback of this particular solution is that the desire of separate bureaucracies for what economists call product-differentiation—a normal organizational proclivity—encourages dissenting estimates for the wrong reasons. Dissent for the wrong reason can also result when different intelligence groups have different institutional customers with competing vested interests. A third danger is that the different groups seek to limit competition by negotiating informally about the degree and nature of estimative disagreement. Remedies (2), (3) and (4) mean that the consumer will not receive a single clear-cut estimate. In principle, this result is to be welcomed because the consumer should understand the limited reliability of all estimates, and should not be allowed to escape facing up to uncertainty. Indeed, he should recognize that firm prediction is not only the most risky but also the least important function of intelligence.[14] There is the danger, however, that the supply of alternative estimates will let the consumer follow his predispositions and simply pick the one he likes best because it permits him to do what he wants to do anyhow.

(5) To evaluate intelligence predictions after the event is critical to organizational learning. But to make sure that post-mortems are done thoroughly and without prejudice, they must be undertaken by an independent group, as has been the case in the CIA since 1972, and making estimating staffs react to the reviews in detail would be necessary in order to assure that feed-back generates learning. The review process should include estimates that turn out to have been correct because they

---

*According to newspaper reports, the Director of Central Intelligence experimented recently with appointing an outside team for estimating Soviet intentions as a check on its own 'in-house' estimate. The outside team was rumoured to have been one of 'hard-liners' and in any case came to the conclusion that the Soviet threat to the United States was greater than the one presented by the regular CIA team. The value of this practice would seem to depend on who picks the teams, on which criteria of selection. For a description of this experiment, see Lee, op. cit., Appendix B.

may have done so for the wrong reasons, and therefore have just been lucky.

(6) Intelligence services sometimes become reluctant to alert governments to disruptive events they think might occur because the same warnings have been expressed repeatedly before when nothing of the kind ensued. Intelligence officers may be afraid of being blamed when their government leaders react to warnings in costly ways (e.g. a partial mobilization of military forces) and then nothing happens. They may fear that the value of warnings will depreciate when they seem repeatedly to have been unpredictive of actual events: and they may be afraid that policy-makers will overreact to a particular warning. The 'cry-wolf' syndrome is obviously dangerous when the events in question are of grave consequence, and intelligence officials should not be deterred from reissuing such warnings with a considered indication of probabilities. If the warning problem is properly understood, intelligence consumers in the government will accept the necessity of repeated estimates that, expressed in probability terms, warn of events that do not later take place (possibly because of a state of alertness produced by the warning).

(7) Because the behaviour of other countries commonly depends on the policies pursued by one's own government, it seems advisable that intelligence estimates take such policies into account. This is especially important because foreign governments may operate on the basis of multiple options, effecting surprise being only one of them, and the ultimate choice may depend on one's own policy behaviour. Such co-operation may not be easy to arrange and even be frowned upon when the policies are still secret and the intelligence service is institutionally separated from policy-making. But this objection would be less weighty if intelligence producers were occasionally requested to respond to sets of different scenarios involving a series of 'if . . . then' propositions.

(8) As already mentioned, reliance on new technologies for processing information has serious problems. Perhaps it is possible to reduce the extent to which specialization developed, for dealing with the flood of information impedes the reintegration of inputs at the top of the estimating effort. It seems also advisable not to depend on computers for complex judgmental tasks. Given the difficulties of using ambiguous information in matters of threat-perception, computers are useless for the larger analytical tasks. How do we programme them for the simulated enactment of real-life sequences? How do we programme computers for processing ambiguous information? To hope for the discovery of indicators that remove ambiguity seems extremely far-fetched at this stage of knowledge. No doubt, computers are and will be useful in accomplishing clear-cut subsidiary functions. But the central problems in international threat-perception are not susceptible to technological solutions.

Evidently, none of the remedial practices we have listed is without problems of its own. It is possible that some will be counterproductive in the real bureaucratic world. At this point, therefore, the question is one of experimenting with various remedial procedures in order to discover their cost-effectiveness.

Yet, in any case, the introduction of such practices that promise improvement is unlikely to yield good results, and might not even take place, in the absence of proper professional doctrines among intelligence producers and consumers alike. Professional self-indoctrination among producers would encompass a sense of responsibilities that is realistic in terms of all the grave difficulties that beset international threat-perception. The preceding discussion of practices indicates the specific issues which doctrine should engage. However, there is, in my opinion, one pre-condition that must be met squarely before sound doctrine can develop. This is a full understanding of the historical record of statecraft concerned with international threat-perception—a record that now exists only in fragments and demands more analysis as well as completion. Only historical knowledge and analytical penetration can give intelligence officers a realistic conception of the daunting difficulties they must professionally face, the pitfalls to be avoided as much as possible, and the approaches to be cultivated.

If knowledge about the problems of intelligence production has only begun to develop, even more needs to be done about understanding the problems of intelligence consumption and of bridging the gap between output and consumption by means of proper recognition and guidance.

For reasons we have spelled out, trouble is inevitable if the main production of intelligence is closely integrated with the design of foreign policy. The temptation to tailor intelligence estimates to the desires of the policymaker is then exceedingly hard to resist. Separation, however, also creates problems. One is that intelligence production may not be properly directed toward the issues that are important to policy-making. The intelligence people therefore need guidance to make their work sensitive to consumption needs. This does not mean that intelligence should be dominated by policy. All that is needed is sufficient co-ordination. Even if this separation of functions is adopted, the policy-maker and especially top leaders should not rely exclusively on the output of the main intelligence organ because, as we have shown, even the most carefully made estimates can turn out to be seriously misleading. Consumers, therefore, should also have access to smaller intelligence units in the government structure as a check on the dangers of intelligence monopoly. In the United States, for instance, intelligence groups in the Department of State and Defense Department, and—closer to the White House—attached to the National Security Council, are available in addition to the CIA. Such pluralism also entails drawbacks. If conflicting estimates are produced, consumers have a choice and may well pick the one that fits their own predispositions. Yet the disadvantage of relying on one single source seems to be even greater. In addition, top consumers should insist on estimates (concerning questions of great consequence) in which the one favoured by the producer is bracketed by competing interpretations of the available information that are rejected. If it is objected that this would overburden the consumer, the answer surely is that to accept any lesser burden—a short and single and supposedly reliable estimate—is to have surrendered to illusion.

Such practices will not be instituted unless intelligence *consumers* are properly indoctrinated in the uses of estimates. Consumers also require considerable education in the problems that are inherent in international threat-perception. Once they have internalized this knowledge, they will be less likely to substitute their own estimates, for intelligence products that frustrate their expectations, will tolerate the fact that no one estimate is sure to be correct, will accept intelligence warnings for what they are, and will appreciate and yet not abuse the presentation of diverging products. In the light of past performance and of analysis, there can be no excusable expectations of perfect intelligence and no justification for expecting the resolution of uncertainty about the future.

It is perhaps unfortunate that, in the improvement of intelligence, we must place so great a burden on the consumer, on his ability to formulate and guide intelligence tasks and to make proper use of the results. Certainly, top decision-makers usually reach their positions on the basis of talents and careers that leave them disinclined to give priority to a true understanding of these problems. Even the more numerous bureaucratic consumers, especially in foreign and military services, may prefer to remain unfettered by the constraints of such understanding. But without challenging this preference, statecraft in this area is incapable of more than marginal improvement.

The acceptance of unavoidable uncertainty greatly complicates the conduct of foreign policy, but need not paralyse it. If we understand that all forecasts have a substantial chance of proving faulty, we have accepted the real possibility of surprise and we are free to make provision for minimizing its ill consequences. Such provision may be costly in terms of resources, as insurance always is, and even in terms of downgrading or abandoning policy options that look too risky. But to make such provision would seem to be prudent and conducive to national interest in an insecure world.

APPENDIX

SELECTIVE LIST OF LITERATURE
(with Selective Annotations)

Belden, Thomas G., 'Indications, Warnings, and Crisis Operations', *International Studies Quarterly*, XXI, March 1977, pp.181-198.
A thoughtful analysis of the problem of indicators to be used in the warning process.

Betts, Richard K., 'Analysis, War, and Decision: Why Intelligence Failures are Inevitable', *World Politics*, xxxi (Jan. 1979).
A sophisticated examination of the entire range of intelligence problems.

Commission on the Organization of the Government for the Conduct of Foreign Policy, Appendices, Vol. VII, Washington, D.C., Government Printing Office, June 1975.
Several papers of interest on many problems of foreign intelligence, but mainly on organization matters.

George, Alexander L. and Richard Smoke, *Deterrence in American Foreign Policy: Theory and Practice*, New York, Columbia University Press, 1974.
The case studies on deterrence failure are also case studies on inadequate threat-perception. The theoretical part researches especially attitudinal barriers to correct threat-perception.

Handel, Michael I., *Perception, Deception and Surprise: The Case of the Yom Kippur War*, Hebrew University of Jerusalem, Jerusalem Papers on Peace Problems, 1976.
A rich study of the previous literature and a detailed examination of the Israeli intelligence failure in 1973.

Hilsman, Roger, *Strategic Intelligence and National Decisions*, Glencoe, Ill., Free Press, 1956.
A formulation of intelligence doctrines based on interviews with intelligence operators.

Jervis, Robert, *Perception and Misperception in International Politics*, Princeton, Princeton University Press, 1976.
The most systematic analysis of problems of international perception.

Kent, Sherman, *Strategic Intelligence for American World Policy*, Princeton, N.J., Princeton University Press, 1949.
One of the earliest American introductions to the subject, written by an academic historian who subsequently became a high-ranking intelligence officer.

Knorr, Klaus, 'Failures in National Intelligence Estimates: The Case of the Cuban Missiles', *World Politics*, XVI, 1964, pp.455-467.
The influence of preconceptions and assumptions on intelligence production is examined in this case study.

—————, *Foreign Intelligence and the Social Sciences*, Research Monograph No. 17, Center of International Studies, Princeton University, June 1964.
In addition to discussing the relevance of social science knowledge to intelligence work, this paper emphasized the need for a descriptive and normative theory of intelligence.

—————, 'Threat Perception' in Klaus Knorr (ed.), *Historical Dimensions of National Security Problems*, Lawrence, Ka., Kansas University Press, 1976, pp.78-119.
A historical assessment of the record of threat-perception and an analysis of its problems, including predispositional factors.

Lee, William T., *Understanding the Soviet Military Threat* (National Strategy Information Center, Agenda Paper No. 6, New York, 1977).
An examination of faulty C.I.A. estimates on the Soviet defence budget.

Leites, Nathan C., *The Operational Code of the Politburo*, New York, McGraw Hill, 1956.
  A fascinating attempt at identifying systematically the doctrines that govern foreign policy-making in a major country.
Morgenstern, Oskar, Klaus Knorr and Klaus Heiss, *Long-Term Projections of Power: Political, Economic, and Military Forecasting*, Cambridge, Mass., Ballinger, 1973.
  A critique of several techniques of forecasting.
Shlaim, Avi, 'Failures in National Intelligence Estimates: The Case of the Yom Kippur War', *World Politics*, XXVIII, 1976, pp.348-380.
  An excellent case study placed within a conceptual framework and illustrating several key hypotheses. Also good on remedies.
Whaley, Barton, *Codeword Barbarossa*, Cambridge, Mass., MIT Press, 1973.
  A detailed case study of Stalin's failure to foresee the German attack in 1941. It adds to the study of Roberta Wohlstetter by emphasizing the factor of deception.
Wilensky, Harold L., *Organizational Intelligence* (New York, Basic Books, 1967).
  Fine analysis by a sociologist of the intelligence function in all organizations.
Wohlstetter, Roberta, *Pearl Harbor: Warning and Decision*, Stanford, Stanford University Press, 1962.
  The classic case study on strategic surprise.

OTHER WORKS

Axelrod, Robert, 'The Rational Timing of Surprise', paper to be published in *World Politics* in 1979.
Ben-Zvi, Abraham, 'Hindsight and Foresight: A Conceptual Framework for the Analysis of Surprise Attacks', *World Politics*, XXVIII, 1976, pp.381-395.
————, 'Misperceiving the Role of Perception: 'A Critique', *The Jerusalem Journal of International Relations*, II, 1976-77, pp.74-93.
Bittman, Ladislav, *The Deception Game: Czechoslovak Intelligence in Soviet Political Warfare*, Syracuse, N.Y., Syracuse University Research Corp., 1972.
Cooper, Chester, 'The C.I.A. and Decision-Making', *Foreign Affairs*, Vol. 50, Jan. 1972, pp.223-236.
de Sola Pool, Ithiel, 'Content Analysis for Intelligence Purposes', *World Politics*, XII, 1960, pp.478-485.
Dulles, Allen W., *The Craft of Intelligence*, New York, Harper, 1963.
Evans, Allan, 'Intelligence and Policy Formation', *World Politics*, XII, 1959, pp.84-91.
Harris, William R., *Intelligence and National Security: A Bibliography with Selected Annotations*, Cambridge, Mass., Harvard University Press, 1968.
Ransom, Harry H., *Central Intelligence and National Security*, Cambridge, Mass., Harvard University Press, 1958.
————, *The Intelligence Establishment*, Cambridge, Mass., Harvard University Press, 1970.
Schelling, Thomas C., *The Strategy of Conflict*, Cambridge, Mass., Harvard University Press, 1960.
U.S. Congress, House, Select Committee on Intelligence, *Hearings, U.S. Intelligence Agencies and Activities: The Performance of the Intelligence Community*, 94th Cong., 1st sess., 1975.
U.S. Congress, Senate, Select Committee to Study Governmental Operations with Respect to Intelligence Activities, *Final Report*, Book I: *Foreign and Military Intelligence*; Book IV: *Supplementary Detailed Staff Reports on Foreign and Military Intelligence*; 94th Cong., 2nd sess., 1976.
Wohlstetter, Albert, 'Is there a Strategic Arms Race?,' *Foreign Policy*, No. 15, Summer 1974, pp.3-20.
————, 'How to Confuse Ourselves', *Foreign Policy*, No. 20, Fall 1975, pp.170-198.

4

The Post-War Strategy of Limited War: Before, During and After Vietnam

by Robert E. Osgood

The Historical Context

Limited wars are as old as the history of mankind, as ubiquitous as armed conflict. In the history of international conflict the wars that have been truly momentous and rare are those fought to annihilate, to completely defeat or dominate, the adversary. These wars have been the principal stimulus of theories and doctrines of how to limit and fight wars as rational instruments of national policy. In the period since World War II the detailed elaboration of strategies of limited war and the prominent role these have played in international politics and military policies are derived particularly from the fear of nuclear destruction and the exigencies of the Cold War.

One strand of limited-war strategy, inspired by the concepts of Clausewitz and propounded by Western political scientists and defence specialists, sought to make force, in both war and deterrence, an effective instrument of containment against the Soviet Union, China, and the international communist parties aligned with them. The other strand, inspired by Mao Tse-tung and Third-World nationalism and propounded by revolutionary nationalists, sought to use guerrilla warfare to abolish Western colonialism and hegemony and establish new nations ostensibly dedicated to social justice. The first strand of theory looks to the deliberate restraint and measured use of force in order to deter or defeat communist military expansion without running an unacceptable risk of general war. The second strand envisages the use of limited means—the strategy of insurgency—to achieve total political conquest. This essay is concerned primarily with the former and only secondarily with the latter as it became a concern of the former.

The Western post-war theory of limited war raised the question of how to distinguish limited from general or total war, since it was developed specifically as an alternative to a third world war, which, in the nuclear

93

age, was believed to be disastrous to the victor as well as to the vanquished, and as a counter to the Western (and pre-eminently American) concept of war as the use of maximum force to overwhelm the enemy and compel his unconditional surrender. In the generally accepted definition that emerged in the West in the 1950s, a limited war must be limited in both means and ends. It is fought for ends far short of the complete subordination of one state's will to another's, by means which involve far less than the total military resources of the belligerents and which leave the civilian life and the armed forces of the belligerents largely intact. According to a strict application of this definition, limited war is not only a matter of degree but also a matter of national perspective, since a local war that is limited from the standpoint of external participants might be total from the standpoint of the local belligerents, as in the Korean and Vietnam wars. Clearly, the Western definition of limited war, like the theory, reflects not some universal reality but the interests of the Western allies, and especially of the United States, in a particular period of international conflict.

In this period—the Cold War—international conflict has been punctuated by numerous local limited wars. Most of them have been 'internal wars'—dozens of insurrections and rebellions and a number of larger-scale civil wars within the boundaries of a state or between the two parts of a divided state.* The political significance of several of these internal wars, although they arose essentially from indigenous conflict, has been enhanced by material or political support from the Soviet Union, the Peoples Republic of China, or other communist states and by countervailing intervention, directly or indirectly, by the United States or its European allies—most notably, in Greece, 1946-1949; China, 1946-1950; Indochina, 1947-1954; Malaya, 1948-1958; the Philippines, 1949-1955; Korea, 1950-1953; Guatemala, 1954; Algeria, 1954-1962; Cuba, 1957-1959; Lebanon, 1958; the Congo, 1960-1963; Dominican Republic, 1965; and in Vietnam, 1959-1975. Relatively few local wars, discounting a great number of border clashes, were direct armed encounters between states. Those that were included the Suez War of 1956, the Arab-Israeli wars of 1948-49, 1967, and 1973, the India-Pakistan wars of 1965 and 1971, and the India-China border war of 1959-62. Except for the last, these did not originate in a conflict between communist and anti-communist forces, nor did they entail American intervention or a U.S.-Soviet confrontation (although there were competing military assistance and veiled threats of intervention in the 1973 Arab-Israeli war).

Almost all of these two kinds of local wars were limited for reasons that need no special explanation. As in previous periods of international conflict, they were limited by the nature of the political stakes and/or the limited military capacity of the belligerents.

---

*Seymour J. Deitchman lists 12 'conventional' and 16 'unconventional' wars in the period 1945-1962. *Limited War and American Defense Policy* (Cambridge, Mass: M.I.T. Press, 1964), p.27. I would classify at least two in the first category—the Congo and Yemen civil wars—as 'internal'.

Why, then, did limited war become such a lively conceptual and operational concern in the Cold War? First, because of the fear in the United States and among its major democratic allies (in lesser degrees except where they were directly involved) that local wars might become an instrument of communist expansion which could not be contained, since indigenous local resistance would be inadequate and since American intervention would be either ineffective in shoring up weak governments or else entail too big a risk of Soviet or Chinese counter-intervention and nuclear war. Secondly, because of the fear that America's nuclear forces might be an ineffective deterrent, since they would be incapable of preventing local wars in which the major communist powers did not directly participate and since the growth of the Soviet capacity to devastate the United States and its allies would erode the credibility of nuclear intervention or retaliation.

The lesson derived from these twin fears, which dominated strategic thought before the last years of the Vietnam War, was that the military containment of communist expansion, in order to preserve international order against the prospect of a chain of local aggressions leading to World War III, depended on the United States' capacity to help the actual and prospective victims of communist aggression withstand local aggression and to intervene in their interests by effective non-nuclear means that would minimize the risk of Soviet or Chinese counter-intervention. The subsidiary lesson drawn by some strategists was that in order to strengthen deterrence and avoid a catastrophic war if deterrence should fail, it was also necessary to enhance the capacity of the United States to use tactical and even strategic nuclear weapons within tolerable limits of physical and human destruction for limited ends.

All the Western post-war theories of limited war are designed to carry out these lessons. All are derived from the interaction of the Cold War and local conflicts with the fears of nuclear war and the impact of a changing military technology. Looming behind all of them and driving the logic of limitation—within the limits of defence budgets, organizational flexibility, and the bounds of plausibility—has been the steadily growing Soviet capacity to devastate Western Europe and the United States with nuclear blows.

As early as 1949 American defence analysts and statesmen began to develop the outlines of the limited-war strategy that finally came into office with the Kennedy administration. But it was the Korean War that served as the great catalyst of limited-war thinking and touched off the creative surge of strategic concepts, and their accompanying dilemmas and ambiguities, which remain a part of our intellectual baggage on an international voyage that has taken surprising turns.

The great impact of the Korean War on Western strategic imagination springs from the fact that it undermined the preoccupation of strategic thought and plans with general war and challenged the basic premises underlying that preoccupation. The war was a major but local war, which occurred in a politically and strategically peripheral point when strategic concepts and plans were dominated by the vision of another general war starting in Europe and by confidence that nuclear deterrence would prevent such a war. Contrary to the whole American conception of fighting a war to completely defeat the enemy with maximum force, the United States government found itself seeking only a partial victory while deliberately restricting the nature and scope of its intervention in order to avoid a direct armed encounter with the Soviet Union or a protracted war on the mainland of Asia.

The Korean War, therefore, compelled the proponents of containment to cope with a form of warfare—local conventional war by Soviet proxy— that might not be deterred and could not be won by America's central-war capacity. And it did so when the Western allies were just beginning to anticipate the long-run erosion of American nuclear deterrence by the growth of the Soviet Union's capacity to reach the United States with nuclear weapons. The Korean War raised the spectre of a series of local communist proxy aggressions all round the periphery of the Sino-Soviet bloc, and for a moment it raised active fears in the United States and among its European allies that Western Europe might also become the victim of conventional aggression unless the allies greatly strengthened their capacity for local conventional resistance. Although the fear of local proxy wars rapidly diminished and economic stringencies drove the NATO powers to stress nuclear deterrence as a substitute for local resistance and building up conventional forces, the rationale of a Western limited-war strategy persisted. Indeed, thriving on its opposition to the prevailing Eisenhower-Dulles strategy of increased reliance on nuclear deterrence bolstered by military alliances, limited-war strategy entered its great period of intellectual creativity, cultivated in the United States and England by a host of academic analysts, army and navy strategists, civilian military planners, and research organizations.* When President Kennedy came into office, he made the build-up of limited-war capabilities a major part of his foreign policy of restoring American power and prestige around the world and adapting it to the new necessities of containment in a new phase of the Cold War, in which the Third World was regarded as the decisive arena of competition between the Free World and International Communism.

---

*By 1960 the basic themes of limited-war strategy had been expounded by William W. Kaufmann (in 1954 and 1956), Bernard Brodie (1954, 1956, 1959), Basil H. Liddell Hart (1956, 1960), John C. Slessor (1954-58), Anthony Buzzard (1956), Denis Healey (1956), Raymond Aron (1956, 1959) in France, Paul Nitze (1956, 1957, 1958, 1960), Arnold Wolfers (1956), Maxwell D. Taylor (1956, 1959), Robert E. Osgood (1957), Henry A. Kissinger (1957), James E. King, Jr. (1957), Thomas C. Schelling (1957, 1959, 1960), James Gavin (1958), Glenn H. Snyder (1959, 1960), Alastair Buchan (1959, 1960), and Herman Kahn (1960). For a brief bibliographical essay on this period of limited-war writing, see Morton H. Halperin, *Limited War* (Cambridge, Mass.: Harvard Center for International Affairs, 1962).

The Theory and Rationale

At the height of limited-war thinking and planning in the United States during the Kennedy period, the theory of limited war was applied to three kinds of wars: local or theatre wars between states; unconventional or internal war; and strategic or central war, involving the homelands of the United States and the Soviet Union. In each kind of limited war the theory addressed three functions of military strategy: deterrence (the prevention of a military attack and war), denial (the defeat of a military attack), and political support (the support of national policy in situations short of war, ranging from crises to allied relations and the diplomacy of containment). With respect to each kind of limited war a rough consensus developed, though not without significant differences of opinion and emphasis within the United States and between the United States and its European allies that remained unresolved. In each case strategic consensus was accompanied by a good deal of uncertainty, ambiguity, and controversy.

The strategic uncertainties, ambiguities, and controversies were fundamentally the result of the multiple and often conflicting purposes that limited-war strategy was supposed to serve: credible deterrence based on the threat of local war expanding to general nuclear war, but also maximum limitation of war and assured control of escalation; effective denial through conventional defence, but economy of defence expenditures and manpower; the geographical restriction of local war, but the minimization of damage to the countries defended in a local war; retaining the confidence and co-operation of allies by convincing them that local defence will be coupled to America's strategic nuclear deterrent, but reducing the risk that a local war to defend allies will become a central war involving the super-powers; exploiting new technology to save manpower and facilitate limitation, but avoiding weapons innovations that might jeopardize arms control agreements and stimulate the arms race. Strategic theories aspire to serve all of these purposes but obviously must choose and compromise among them.

In choosing and compromising among objectives that are equally valid in logic, moreover, strategists operate in a field of human interaction that is full of hypotheses untested and largely untestable by experience. Thus no one knows what would happen if tactical nuclear weapons were used in various ways under various conditions. No one can prove the validity of a strategy of deterrence if the event to be deterred does not occur; no one can prove that an alternative would be better if it is not tried; and if the event occurs, no one can be sure that a particular deterrent failed (since the event might have occurred anyway) or that an alternative would have succeeded. Furthermore, as a test of war-fighting theories, an actual armed conflict is likely to be as inconclusive as, and, possibly more misleading than, the absence of war, since each war is the result of a multiplicity of factors combined in ways that are unique to that conflict, and the strategy that may or may not have worked under one set of circumstances might produce a different outcome under other circumstances. Consequently, the rough consensus on limited-war strategy that has emerged over the years represents logical speculation and inference, shaped more by politics and psychology than by science and evidence; and therefore it permits the claims of competing strategic objectives and theories continually to reassert themselves in new forms, always plausible in logic and unverifiable in practice.

One broad division among limited-war strategists, operating in this clouded realm of logical speculation, is between those who emphasize the value of effective denial within controlled limitations and those who emphasize deterring the adversary or bringing him to terms by punitive threats and blows that impose unacceptable costs. Strategic controversies have often turned on this difference of emphasis. The first emphasis has generally prevailed but has never resolved the doubts inherent in its triumph. As a guide to military policies, denial strategies have been afflicted with the problem of coping with growing Soviet war-fighting capabilities. Both denial and punitive strategies have been troubled by the apparent unresponsiveness of Soviet doctrine to the logic of controlled limitation.

Among the proponents of denial strategies there is another broad division between those who emphasize the limitation of war and those who emphasize winning it, with academic theorists foremost in the first group and professional military men in the second. The 'limiters', fearing the natural tendency of military objectives to follow their own logic, have stressed the elaboration of measures of control and mutual restraint designed to keep war from becoming catastrophic. The 'winners', relying principally on geographical and political limitations, have stressed the need to be able to defeat enemy forces at every level of war.

In one crucial respect, however, the theory of limited war was largely taken for granted by all strategists of limited war before Vietnam: its political rationale as an instrument of containment. It is remarkable that this rationale should have become so generally accepted under the Kennedy administration's aegis, whereas it had aroused such strong opposition during the Korean War and in the Eisenhower-Dulles administration that followed. Perhaps acceptance came so readily because, as an abstract theory designed to deter and cope with future contingencies, the strategy of limited war seemed to cost little while promising simultaneously to strengthen containment and reduce the danger of nuclear war.

The war in Vietnam revived some of the original doubts and controversies about the utility of limited war. It called into question in the 1970s some of the basic assumptions about American interests and power and about domestic political support that underlay the ascendance of limited-war strategy in the 1960s. Yet in many significant ways the strategy transcended the Vietnam War and not only survived it but continued to expand in application and acceptance because its basic rationale was rooted more deeply than in the fertile soil of containment.

Although the principal stimulus to limited-war strategy was the perceived imperatives of military containment in the nuclear age, the underlying rationale, as expounded by academic analysts and public leaders, transcended the Cold War. It rested on the Clausewitzian principle that armed force must serve national policy and therefore, lest it follow its own rules to the physical limits of violence, must be restrained and controlled in order to serve specific political objectives of the state by the use of means proportionate and appropriate to the political stakes and circumstances. The purpose of war, according to this principle, could not be simply to apply maximum force toward the military defeat of the adversary; rather, it must be to employ force skilfully in order to exert the desired effect upon the adversary's will along a continuous spectrum from diplomacy, to crises short of war, to an overt clash of arms.

This principle held an appealing logic for the new breed of American liberal realists who had discovered the duty of managing power shrewdly in the interests of world order. It promised to make American power more effective, yet safer. But the fear that a local crisis or war might expand into a nuclear holocaust also provided a compelling motive for limiting warfare to those who were not attracted by the enhancement of military security. In either case, the rationale called for developing alternatives to the strategy of general war, which had dominated American experience in the twentieth century. In the context of the 1960s this meant developing armed forces capable of flexible and controlled responses to a variety of possible political and military contingencies. It meant providing the American President with a reliable communications, command, and control system that would enable him to tailor force to serve specific political purposes under varied conditions of combat.

This basic rationale, driven by its inner logic and the continued growth of Soviet nuclear striking power, was extended to the calculated, measured use of force throughout the whole spectrum of conflict from armed crises to central nuclear war. The conduct of limited war came to be seen as part of a general 'strategy of conflict', in which adversaries would bargain with each other through the medium of graduated military responses, within the boundaries of contrived mutual restraints, in order to achieve a negotiated settlement short of mutual destruction.* The 'escalation' of war—that is, the graduated increase of its scope and intensity—although originally feared as an uncontrollable danger, came to be regarded as a controllable and reversible process by which

---

*The most influential exponent of the concept of limited war as a game-like manifestation of a general strategy of conflict was Thomas C. Schelling in *The Strategy of Conflict* (Cambridge: Harvard University Press, 1960) and *Arms and Influence* (New Haven: Yale University Press, 1966).

adversaries would test each other's will and nerve in order to resolve their conflict at a cost reasonably related to the issues at stake.* In its outer theoretical reach, this logic was applied to nuclear exchanges in central war.

The Disparity between Concept and Capabilities

The rationale of limited-war strategy and strategic theories derived from it have, in essence, become ever more widely accepted over the years, notwithstanding the doubts and reservations arising from Vietnam. Ever since the Korean War, however, there has been a gap between the strategic consensus and the operational plans and capabilities for carrying it out. The Kennedy administration made a determined effort to close this gap but only partially succeeded—succeeded enough, perhaps, to encourage intervention on an expanding scale in Vietnam but not enough to make the mode of intervention appropriate to the circumstances.

The basic reason for the disparity between theory and practice is easy to understand but the disparity itself is hard to overcome. Strategic theory is relatively free to respond to perceptions of national interests, the military balance, and domestic and foreign political imperatives. Operational plans and capabilities, however, are constrained by the limits of the defence budget, the rising cost of conventional manpower, and the inertia of military organization, training, and missions.

The danger of this disparity is that it encourages the commitment of American power to support national interests in contingencies for which the forms of available power are inadequate or inappropriate. The gap between strategy and capabilities may therefore weaken deterrence, undermine the will to fulfil commitments, or lead to military failure.

Logically, if capabilities cannot be made adequate and appropriate, the disparity between strategic theory and practice can be overcome in the following ways: (a) by altering military strategy to make its requirements commensurate with capabilities (for example, by increasing reliance on nuclear deterrence instead of conventional or unconventional resistance); (b) by contracting the scope and demands of military containment (as through a more selective definition of vital interests or a greater tolerance of an adversary's efforts to expand his sphere of influence at the expense of these interests); (c) by relying more heavily on other countries to support containment; (d) by relying on diplomacy, supplemented by the levers of economic and arms transfers or arms control, to diminish the threats to containment. To one degree or another, at various times, the United States has resorted to these methods; but they have never completely closed the gap between strategy and capabilities in the past, and there is no assurance that they will succeed in the future.

*The most striking exposition of controlled escalation was Herman Kahn's *On Escalation: Metaphors and Scenarios* (New York: Praeger, 1965).

The growing strength and reach of Soviet conventional power, combined with the deepening inhibitions in the West against relying on nuclear responses to supplant conventional ones, tend to preclude the adjustment of strategy to suit capabilities. The reaction of the military establishment to the frustrations of Vietnam, the mounting costs of military manpower, and the diminished public support for armed intervention obstruct the adjustment of capabilities to suit strategy. The proliferation of local conflicts and of other threats to regional stability and international order bode ill for narrowing the disparity between the theory and practice of limited-war strategy by diplomatic means. What devolution of military power and initiative has taken place seems as likely to complicate as to facilitate containment. The post-Vietnam relaxation of containment is challenged by rising turbulence in the Third World and the evident determination of the Soviet Union to exploit it, for such relaxation evidently depends more on hopeful assumptions about the limits of Soviet intentions and ability to exploit opportunities for aggrandizement than on tolerance of Soviet success.

Local War

Limited-war strategy in the early 1960s applied pre-eminently to local conventional war, since this was a kind of limited war which the United States had experienced in Korea, which was congruent with the American emphasis on firepower and attrition in military doctrine and organization, and which was integrally related to the West's most important security interests in Western Europe.

The strategy of local conventional war started with the premise that the growth of the Soviet capacity to devastate the United States with nuclear weapons would lead to a situation of strategic parity in which the Soviet Union and the United States could inflict unacceptable damage upon each other no matter which struck first. In this situation, which was perceived to be as much a matter of psychology as capabilities, the credibility of the United States using nuclear weapons to protect even its most important allies, if they could not be protected conventionally, would be bound to erode.

Not only would this situation undermine deterrence and make local conventional aggression more likely, it would also weaken NATO, the most important international sinew of containment, by raising doubts that the United States would defend its allies by retaliating with nuclear strikes against Soviet forces at the penalty of a Soviet nuclear assault against the United States, and by raising fears that the allies would become a nuclear battleground if the United States did use nuclear weapons. If the President, therefore, had no choice but humiliation or holocaust, he might lack the nerve for tough bargaining in crises, or he might run improvident risks of war. Finally, if the United States or its allies and other friendly countries became involved in a local war because deterrence was ineffective or inapplicable, as would be most likely in the so-called 'grey areas' not clearly protected by American military alliances, the West, unable to deny the aggressor a victory by conventional means, could only face defeat or resort to a desperate nuclear response.

It followed, according to the strategic logic of the Kennedy administration, that the United States, in order to avoid these military and political dangers, must have forces that could raise the 'nuclear threshold' in Europe by helping raise NATO's level of conventional resistance and provide a range of conventional military options to cope with a variety of contingencies, from the 'management' of crises, to the containment of 'brush-fire' wars, to the waging of a large-scale war in Europe. Achieving these options would put a premium on mobility, readiness, and command and control. Conventional forces, according to projections of a 'two-and-a-half war' capability that was never achieved, would have to be powerful enough not only to fight a large-scale protracted war in Europe but also—because of assumptions about a Sino-Soviet bloc that were already out-moded in the 1960s—to cope with a major local war in Asia and have something left over for a crisis or brush-fire war in the Caribbean or some peripheral area.

The strategy of conventional local war raised several questions to which there could be no definitive answer in the absence of an empirical test—and probably not then. One question concerned the relation of deterrence to denial. If the conventional denial capabilities of NATO were strengthened, would this weaken their deterrent effect by indicating to the adversary that the United States was afraid to use nuclear weapons? Or would this strengthen deterrence by convincing the adversary that he would have to fight a large-scale war, which would entail a larger risk of nuclear war than a small encounter or a quick military *fait accompli*? The European allies, aware of their relative geographical vulnerability, hard-pressed politically to maintain conventional force levels (particularly because of rising manpower costs), and anxious to do nothing to diminish the credibility of their American nuclear umbrella, posed the first question. Yet they more or less acceded to American pressure for defence contributions as long as Washington buttressed its affirmative answer to the second question by repeated assurances that American troops would stay on NATO's central front to guarantee that the United States would regard an attack on its allies as an attack on itself.

On paper and in doctrine the American strategy of flexible response and enhanced conventional capabilities to raise the nuclear threshold prevailed and was finally embodied, with numerous concessions to allied anxieties, in NATO's official strategic posture statement (MC 14/3) in

December, 1967.* In reality, however, this did not resolve the question about the effect of denial capabilities on deterrence, which continued to underlie the issue of how much and what kind of conventional capabilities NATO needed or could be expected to get. Since this controversy could never be settled in logic, both sides of the issue showed some ambivalence, and the resulting compromise reflected domestic and international politics more than theoretical speculation.

Closely related to the question about the relation of deterrence to denial were doubts about the feasibility of offsetting the Warsaw Pact's advantages of geography, military initiative, and mobilized manpower with conventional forces. For if the presumed East-West imbalance of forces could not really be significantly redressed, the NATO allies would be no more secure after going to the great trouble and cost of a fruitless competition in conventional forces. American defence officials in the 1960s tried to convince allied governments that the estimates of the East's inherent combat superiority that had been publicized in the 1950s were inflated and that raising the relative level of NATO's conventional capabilities was feasible. At the same time, defence planners worried about ways in which NATO—with its huge military overhead and logistical tail, illogical deployment of national forces, duplication of weapons systems, and vulnerable communications network and airfields—might fulfil this promise by getting more fighting power for its money.

The feasibility of a large-scale local war was not only a question of military effectiveness, however; it was also a question of whether such a war could be limited. The Korean War demonstrated, contrary to prevailing Western strategic concepts and plans, that even a major clash of regular military units—World War II writ small—could be limited geographically, militarily, and politically, despite the direct participation of the United States and China and the indirect participation of the Soviet Union. But after the sudden fear in the West that the North Korean invasion might be the model for aggression in Central Europe had quickly subsided, there remained considerable doubt—especially in Western Europe, where the difference between a Korean-type limited war and another general war seemed less significant than in the United States—that a war on this scale in an area of such decisive interest to the super-powers could remain significantly limited even if both sides wished to avoid another world war. This doubt reinforced the question, with very practical implications for defence expenditures and manpower policies: If

---

*Curiously, in their preoccupation with raising the nuclear threshold and distinguishing between conventional and nuclear weapons, western strategists ignored, and largely continue to ignore, the possible role of chemical weapons. While Soviet doctrine, training, and equipment reflect the view that chemical weapons are integral to military operations, the NATO countries have largely avoided the subject, presumably on the assumption that even if the Soviet Union does not regard such weapons as part of a tactical nuclear war, the United States must, pending the achievement of a comprehensive treaty to ban chemical warfare.

a large-scale limited war in Europe is unlikely, why go to the cost and political trouble of preparing for it and incur the risk of weakening the deterrent effect of the prospect that such a war would rapidly escalate to central war?

Although some strategists, particularly in the United States, preferred to rely on NATO's ability to fight a large-scale local conventional war rather than depend on any strategy of limited options beyond the nuclear threshold,* the prevailing strategic concept in the United States and Western Europe envisaged a Korean-type war in Europe escalating to a general war within a few weeks. (Whether NATO's plans and capabilities were any more appropriate for a general nuclear war than for a large-scale conventional war was another question, but this was a question that was easier to ignore when the United States retained a significant superiority in intercontinental striking power, before the 1970s.) The prospect of such escalation, not the avoidance of it, remained the crux of NATO's deterrent strategy. At most, NATO's conventional forces, if confronted by a major attack, might enforce a 'pause' for negotiating a termination of the war before ascending the escalation ladder. How this pause differed from a 'trip-wire' on American nuclear retaliation, which had been a popular concept in the 1950s, depended on how long NATO forces might be expected to withstand a determined Warsaw Pact attack; and on this question, estimates ranged widely from a few days to a couple of months.

To keep local wars of various magnitudes limited in areas outside the protection of NATO or the Security Treaty with Japan would depend, according to the prevailing view, on limiting the political objectives of the war (principally, to preserving the independence and territory of the country attacked) and carefully relating these objectives to limits on the war's geographical extent and its weapons and their targets. Above all, these limitations should be designed to avoid direct Soviet or Chinese intervention, even at the price of granting local aggressors military sanctuaries. Apart from geographical restriction, the clearest and most compelling standard of limitation was believed to be the non-use of nuclear weapons. In Europe, just where this dividing line (or 'fire-break', as its advocates called it) should be drawn was the source of strategic doubts and controversies that persist to this day. Outside Europe the credibility (in American eyes) of initiating the use of nuclear weapons under any circumstances seem to reach its high point in 1954, during the Quemoy and Matsu crisis and the fall of Dienbienphu, and has steadily declined ever since.

Integrally entangled with both the question of the relation between

---

*See, for example, the argument for this strategic preference by Alain Enthoven, who was an influential systems analyst for Secretary of Defense McNamara. Alain C. Enthoven and K. Wayne Smith, *How Much Is Enough?* (New York: Harper & Row, 1971), chap. iv. Helmut Schmidt applied the American case to German interests, in *Defence or Retaliation: A German View* (London: Praeger, 1962).

deterrence and denial and the question of feasible limitation was the chronic question about the role of tactical, or battlefield, nuclear weapons (TNW). In the 1960s this question, too, was primarily addressed to the European theatre, although the option of using tactical nuclear weapons against staging bases and other military targets in Korea and elsewhere, which was part of Secretary of State Dulles's supposedly rejected strategy of avoiding future Korean Wars, remained alive.

Tactical nuclear weapons were originally adopted in 1953 as part of NATO strategy in order to compensate, by substituting firepower for manpower, for the shortfall in meeting the post-Korean force goals that were projected for an effective forward defence.* Any war in Europe was expected to be nuclear, so TNW were to be used from the outset. As late as 1960 operational plans for using the several thousand TNW that had been deployed in Europe still treated them pretty much as conventional weapons. However, with the rising consciousness of the destructive effects of nuclear weapons and of growing Soviet nuclear strength in the late 1950s, TNW have generally been regarded more as weapons of deterrence—slightly less dangerous and therefore more credible than strategic nuclear weapons—than as an adjunct to conventional denial. They have seemed to provide a necessary step between a conventional local war and nuclear central war, but there has never been an agreed plausible doctrine for keeping a nuclear local war limited. So, although TNW are regarded as a necessary step up the nuclear escalation ladder, they have suffered from the same growing inhibitions against the first use of nuclear weapons that have steadily diminished the credibility of strategic nuclear retaliation against a conventional attack.

The effort of strategists to harness TNW to local war reached its logical extreme in the theories of limited tactical nuclear war propounded by Admiral Sir Anthony Buzzard in 1956 and Henry Kissinger in 1957.†But confidence in tactical nuclear warfare as a more effective form of local resistance soon waned and was never widespread or officially implemented.

Most official studies and war games indicated that, even if it could be limited geographically, a tactical nuclear war in Europe would probably

---

*Robert E. Osgood, *NATO: The Entangling Alliance* (Chicago: University of Chicago Press, 1962), Chap. V ('NATO Goes Nuclear').

†In *On Limiting Atomic War* (London: Royal Institute of International Affairs, 1956) and 'Massive Retaliation and Graduated Deterrence', *World Politics*, VIII (Jan. 1956), 228-37, Buzzard presented the case for distinguishing between tactical and strategic weapons within a strategy of 'graduated deterrence' in order to make local defence effective. In his influential *Nuclear Weapons and Foreign Policy* (New York: Harper & Bros., 1957), especially Chap. vi, Kissinger propounded a limited nuclear war strategy featuring special force structures, tactics and reciprocal restraints that would enable NATO to capitalize on its superior industrial and technological capacity without necessarily causing greater destruction than conventional war. By 1960, however, Kissinger had reappraised his views and joined the consensus that the United States should rely primarily on conventional war for local resistance, leaving tactical and strategic nuclear weapons as deterrents of last resort. 'Limited War: Nuclear or Conventional—A Reappraisal,' in Donald G. Brennan, ed., *Arms Control, Disarmament and National Security* (New York: George Braziller, Inc., 1961), 138-52. Originally published in *Daedalus*, LXXXIX (Fall, 1960), 800-17.

produce such chaos as to be beyond predictable control, that it would devastate the European allies, and that it would require more rather than less manpower. Moreover, given the growing Soviet TNW force, NATO's ports, airfields, supplies, and logistics seemed particularly vulnerable in a tactical nuclear war. Nor could the presumed advantage of TNW for defence be counted on to help NATO, since the defending countries would be faced with the task of going over to the offensive in order to remove the attacking forces from allied territory.

The elaboration of nuclear local-war strategies, therefore, was left largely to the ingenious but esoteric theories of bargaining, controlled escalation, reprisals, 'shots across the bow', and demonstrations propounded by Herman Kahn and Thomas Schelling. But, considering West European nuclear fears, the constraints on democratic governments, and the problems of co-ordinating nuclear decisions among allies, there was no reason to think that the NATO powers would have the advantage in nuclear bargaining, particularly since the Soviet Union would probably follow a nuclear demonstration with nuclear retaliation aimed at exerting a military effect.* Since there was an equal lack of confidence in NATO's ability to either limit or win a large-scale conventional war in such a vital area as Western Europe, the function of TNW became primarily one of deterrence through threat of escalation. As such, TNW became the source of a certain tension of strategic emphases between the United States, which alone could authorize the use of nuclear weapons, and America's allies. For Americans were bound to become more interested in reducing the risk that the use of TNW would lead to a central nuclear war, and the allies were bound to be more concerned that the 'decoupling' of TNW from America's strategic forces would reduce their credibility as a deterrent.

Some concluded that the dilemma of NATO's relying on a great quantity of battlefield weapons which were an indispensable supplement to conventional resistance but an unreliable instrument of local war, and which were a necessary step short of strategic nuclear retaliation but an increasingly incredible step as a prelude to central war, could only be mitigated by technological innovations that were making tactical nuclear weapons less destructive and more discriminating through lower explosive yield, reduced radiation, or reduced blast. But these innovations, on the other hand, encountered the objection that they would tend to cloud or eliminate the fire-break between nuclear and conventional weapons, which, it was argued, is the clearest and the indispensable criterion for preserving mutual limitations on war, especially when one or both of the nuclear powers are belligerents.

---

*Thus, according to American officials involved in considering military contingencies at the time of the Berlin crisis, the United States government considered and rejected the resort to demonstrative uses of tactical nuclear weapons if conventional resistance were to fail in a local war, even though the United States enjoyed a considerable superiority in nuclear weapons at the time.

One trouble with all strategies of local war in Europe was that the Soviet Union showed virtually no inclination to be a partner to them. Rather, Soviet doctrine, published sources, and war manoeuvres, seemed rigidly geared to a strategy of blitzkrieg—a sudden offensive strike with conventional and nuclear (both battlefield and strategic) weapons intended to defeat and disorganize the NATO powers. Although Soviet military writings in the late 1960s envisaged the possibility of limited non-nuclear exchanges, they remained as hostile as ever to ideas of controlled escalation and intra-war bargaining by limited options of any kind, and especially by nuclear options.

One could argue, of course, that Soviet declaratory strategy was a form of psychological warfare and that Soviet leaders, being rational and cautious in the use of force, would follow the logic of limitation when actually faced with war rather than incur the extravagant costs of a general nuclear war. But given the evidence that Soviet strategy followed a different logic, dominated by the 'winners'' objective of defeating enemy forces by all available means, all the Western strategies of local war in Europe suffered from the implication that they served primarily to ameliorate the NATO countries' own psychological and political problems rather than to induce the principal adversary to observe the rules of limitation. Since one could argue that allied cohesion, on the basis of whatever strategic compromise, enhanced deterrence, there was something to be said for formulating strategy to suit the allies even if the Warsaw Pact would not play the game. But if Soviet relative military capabilities continued to increase at every level of warfare—nuclear as well as conventional and theatre as well as central war—there was a danger that allied acceptance of the American logic of limitation would simply undermine the credibility of an inexorably escalating nuclear first-use strategy while NATO's capacity to win *any* kind of war declined.

Unconventional War

The strategy of local resistance, despite or because of its ambiguities, the unanswered and probably unanswerable questions it raised, and the disparities between strategic concept and operational plans and capabilities, did, in its essentials, become an enduring aspect of the broad policy of containment, transcending the particular phase of the Cold War in which it emerged. It even survived the Vietnam War, although the international political environment and some of the key assumptions about it have changed, and, with this change, have left confusion and uncertainty about the contingencies in which the United States or its allies might engage in such a war.

By contrast, the intense American preoccupation in the 1960s with unconventional internal war and a strategy of counter-insurgency quickly dissolved in the agonies of the war in Vietnam, where it was overshadowed by a large-scale conventional war of attrition. As in the case of strategies of local interstate war, the strategy of counter-insurgency attained prominence as a reflection of the interests of the United States—and, before that, of France—in a particular period of history. It declined into obscurity for the same reason, when the United States lost confidence in counter-insurgency as an instrument of containment.

There have been a great many internal wars since World War II—that is, wars fought within a state (though usually assisted from outside) for the control of a people and government, through guerrilla warfare, terrorism, insurrection, and subversion—but until recently relatively few interstate wars between regular military units. Nevertheless, internal wars did not concern American strategists until the 1960s. Their concern, however, was foreshadowed by French and (more in a tactical sense) British strategists who were generalizing their countries' experience in fighting insurrections in Burma, Malaya, and Indonesia (in the case of Great Britain) and in Indochina and Algeria (in the case of France).

In France the theorists of *la guerre revolutionnaire,* who were mostly professional military officers, expounded a strategy of fighting revolutionary war, which they saw as an instrument of communist expansion, based on the theory of Mao Tse-tung, serving Soviet interests and designs.* Indirect aggression by revolutionary war, they contended, was an insidious substitute for *la guerre classique.* If it were not contained, it would lead to Soviet hegemony or World War III, just as the chain of fascist aggression led to World War II.

Despite the similarity of their conceptual frameworks, these French strategists had practically no influence on American strategic thinkers, who were predominantly political scientists reacting to the lessons of the Korean War. In the United States the lesson drawn from the French experience by Senator John F. Kennedy and a few others was only that counter-insurgency had failed because it was not sufficiently responsive to the need to build an indigenous nationalist anti-communist base of operations. Nor did the American experience of assisting counter-insurgencies in Greece, the Philippines, Guatemala, or Cuba affect American strategic theory until the 1960s, when counter-insurgency came to be seen as a major means of combating a grave threat to American security. The American strategy of counter-insurgency arose from the perception of American statesmen and strategists in the mid-1950s that the Sino-Soviet bloc, having been contained on the level of regular local interstate war, was actively exploiting less risky, more effective means of communist expansion through 'indirect aggression' based on the support of local guerrilla action and subversion. But whereas Secretary of State

---

*Raoul Girardet, 'Civil and Military Power in the Fourth Republic', in Samuel P. Huntington, ed., *Changing Patterns of Military Politics* (New York: Free Press of Glencoe, Inc.), 221-49.

Dulles had merely identified this form of aggression as part of a new and dangerous phase of the Cold War, President Kennedy came into office determined to do something about it.

From the beginning the President and his brother Robert personally took the lead in developing and implementing a strategy of counter-insurgency in order to prevent and defeat 'wars of national liberation', as the Communists called them. Chairman Khrushchev's declaration just before Kennedy's inauguration that these wars, unlike a general nuclear war, were inevitable and that communists must support them as 'just wars' may have been primarily a response to increasingly strident Chinese criticisms of Soviet unwillingness to provide moral and tangible support to the needs of foreign communist parties. But coming in the wake of revolutionary wars in South Vietnam, Cuba, and Algeria, not to mention lingering memories of the 'loss of China', and coinciding with a presidential campaign that promised to arouse the United States from the lethargies of the Eisenhower regime and mobilize its power to meet the communist challenge in the Third World, Khrushchev's pronouncement became the catalyst for a new departure in strategic doctrine and plans.

This doctrine, as publicly espoused by Walt Rostow, Roger Hilsman, and U. Alexis Johnson and officially promulgated in National Security Memoranda (NSAMs) 124 and 182 of August, 1962,* postulated a co-ordinated Sino-Soviet strategy of advancing communist power in the Third World. Avoiding the risk of a direct military confrontation, the Sino-Soviet bloc, according to this analysis, had conspired to exploit the political and economic dissatisfactions and the indigenous nationalist ambitions of peoples who, seized by the 'revolution of rising expectations', were determined to modernize their countries and free them from foreign domination. To defeat this threat to American security, democratic principles, and international order the United States would have to adopt a strategy of integrating economic and political development on democratic lines with counter-insurgency measures in order to enable threatened governments to eliminate the roots of popular discontent and suppress guerrilla attacks upon their freedom.

This might require the United States to strengthen beleaguered governments—even to reform them—by giving them economic, administrative, and internal security assistance; but there was no expectation that Americans themselves would be involved in counter-insurgent wars except as advisers, trainers, and, if necessary, adjuncts to local forces. For American forces to assume direct responsibility for combat would be to fall into the fatal French misconception that external forces could defeat insurgencies. Yet President Kennedy insisted upon a wide array of counter-insurgency programmes throughout the armed

---

*Douglas S. Blaufarb examines the origins, development, and application of the American strategy of counter-insurgency in the 1960s in *The Counterinsurgency Era: U.S. Doctrine and Performance* (New York: The Free Press, 1977). On the Kennedy administration's strategic concept, see chap. 3.

services, which' required a radical revision of weapons, tactics, and organization in order to meet the new challenge. Although the regular armed services, with the possible exception of the Marines, never in fact came close to this kind of revision, the confidence and enthusiasm of the time, inspired by the President's leadership, infected civilian security leaders and some military officers who shared their outlook with a determination to demonstrate that the United States could cope with this form of aggression too within the constraints of limited war.

Central War

The general rationale for limited war received its most ambitious application in the strategies of limited central war popularized by Herman Kahn and a few other academics and partially applied, then substantially abandoned, by President Kennedy's Secretary of Defense, Robert W. McNamara, in the 1960s. In a sense, the logic of limitation as applied to central war, whether in order to enhance deterrence or limit damage, was more compelling than as applied to any lesser use of force, since basing security on a threat that would quite probably result in retaliatory destruction so extreme as to call into question the practical and moral justification of carrying it out—the threat of countering a nuclear assault on the homeland or a major conventional attack on allies with nuclear retaliation against an adversary approaching parity in destructive power—posed the most severe dilemma of military containment. On the other hand, logic aside, central war was obviously also the most difficult kind of war to limit in practice, especially if winning such a war were to be given equal weight with limiting it.

Although neither Soviet nor allied strategic views acknowledged the practicability of limiting central war, and the strategy found virtually no reflection in American operational plans, the Kennedy and Johnson administrations kept alive the strategy of limited central war as at least an option not to be excluded. In the 1970s the strategy was revived, elaborated, and translated into operational plans by Secretary of Defense James R. Schlesinger, by which time the growth of Soviet strategic striking power had made its logic even more compelling and the improved accuracy and targeting flexibility of missiles, along with the advanced technology of command, control, and communications (C^3), had made it seem more feasible.

Other analysts in this book examine the efforts and problems of formulating and implementing strategies of limited central war. Suffice it to note here that the American effort to refine and implement a strategy so unlikely to be carried out successfully is testimony to the compelling appeal attained by the general rationale of limited war in the country that began to adopt it, wholly against the grain of its traditional approach to war, only after it found itself engaged in a limited war in Korea.

Lessons of Vietnam

If the early 1960s saw the height of enthusiasm for limited war as an instrument of American policy, the late 1960s witnessed the greatest blow to that enthusiasm in Vietnam. The impact of the blow was accentuated by the fact that it came in the Third World, where the Kennedy administration saw the greatest danger to American interests and the greatest opportunity to protect them by applying a strategy of limited war.

The failure of limited war in Vietnam was bound to affect America's strategic outlook, just as the success of limited war in Korea had shaped the strategic outlook that contributed so much to America's intervention in Vietnam.* But the nature and scope of the strategic reaction to the Vietnam War, like that to the Korean War, would be determined not only by the experience of the war itself but also by the impact of the changing international environment on perceptions of American security interests, the external threats to these interests, and the role of American military power in countering these threats.

Ten years after America's disaffection with the war in Vietnam, marked by North Vietnam's Tet offensive in 1968, the war's impact was profound, yet by no means as drastic as many observers predicted at the time of American withdrawal. The impact on limited war strategy was concentrated on the use of limited war as an instrument of containment in the Third World, and here the political conclusions drawn from the experience, though by no means definitive, were much clearer than the military lessons. This is appropriate enough since it was the general rationale of the Kennedy strategy of limited war, not the specific military tactics of counter-insurgency, that was most clearly applied, and since it was the political constraints in Vietnam, the United States, and abroad that most clearly affected the outcome of the military operations.

The lessons drawn from the war fall predominantly into two views, which ascribe the unhappy outcome to two different kinds of errors. Some critics, accepting the rationale of American intervention and taking the local political and military conditions as given, believe that the outcome might have fulfilled the rationale if certain mistakes of strategy and execution had been avoided. Therefore, they conclude that the United States might have conducted the war differently and won; that is, it might have defeated North Vietnam and achieved the independence of South Vietnam sooner at an acceptable cost. It follows that either the United States should have fought the war differently or it should not have intervened at all. Other critics, however, believe that, given the political and military conditions in Vietnam, the rationale for intervening was

---

*Failure and success are measured here by the achivement or non-achievement of the most limited objective of these wars: to establish the independence of the attacked country within its pre-war boundaries at a political and material cost to the United States that was considered worth the objective.

wrong (that is, contrary to American interests and principles) and could not have been achieved at a reasonable cost by a different strategy and execution even if it had been right. They conclude that the United States could not have won the war and probably should not have tried.

Actually, neither of these lessons is more plausible than its obverse; namely, that the rationale of American intervention was misconceived but the United States might nonetheless have won the war with greater boldness, skill, or willingness to make a greater effort; or that the rationale was valid but there was no way to win the war, given the weakness of South Vietnamese government and society and the limits of American interest and power in the area. Psychologically, however, the contradiction and irony of these positions is less appealing. In any case, whether either verdict is right or both are wrong, no lesson can tell us much, if anything, that is definitively relevant to future local wars in which the political and military conditions might come closer to justifying intervention and be more conducive to success. Significantly, neither view categorically rejects containment, or intervention in some form to support containment, by means of a limited war.

Several key military issues arise from the Vietnam War from which some lessons that transcend Vietnam may be derived. They pertain to the strategy and tactics of counter-insurgency, early escalation versus gradualism, controlled and graduated escalation, sanctuaries and other limits, and the dynamics of large-scale conventional war in Third World insurgencies. Cutting across these military issues are the political issues arising from the effects of political constraints in South Vietnam and the United States on the conduct of the war and pertaining to what, if anything, could have been done about them. Underlying all these issues is one ultimate question with the broadest relevance to the future of limited-war strategy in the Third World: did United States interests justify intervention in Vietnam?

This is not the place nor is it yet the time to try to appraise the errors and successes of Vietnam in a detailed and authoritative way.* Yet since appraisals are being made and general lessons are being derived from them, we may suggest some tentative conclusions as part of a process of historical interpretation that will go on for decades. The search for lessons naturally begins with the reasons for failure.

Four principal reasons for the failure in Vietnam emerge from the data and analyses available:

1. The government (GVN), political system, and society of South Vietnam were too vulnerable to insurgency to preserve their

---

*The documents are voluminous, even in unclassified form. The experience of participants, recorded and recordable, is superabundant. There may soon be a flood of literature on Vietnam, but intensive monographs and comprehensive studies are still scarce. The military are just beginning to undertake the painful process of appraisal and self-appraisal. Among the few serious studies of the war based on more than personal experience and the *Pentagon Papers*, I found Douglas S. Blaufarb, *The Counterinsurgency Era*, cited before, most useful.

independence by themselves or to be rescued by the United States, except at the cost of massive intervention and perhaps an American protectorate.

Neither the strategic hamlet programme (when the GVN carried the main military effort) nor the much larger pacification programme (when the United States dominated the military effort) fostered the base of popular support and discipline that might have enabled South Vietnam to win the *political* war, even though they helped nearly to defeat North Vietnam militarily. Whatever the deficiencies from which such programmes may have suffered, it is hard to imagine the most sophisticated and skilful efforts transforming South Vietnam into the kind of polity that could have mobilized popular support to win the protracted war of insurgency and establish a secure government. For South Vietnam was a fractured society with no experience in self-government and no unifying traditions or sense of nationality, governed by urban élites and a military junta with no broad base of political support and out of touch with the villages. Under the circumstances, it is unlikely that any improvements in counter-insurgency (such as those modelled on the operations in Malaya) or in regular military operations (such as those advocated by critics of the self-imposed limits on combat) could have won the war without massive infusions of American armed force and an American military protectorate to preserve the fruits of victory.

2. The American Military were not properly trained, organized, or equipped to fight an insurgency; and therefore they transformed the war into an expanding conventional war, which, even though it virtually defeated North Vietnam militarily, the public was not willing to sustain.

Despite the Kennedy administration's extensive introduction into the armed services of military and civic action programmes, special units, and tactical training oriented toward counter-insurgency, these activities were added on to the missions of regular combat units. They did not prepare U.S. armed forces to fight a large-scale guerrilla war. When the regular units became involved, counter-insurgent activities were overshadowed by the mode of fighting which American armed forces had been trained, equipped, and organized to fight in Europe and Korea, a mode which emphasized the most modern weapons, technical mobility, and concentration of firepower. And Americans trained the South Vietnamese forces (ARVN) to fight the same way. Consequently, when the American government raised the level of military activity and introduced its own forces, following the failure of the strategic hamlet programme and the demise of the Diem regime, the war became a strange amalgam of guerrilla warfare within an escalating conflict of regular combat forces and aerial bombing.

In this expanded war the US/ARVN forces inflicted substantial costs on the North Vietnam Army (NVA) in big-unit combat as well as on the

Vietcong (VC) in guerrilla operations. In desperation North Vietnam unleashed the risky Tet offensive of 1968, in which the VC launched massive attacks against Saigon and other cities. As a result of Tet the VC were devastated. The war reverted to guerrilla patterns with occasional surges of regular military action. When the VC seemed in danger of losing its hold on the southern countryside, the NVA staged a conventional invasion of South Vietnam in 1972.

Waging the kind of war they were prepared to fight, American forces in the South, together with aerial assaults against North Vietnam, clearly gained the upper hand in the conventional war. In the villages, too, Hanoi was losing the war. On the other hand, the GVN was not clearly winning it. Alienation of the countryside from the VC did not enable the GVN to gain a solid base of popular support. In any case, the decisive feature of the war was that Tet—as televised disproof of official optimism—convinced the American public, many of the policymakers, and President Johnson himself that the objectives of the war could never be obtained militarily at an acceptable cost.

3. Incremental expansion of the war was inefficient militarily and fatal politically, but it does not necessarily follow that rapid escalation would have been more successful.

'Gradualism', as critics came to describe the incremental approach, resulted from the fear that sudden and extensive escalation might lead to direct Chinese or Soviet intervention, the reluctance of Presidents either to lose the war without a greater effort or to fight it at any greater cost than necessary, and the repeated underestimation of the effort that would be needed to win the war. Gradualism was, moreover, rationalized by the theory of limited war, which called for the restricted, flexible, controlled, proportionate use of force in order to persuade the adversary to terminate the war for limited objectives.

The result of gradualism in Vietnam was to permit the war to drag on at increasing cost and public opposition without the satisfaction of anticipating a clear-cut victory. North Vietnamese forces were given time to adjust the scale and tactics of their operations to each successive increment while enjoying the protection of geographical sanctuaries that the United States imposed upon its own operations. Under these conditions, the longer the war lasted, the more successful Hanoi was in waging the political side of the war in South Vietnam and the United States, even though it incurred increasing costs in military terms.

Impelled to fight an expanding war of attrition but constrained to fight it incrementally and within cautiously imposed restrictions, some American officials looked to a more psychologically-oriented strategy of graduated punitive escalation in order to persuade the adversary to terminate the war without having to defeat his forces. Frustrated by Hanoi's incursions in the South, the U.S. government, in the spring of 1965, launched ROLLING THUNDER, a highly selective, gradually intensified bombing of targets in North Vietnam on lists authorized by the President, intended to persuade Hanoi through 'signals' and symbolic 'bargaining' to accept reasonable limited terms of settlement under penalty of paying an increasing price for war. Hanoi was not persuaded. After three years the experiment in punitive bargaining was abandoned as a failure.

Perhaps the signals were not clear. Indeed, in response to public protests throughout the world, the U.S. government stressed the purely military objectives of the bombing as though to deny their punitive function. Perhaps the escalation was not undertaken soon enough, by the right means, or in sufficiently big increments; or the cost of the bombing in Hanoi's eyes was overestimated. More clearly, Hanoi was simply determined, after decades of persistence, to achieve its total national aim by any means, over any length of time, and at great cost; whereas the United States, with much more limited aims and interests, was in an inferior position in any contest of wills that entailed a military cost without a distinct military gain. Controlled escalation did not sufficiently affect the balance of military capabilities to alter the balance of will and interests in America's favour. Restrictions on the bombing of industrial, supply, and transportation targets in a broad area around Haiphong and Hanoi were probably interpreted as confirmation of an inferior will to win. In any case, the difficulty of conducting a finely tuned campaign of controlled escalation against a belligerent with total aims in a civil war demonstrated the limits of the more sophisticated theories of limited war.*

Impressed by the disadvantages and failures of gradualism, a number of retrospective critics of America's conduct of the war in Vietnam, like a few participants and observers at the time, have argued that the United States could and should have won the war by earlier and more extensive escalation; or they have argued that if the United States were not prepared to incur the risk and political cost of sudden escalation, it should have stayed out of the war or withdrawn much earlier. There is a strong case, in retrospect, for the contention that sudden escalation, especially as applied against bases and lines of supply in the North and running through Laos, would have crippled North Vietnam's large-scale operations in the South without provoking direct Chinese or Soviet intervention. But it seems unlikely that this would have stopped the guerrilla warfare or enabled the GVN to overcome the political weaknesses that enabled such warfare to continue. Consequently, an

---

*In contrast to ROLLING THUNDER, the eleven-day bombing campaign undertaken in December, 1972, called LINEBACKER, substantially reduced the flow of supplies into North Vietnam and along the lines of communication to the South and heavily damaged supply depots, transportation centres, port facilities, airfields, and military complexes. Opponents of gradualism see a direct connection between the resulting effect on Hanoi's fighting power and its resumption of serious negotiation. More dubiously, some enthusiasts of airpower contend that an earlier bombing campaign like this could have brought the war to a successful conclusion in 1965 in a matter of weeks.

early military success would not have enabled the United States to escape the frustrations and dissatisfactions of a protracted war unless sudden escalation had induced the PRC and the USSR to compel North Vietnam to sue for peace or had enabled the President to withdraw American forces with the national honour and prestige intact.

4. The national interests at stake were not sufficiently compelling to Americans to have justified a scale and duration of combat necessary to win the war of attrition.

Whether by an intensified and protracted effort the United States could have won the war of attrition, whether it could have consolidated its post-Tet military advantage and have established a lastingly independent South Vietnam, must remain an unanswerable but doubtful supposition, given the historic persistence of North Vietnam and the political weakness of the GVN. It is clear, however, that both the intensity and the duration of the American effort were diminished by popular disaffection with the war. This disaffection was not due to extraordinary material, human, economic, diplomatic, or moral costs, by themselves. The Korean War was more costly and just as unpopular (before the United States began winning it). The costs in Vietnam seemed excessive because they bore so little promise of victory and because, despite the hyperbolic justifications of the American effort as indispensable to the protection of the Free World from communist expansionism everywhere, neither the American public nor its leaders really believed that the stakes of war were as important to American security interests as in the Korean War and, of course, not remotely as vital as in World War II. By 1968 the overriding justification had become simply the maintenance of American prestige, which meant, especially, the country's reputation for defending its allies under hardships. Indeed, the claim that the United States had honourably upheld its prestige eventually became a justification for withdrawing under the formula of 'Vietnamization'. Lacking any more tangible and convincing connection between the war and U.S. security, the costs of the war—particularly the domestic ones—were bound to seem excessive.

Just as the costs of continuing the war came to seem excessive, the costs of waging it more intensively seemed to be unjustified. Consequently, American leaders felt constrained to escalate the war on a piecemeal basis, reluctantly approving increased allocations of combat manpower in increments that seemed to be the minimum needed to avoid losing the war and the maximum the public would accept. When the increments caused a sharp rise in military spending in late 1965, President Johnson declined for three years to increase taxes in order to offset the resulting inflation. He also declined to call up reserves. And when his military advisers eventually recommended an increment of additional combat forces that could not be met without mobilizing the reserves, he decided to call a halt to the process and resign. To be sure, there were other reasons for not putting the nation on a wartime footing, but all of them could have been overcome if the objectives of the war had really been as compelling in tangible terms as its high-flown rationale implied.

Thus the Vietnam War posed acutely the issue that the Korean War had raised in a different form: How long and at what cost would the United States be willing to sustain a limited war? In Korea the issue was raised by those who urged escalation beyond the official geographical and weapons limitations rather than accept stalemate. In Vietnam it was raised by those who preferred stalemate or defeat to escalation. It is significant, none the less, that in both cases the nation did fight a large-scale, protracted war within self-imposed restraints and in accordance with the theory of political limitation and proportionate force, which is at the heart of limited-war strategy. One basic reason for the acceptance of self-imposed limitations under adverse military conditions is that in neither case did the interests at stake seem worth the risks of expanding the war. In this respect, cautious gradualism, as opposed to sudden and bold escalation in order to achieve the maximum military effect as soon as possible, seems intrinsic to the phenomenon of large-scale limited wars as the United States is disposed to fight them. Although the critics of gradualism who would opt for sudden escalation may be right on military grounds, they are almost certainly wrong on domestic political grounds.

* * *

If there are any lessons of general applicability that emerge from the American experience in Vietnam, they are highly contingent, since so many of the military and political features of another local war might be different or occur in different combinations. Moreover, the general lessons must be largely confined to the most salient characteristic of the war: that it was a large-scale, protracted local war in the Third World at a place of minor intrinsic national interest.

What should be America's or any other Western country's interest in intervening directly or indirectly in such a war? Considering the variety of conditions that might characterize such a war, one can prudently generalize only to the extent of saying that henceforth U.S. interests or the interests of other Western countries must be assessed not only in terms of a general commitment to stopping the expansion of communism or defeating communist aggression but also in terms of intrinsic economic, political, and security interests and a sober estimate of both the prospect of local communist victory—or, one must now add, the victory of any unfriendly country or faction—and its consequences for the broader balance of power with the Soviet Union.

As for the feasibility of intervening successfully to support a government against an insurgency or to support one faction competing for power against others, it is bound to be difficult to estimate (before it is too late) the prospect of the government or a faction gaining a sufficient base of political support to be capable of being rescued. If they had that kind of support to begin with, there would either be no war or no need for much external help. It is somewhat clearer from the Vietnam example that if indirect assistance is not sufficient, the direct participation of foreign troops is not likely to succeed either, although it could well make the situation worse. At least it is not likely to succeed except at the cost of a protracted large-scale local war, unless the opposing foreign conventional intervention is weak or nonexistent.

If the intervention of American armed forces on a large scale is needed to prevent the defeat of a government or a faction engaged in an internal war, the United States will have great difficulty avoiding a war of such cost and duration as to become unacceptable domestically. Rapid and intense escalation probably will not avoid this situation at an acceptable risk of expanding the war, but gradualism may be equally costly and will tend to jeopardize the domestic base of support. In any case, graduated escalation is not likely to persuade the adversary to negotiate for peace except in proportion to the military effect it exerts, unless it persuades the adversary's nuclear protector that the risks of expanding the war are not worth running and the protector is in a position to persuade the protected to desist.

On the basis of the Vietnam experience one is tempted to conclude, as many military men do, that the United States—and the rule applies even more to its major allies—should not intervene in any kind of local war unless it can defeat the enemy and restore the status quo within a year or two by applying maximum military force within the geographical boundaries of the nation attacked. Some would add that American armed forces should also refrain from intervening if the adversary is going to be permitted to enjoy adjacent sanctuaries outside the nation attacked. By implication, therefore, the United States should intervene only if it can attack such sanctuaries—unless, perhaps, this would create a clear and present danger of a direct encounter with Soviet forces. But even if these guidelines are sound, acting upon them presupposes advance knowledge about a complicated interaction of military and political factors that no one can predict or guarantee. And although the tendency of Vietnam is to reinforce the arguments of the 'winners' over the 'limiters' among limited-war strategists, the nature and scope of prudent limitations that even the 'winners' would impose on efforts to defeat enemy forces will depend very much on such intangible factors as the importance of the interests at stake and the balance of interests between the United States and the Soviet Union as well as upon tangible factors like the local balance of military power and the proximity of Soviet forces. The difficulty of generalizing about such factors is illustrated by imagining the differences between the war in Vietnam and possible wars in the Near East.

Clearly, the gross lessons about limited-war strategy that can be derived from the Vietnam experience are so subject to qualification and elaboration as to be no more than cautionary items on a very long agenda of relevant considerations. At best they are antidotes, if we need any, to the grand simplifications and stylized stratagems of the Kennedy era.

In the short run, at least, it is somewhat easier to generalize about the lessons that American statesmen, politicians, and military officers, rightly or wrongly, have in fact already derived from Vietnam. But these generalizations do not go very far, and they may not last very long. Concerning the place of unconventional war in America's strategy of limited war, for example, the dominant lesson at present, according to common wisdom, is simply that the United States must avoid fighting another such war with its own forces. Counter-insurgency remains a task for special forces, but it has ceased to be a doctrinal imperative or a practical concern for the regular armed services.

The trauma of Vietnam has also affected the place of conventional local war in American strategy in the Third World—we shall revert to this in the final section. It has apparently ruled out large-scale protracted local war, for example. Yet the essential rationale of limited war and the doctrinal propositions, as well as the ambiguities, doubts, and controversies surrounding them, persist.

In any case, along with the effect of Vietnam on the American approach to limited war, there are a number of factors shaping strategic thought in the period since Vietnam which are independent of the Vietnam War's effects. Among these are the evolution of detente, the outbreak of local conflicts in the Third World, the consolidation of strategic parity, the relative growth of Soviet military strength in both nuclear and conventional capabilities, financial and manpower constraints on Western forces, and the prospect of new weapons technology.

Limited-War Strategy in Europe

In the later 1970s a number of developments merged to revive the efforts of analysts and governments to cope with the familiar strategic problems of NATO: the codification of strategic parity in the SALT agreement and negotiations, the continued absolute and relative growth of the Soviet nuclear striking force, the concomitant modernization and expansion of Soviet forces in Europe, the further development of more accurate, flexible, and mobile conventional as well as nuclear weapons, the persistence of pressures to hold down manpower expenditures in defence budgets, and the end of the distractions of Vietnam. NATO also became the locus of the only significant effort to implement limited-war strategy with new forces and weapons. But the basic strategic issues underlying this renewed effort remained the same, and neither new tactics nor new technology seemed likely to resolve them.

On paper the allies have never been more solidly committed to a strategy of flexible and controlled response and to the prerequisite of raising the nuclear threshold, but there is no commensurate increase of conventional capabilities. Indeed, the significant change in European military capabilities has occurred not in NATO but in the Warsaw Pact, where the modernization and full manning of Soviet divisions over the last decade compound the difficulty of NATO's achieving a forward defence. Soviet conventional forces, some fear, could launch a blitzkrieg without mobilizing and with only a few days' warning instead of the 23 to 30 days mobilization posited in NATO plans.* Using only conventional weapons, these forces might occupy much of Germany and leave NATO in the predicament of launching a counter-offensive with nuclear weapons that would devastate Germany. At the same time, the great advance in Soviet TNW would deter NATO from responding with nuclear weapons, while Soviet striking power would deter the United States from turning a theatre war into central war.

The proper response to this danger, most strategists believe, is to build up NATO's capability for forward conventional defence. Indeed, in the light of the relative advantage that Soviet forces may now enjoy in theatre nuclear war and the parity they have achieved in strategic capabilities, NATO's best strategy could be conventional war, while the Warsaw Pact has the advantage in initiating nuclear war if its objectives are not achieved by conventional means. But achieving an effective forward defence will require money, a host of remedies for specific deficiencies, and perhaps some basic structural reforms.

A few strategists, convinced that the inadequacy of NATO's forward conventional defence is inherent in the facts of geography and relative military resources, have argued for repulsing a Warsaw Pact invasion at the border with the early use of low-yield, discriminating TNW.† But the explicit revival of the strategy of substituting TNW for conventional responses no longer finds much favour in the absence of any new reason, other than more discriminating nuclear weapons, to believe that a tactical nuclear war could either be significantly limited or won at a reasonable cost. Although Soviet military doctrine and policies could now be construed to support the contingency of a theatre nuclear war excluding the Soviet Union and the United States from the combat zone, there is no reason to think that Soviet forces, still oriented towards a blitzkrieg offensive, would employ TNW for any objectives other than defeating the

---

*This fear was publicized and substantiated in detail by the investigation and report of Senators Nunn and Bartlett. U.S. Congress, Senate, Committee on Armed Services, *NATO and the New Soviet Threat*, Report by Senator Sam Nunn and Senator Dewey F. Bartlett, 95th Congress, 1st Session (Washington, D.C.: U.S. Government Printing Office, 1977).

†Several proponents of this strategy have written in *Orbis*: W. S. Bennett, R. R. Sandoval, and R. G. Shreffler, 'A Credible Nuclear-Emphasis Defense for NATO', *Orbis*, XVII (Summer, 1973), 463-79; Samuel T. Cohen and William C. Lyons, 'A Comparison of U.S.-Allied and Soviet Tactical Nuclear Force Capabilities and Policies', *Orbis*, XIX (Spring, 1975), 72-92; Marc E. Geneste, 'The City Walls: A Credible Defense Doctrine of the West', *Orbis*, XIX (Summer, 1975), 477-90. See also Robert M. Lawrence, 'On Tactical Nuclear War', Parts I and II, *Revue Militaire générale* (January and February, 1971), pp.46-59, 237-61.

adversary as quickly and thoroughly as possible or that NATO could win such a war without incurring enormous devastation of allied territory.*

A more optimistic view of the conventional balance holds that the overall quantitative war-fighting capabilities of NATO and the Warsaw Pact are fairly equal, doubts the reliability of East European contingents, and questions the plausibility of the blitzkrieg scenario from the standpoint of Soviet interests or the deployment of Soviet forces. Moreover, in this view, creating the kind of force that could fend off such a blitzkrieg would cost far more than NATO countries are willing to spend and could be offset, in any case, by the deployment of more Soviet forces near the forward line. The conclusion drawn from this view is not that the nuclear threshold should be lowered—the time for this logic has passed—but that the West must continue to seek an arms control agreement that will create a more stable military balance through mutual balanced force reductions (MBFR).† Although hopes for solving NATO's military problems through MBFR seem dim, the fear of worsening this prospect has reinforced arguments against substantial expenditures for improving NATO's military posture.

Whether optimistic or not about the prospect of increasing conventional forward defence capabilities in Europe, the United States government is bound to stress the priority of this objective, since its inhibitions against using nuclear weapons first are by now so deeply entrenched.‡ Although the government does not dare renounce nuclear first-use for fear of the effect on deterrence and allied confidence, the principal function of TNW, in operational reality, has become the deterrence of, and response to, Soviet first-use of TNW.

Confronted with the new stress on the old problem of achieving an effective forward conventional defence of Germany at an acceptable cost in the face of increasing Soviet conventional and nuclear strength,

---

*Soviet strategic writing and pronouncements have recently acknowledged the need to be able to fight a theatre nuclear war in addition to a small-unit conventional war or a general nuclear war, but they show virtually no recognition of the kind of limitations within such a theatre war that American strategists dwell upon. Rather, Soviet doctrine is oriented toward an offensive (or counter-offensive, in political terms) operation based on surprise, pre-emption, rapid territorial advance, and the employment of nuclear weapons at the earliest propitious moment, while relying on the nature of political objectives and the geographical restriction to limit the war. One can infer from this outlook that in a conventional war in central Europe the first sign of American release of nuclear weapons would trigger Soviet nuclear pre-emption and a full-scale effort to destroy NATO forces. On the Soviet approach to theatre nuclear war see the chapters by William R. Van Cleave and John Erickson in Lawrence L. Whetten, ed., *The Future of Soviet Military Power* (New York: Crane, Russak & Company, Inc., 1976).

†Congressman Les Aspin took this view in response to the alarming report of NATO's weakness by Senators Nunn and Bartlett in 1976. *Congressional Record*, February 7, 1977, pp. H911-14.

‡Secretary of Defense Harold Brown states in his Annual Report for FY 1979 that strengthening conventional forces must be given first priority in NATO's defence programme. Balancing this priority with the imperative of nuclear retaliation, he declares, 'President Carter has already made it clear that the United States does not rule out the use of nuclear weapons if the United States, its friends, or its forces are attacked. However, we continue to believe that we and our allies are best served by basing our collective security on a firm foundation of conventional military power. We cannot depend on tripwire theories or abstract calculations about cool and studied escalation. What we seek in conjunction with our allies is a major conventional capability sufficient to halt any conventional attack.' *Annual Report, Fiscal Year 1979*, p.79.

Western defence analysts and officials have turned once again to technological innovations to alleviate the problem—but this time, in contrast to the 1950s, within the context of the strategy of flexible and controlled response and with no promise of either a technical or a tactical solution to the strategic predicament. Precision guided munitions (PGMs), new guided delivery vehicles (particularly, cruise missiles), and improved C^3 promise to give conventional forces greater mobile firepower, accuracy at long range, concealment and dispersal, and flexibility in the selection of targets, combined with the destruction of targets at long range and the minimization of collateral damage.*

Optimistic assessments anticipate that this technology will enhance NATO's conventional defence and reduce reliance on TNW while facilitating the controlled use of force for specific political effects. However, others point to certain technical weaknesses of PGMs, the vulnerability of C^3 to counter-measures, and the need for new tactics and organization to exploit the new technology effectively. Some analysts calculate that PGMs will accelerate the role of destruction and of weapons consumption and therefore leave less time for pausing to bargain in a local war; that Soviet counter-measures such as area bombing and concentration of destruction on rear-area support facilities will nullify the PGMs' enhancement of controlled limitations; and that Soviet PGMs could facilitate an attack in Europe by enhancing the precise destruction of bases, supplies, ports, and industry at long range.

On balance, the new technology seems to favour a strategy of flexible and controlled response, but it does not promise relief from the problem of achieving an effective forward defence at a politically acceptable cost. Moreover, like TNW, the new conventional military technology introduces new uncertainties into limited-war strategy because it expands the range of hypothetical outcomes of warfare in Europe without any further empirical basis for guessing the real consequences.†

Greater strategic implications may follow from NATO's prospective adoption of long-range cruise missiles with optional conventional or nuclear warheads. These weapons hypothetically offer NATO the opportunity to destroy critical military targets, such as radar sites and

---

*James Digby, *Precision-Guided Weapons*, Adelphi Papers 118, Summer 1975, Richard Burt, *New Weapons Technologies: Debate and Directions*, Adelphi Papers 126, Summer 1976.
†The one example of the use of some PGMs (principally, anti-tank and anti-aircraft weapons) was in the Yom Kippur War of 1973 between Egypt and Israel. Resulting assessments of the effects of PGMs have been inconclusive. Some early analyses rushed to the conclusion that PGMs provide a cheap and preclusive defence against blitzkriegs with modern tanks and aircraft. Subsequent analyses argued that this conclusion is erroneous because it overlooks decisive tactical factors. Jeffrey Record, 'The October War: Burying the Blitzkrieg,' *Military Review*, vol. LVI (April, 1976), pp.19-21. Uri Ra'anan, 'The New Technologies and the Middle East: Lessons of the Yom Kippur War and Anticipated Developments,' pp.79-90 in Geoffrey Kemp, Robert L. Pfaltzgraff, Uri Ra'anan (eds.), *The Other Arms Race: New Technologies and Non-nuclear Conflict* (Lexington, Mass. 1975). Kenneth Hunt, 'The Middle East Conflict 1973: The Military Lessons', *Survival*, vol. xvi, (January/February 1974), pp.4-7. In any case, differences of terrain, weather, geography, the deployment of troops and supplies, the composition and structure of total forces, etc. make doubtful the relevance of the Yom Kippur war to the effects of new weapons technology on war in Europe.

transportation centres, deep in Eastern Europe and in the Soviet Union itself with conventional instead of nuclear warheads. Consequently, they might enhance local denial capabilities and raise the nuclear threshold in theatre and even central war. The promise of this military effect, however, is clouded by speculations about subsidiary political effects. By making conventional strikes at the Soviet Union more attractive might not cruise missiles, in reality, more quickly provoke a Soviet nuclear response, possibly in a pre-emptive attack? And would they not tend to break down the distinction between nuclear and conventional war by virtue of their dual capability? On the other hand, if they succeeded in raising the level of conventional resistance, might they not reduce the credibility of nuclear escalation and so diminish deterrence in West European eyes? Or would they enhance deterrence and increase allied control over the scope of the war by providing allied battlefield commanders with a means of striking at Soviet targets without exclusive American authorization? Might they not therefore create a new European interest in raising the nuclear threshold?

Considering the steady rise of nuclear inhibitions and the search for technology that will raise the level of conventional resistance, the arguments in favour of long-range cruise missiles based in Europe will probably carry the day unless they are rejected on the grounds that they would stimulate the arms race and impede the achievement of a strategic arms limitation treaty and MBFR.* Their real effect on deterrence, however, will be undiscernible and their effect on NATO's war-fighting capability will be unknowable, since neither, one hopes, will be subject to an empirical test.

The same logic—or psychologic—that favours raising the nuclear threshold with more precise and flexibly controlled conventional weapons also favours limiting nuclear war with more precise, flexible, and controllable nuclear weapons once the threshold is crossed, except, some fear, that the new nuclear weapons may obscure the threshold itself. Two kinds of small-yield, so-called 'mini-nukes'—one, based on fission, with reduced blast and radiation, the other, based on fusion, with reduced blast and enhanced short-term radiation (popularly known as the 'neutron bomb')—might exploit the greater military effect of nuclear weapons with less collateral damage. They could thereby enhance the utility and political acceptability of TNW as denial forces while introducing new small steps for escalation—assuming that the Soviet Union would observe compatible limitations. They would not, however, overcome the familiar problems inherent in a nuclear first-use strategy;

---

*The problem that long-range cruise missiles pose for arms control agreements lies not only in the difficulty of verifying limitations but also in that they break down the distinction between strategic and tactical (or theatre) weapons, which underlies both SALT and MBFR. This distinction, however, is also threatened by other weapons, including NATO's 'forward based system' ('tactical' aircraft based in Europe and on aircraft carriers) and Soviet MRBMs (particularly the SS-20), with flight ranges that reach between NATO territory and the Soviet Union.

and if mini-nukes were to be considered a substitute for an enhanced conventional response, they would compound these problems.* They make the most sense, some military commanders and defence officials have plausibly argued, as substitutes for the bulk of the 7000 large-yield TNW that had accumulated in Europe by the mid-1960s—many of them in vulnerable locations, on quick reaction alert, and under uncertain command and control—and as part of a revised NATO military posture to get more conventional power for existing defence expenditures.† So far, however, the efforts of some American defence officials since the mid-1960s to reduce substantially the number of TNW in Europe have encountered strong resistance because of the fear of allies that any such move will weaken the deterrent effect of TNW and lead to the decoupling of TNW from the U.S. strategic force.

Regardless of the strategic issues and political complications raised by new conventional and nuclear weapons, the prospect is that NATO will gradually assimilate them as it has assimilated new weapons in the past. Their utility for limited warfare, however, will depend centrally on tactical doctrines, military missions, and military organization and procedures, which are notoriously much slower to change. Moreover, no improvements due to the introduction of new technology could have as much effect on NATO's capacity to implement a strategy of flexible and controlled response as overcoming the current deficiencies that arise from continued preoccupation of force plans and structure with a war of attrition at the expense of manoeuvre, the lack of standardization (or, more broadly, 'interoperability') of allied weapons and logistics, the illogical deployment of national forces, and the bloated size of NATO divisions.‡

In any event, all these much-studied issues may be less urgent than those arising from political developments on NATO's southern flank. Understandably, the reconsideration of familiar strategic issues in terms of new military technology has taken place almost exclusively with respect to the central front in Europe, since for political reasons this has been the focus of NATO's military concern from the beginning. It is ironic that this focus should be so dominant in the 1970s, when for

---

*On the advantages and disadvantages of mini-nukes from the standpoint of defence and deterrence in Europe, see Laurence W. Martin, 'Flexibility in Tactical Nuclear Responses', Holst and Nerlich, op. cit. *Beyond Nuclear Deterrence* (New York, Crane, Russak & Co. Inc., 1977). Particularly unfortunate in its effects on deterrence and allied confidence in American nuclear protection would be a strategy that tied mini-nukes not only to early first-use of nuclear weapons but also to the geographical restriction of their use to NATO territory in order to enhance the prospect of reciprocal limitation of local nuclear war.
†Alain C. Enthoven presents this argument in 'U.S. Forces in Europe: How Many? Doing What?', *Foreign Affairs*, vol. LIII (April, 1975), 513-32.
‡Steven Canby and Robert W. Komer are foremost among those arguing for almost a decade for the restructuring of NATO's forces in order to get more fighting power out of manpower on the model of the Soviet Union's smaller divisions. See, for example, Canby, 'NATO Muscle: More Shadow than Substance', *Foreign Policy*, no. 8 (Fall, 1972), and Komer, 'Treating NATO's Self-Inflicted Wound', *Foreign Policy*, no. 13 (Winter 1973-74). Neither sees standardization as a panacea. See also, Richard D. Lawrence and Jeffrey Record, *U.S. Force Structure in NATO: An Alternative* (Washington, D.C.: The Brookings Institution, 1974).

political reasons the threat to the central front is generally estimated to have subsided to an unprecedentedly low point, whereas disturbing political changes along the Mediterranean flank of Europe may be confronting NATO with the greatest potential threats to cohesion and strength since its founding.

The reactivation of the old conflict between Greece and Turkey by controversies over the control of Cyprus and petroleum rights in the Aegean, the concomitant loosening of Greek and Turkish ties to NATO and the United States, the possibility that the death of Tito will lead to national strife in Yugoslavia and appeals for outside aid, the ascendance of communist parties to positions of influence and power in countries with serious economic and social problems (notably, Portugal and Italy), the possibly rising influence in several European countries of leftist groups that are likely to be more actively hostile to NATO and the status of American forces in NATO than the communist parties, the latent danger that Soviet suppression of organized East European dissidence might spill over the not-so-Iron Curtain—these developments present a far more diversified, and also divisive, set of threats of direct and indirect Soviet military intervention than the NATO countries have faced before. They call for a more diversified and politically discriminating set of military responses, with implications for conventional weapons systems, rules of engagement, the stationing of forces, naval deployments, bases, and institutional arrangements for bilateral and multilateral military action.* Whether these implications involve military strategy or just military tactics and organization is perhaps a matter of definition, but they certainly involve significant problems of implementing limited-war strategy which the NATO countries have scarcely begun to consider.

Limited-War Strategy in the Third World

In contrast to the strategies of limited central war and limited local or theatre war in Europe, there has been a notable absence in the 1970s of new tactical or technical concerns or even of the revival or reappraisal of old strategic concerns with respect to limited-war strategy in the Third World. It is as though the trauma of Vietnam had suspended creative military thought in this area. Here the most notable developments in military thought have been the virtual disappearance of two features of limited-war strategy that emerged in the wake of the Korean War: reliance on counter-insurgency as a response to wars of national liberation or any other military contingency and reliance on tactical nuclear strikes as a response to direct Chinese or Soviet military intervention. The first feature was a victim of the no-more-Vietnams

---

*Uwe Nerlich, 'Continuity and Change: The Political Context of Western Europe's Defense', and Henry S. Rowen and Albert Wohlstetter, 'Varying Response with Circumstance', in Holst and Nerlich, *Beyond Nuclear Deterrence*. (New York, Crane, Russak & Co. Inc., 1977).

sentiment and the discovery of the obstacles to successful intervention in internal wars. The second declined in favour because of the growing popular and material constraints against initiating the use of nuclear weapons, except perhaps in vital strategic areas, and the growing perception, reinforced by the Vietnam War, that neither the Soviet Union nor China is at all likely to be provoked into large-scale direct intervention anyway.

The problems of applying the general rationale of limited-war strategy to central war and to local war in Europe arise from old issues and new technology that transcend the impact of the Vietnam War and transcend, to some extent, the purely American perspective. The problems of applying limited-war strategy outside the European theatre, where the strategy received its greatest official impetus in the Kennedy period, arise in the first instance because the Vietnam experience has raised fundamental questions about the political premises that provided that impetus. These premises, which underlie the rationale for intervention in local wars in the Third World, are peculiarly American, although they have significant implications for other countries. Basically they concern the nature of American security interests, the threats to these interests, and the efficacy of American forces in coping with them.

As compared to the 1960s, each of these premises has been downgraded and qualified. The chain-of-aggression (or falling dominoes) thesis no longer seems like such an automatically compelling justification for military intervention in support of Third World countries threatened with a local communist take-over. The perceived importance of American security interests in South East Asia has substantially declined. Official confidence in the ability of the United States to intervene effectively in local wars at a cost and duration the Congress and public will support has greatly diminished.

Most consequential, the prevailing estimate of the nature and intensity of the communist threat of expansion has been downgraded. The fear of Chinese aggression, which was so intense after the Korean War and at the onset of American involvement in Vietnam, has almost vanished. The estimate of the threat of armed Soviet intervention in the Third World and the estimate of the Soviet ability to create or exploit the actions of dependencies against American interests in the non-industrial areas have also diminished significantly.

Nevertheless, the general framework and most of the elements of America's security outlook remain in force, and there are plenty of international developments to sustain and even enlarge them. These range from general threats to international order—the prospect of nuclear proliferation, international terrorism, OPEC decisions on oil prices and supply; the fusion of racial, tribal, and ethnic animosity with national rivalries; the new possibility that even small countries in the non-industrial world may constrict American commerce, access to important resources, and the unhampered use of sealanes and straits for commercial and military use—to the more specific threats posed to American interests by the expansion of Soviet naval and air capacity to project forces overseas while impeding the projection of American forces, coupled with the evident Soviet determination and enhanced political ability, now manifest in Africa, to advance Soviet access and influence in the troubled Third World.

More disturbing than the rather remote prospect of Soviet paramountcy in Africa is the prospect of local conflicts in areas that are intrinsically far more important than Vietnam for economic, political, and strategic reasons and which are also close to the central bases of Soviet power. The renewal of Arab-Israeli warfare or a radical revolution in the Near East could confront the United States and its NATO allies with the prospect of Soviet intervention or an economically crippling oil embargo or both. An indigenous Middle East conflict or any further disturbance in Iran might invite Soviet military and political pressure on that country. One cannot dismiss the prospect of another war between North and South Korea, which would threaten to upset the great-power balance of power in the area and make urgent the deterrence of Soviet intervention. In these contingencies the domestic and international political constraints against American armed intervention that have become so conspicuous since the Vietnam War would not necessarily prevail.

Given the spreading realization that the post-Vietnam international environment is anything but peaceful and stable and the persistence of American global interests and of America's broad definition of its security, the once-popular view that military containment is obsolete in the Third World has depended largely on revised assumptions about the improbability and inefficacy of Soviet or Soviet-supported military intervention. Soviet reverses in Egypt, Somalia, and elsewhere have encouraged the hope that even if Soviet military assistance succeeds in advancing the position of a client, the client will eventually turn against its benefactor. But these revised assumptions about the limits of Soviet influence in the Third World are not infallible. Unanticipated events may rather quickly change them. Indeed, the change has already begun in Washington.

All this is not to say that the United States or its European allies will or should find renewed utility in fighting limited wars in the Third World. Hopeful assumptions about the decline of the military threat to vital Western interests in this area may turn out to be valid, not because the Soviet Union is deterred by the United States from intervening in troubled waters but because its interventions are frustrated by local chaos and intrinsic political obstacles to the successful exploitation of tribal, ethnic and national conflicts. America's increased tolerance for disorder in the Third World, as measured by its reluctance to intervene with its own forces or with arms assistance in local conflicts, may reflect a wise and enduring judgment about the limits of American interests and influence as well as about the efficacy of armed intervention during a particularly tumultuous period of history. It is hard to imagine a less propitious political environment for American armed intervention than southern Africa.

In any event, the obstacles to American and western participation generally in local wars are likely to be reinforced by the growing Soviet capacity for counter-intervention and naval interposition in distant places, by the acquisition on the part of less developed states of cheap and easily operated modern weapons with greater accuracy and firepower, by the high cost of fuel and supplies in sustaining a large-scale military operation overseas, and by local restrictions on political access to bases, through narrow straits, and through territorial waters. The Third World has become a particularly inhospitable, costly, and intractable arena for great-power intervention in limited wars of major scope.

Exactly how the multiplicity of actual and potential disruptions of international order may affect the vital interests of the United States and its allies, and whether these disruptions will warrant the limited use of Western military power, are hard to foresee; but for that very reason and because disturbing military and political developments do not warrant the assumption that an American capacity for conventional limited warfare in the Third World is dispensable, common prudence calls for the insurance of flexible military capabilities adapted to serving limited objectives in a variety of contingencies.

What are these contingencies? In Africa, for example, we see not only Western commando raids and rescue operations but the emergence of what used to be called brush-fire wars, in some of which the super-powers are indirectly participating and their allies directly participating. From the standpoint of the super-powers they may play something of the role that insurgency and counter-insurgency were supposed to play in the 1960s.

Recent examples of the limited use of force by major powers in the Third World only begin to illustrate the wide array of low-level military actions involving external powers that may be endemic to the Third World as the patterns of international power and interests grow more complex and diffuse and the sources and means of armed coercion multiply. In this kind of international environment one cannot rely on the constraints against participating in wars like those in Korea and Vietnam to exempt the United States and other Western countries from engaging in a variety of interpositions, naval encounters, blockades, police actions, raids, and skirmishes to support a variety of purposes—from traditional interests, such as asserting territorial and resource rights, to possibly more novel objectives, such as preventing genocide, pre-empting nuclear proliferation, and blocking or pacifying a local conflagration. Nor can one safely rely entirely on the military policies designed to cope with the actual and hypothetical contingencies of the classic period of Cold War to serve national policy in the more complex international environment that is emerging.

Developing military-political doctrine for the expanded range of contingencies that the United States and its major allies must anticipate outside the centres of industrial civilization and tailoring the training, organization, tactics, manpower policies, and weapons systems of armed forces to cope with these contingencies are likely to be the most challenging talks of limited-war strategy in the 1980s. These tasks give a new dimension to the concept of flexible and controlled response. The basic rationale for executing them has convincingly survived the multiple vicissitudes of the last quarter-century in which it was officially established, nurtured, and applied. But the question that bedevils limited-war strategy now, as throughout the post-war period, is whether actual contingency and force plans and actual capabilities to carry them out are commensurate with the demands that spring from the strategy of limited war and the conditions that might call for fighting a limited war. More than at any time since the Korean War, this question arises from the uncertainties about American interests and political will.

Recognizing the variety of small or not-so-small wars that the United States may have to deter or fight in this turbulent period of international relations, the Carter administration emphasized prime reliance upon conventional forces to protect U.S. global security interests. In its defence policies it set the objective of dealing simultaneously with one major and one minor conventional contingency; identified the Middle East, the Persian Gulf, and North-East Asia as areas where the most serious minor contingencies may occur; and reasoned that adequate preparation for 'one-and-a-half wars'—a symbolic formula with which the Nixon administration, in recognition of the Sino-Soviet split, replaced the Kennedy administration's 'two-and-a-half wars'—should be able to cope with brush-fire wars and other lesser eventualities. Actual defence plans and capabilities are more than ever concentrated on deterring and fighting the hypothetical major war on the central front in Europe, and the increased pre-positioning of supplies in Europe reduces the flexibility of American forces in meeting contingencies outside the area. Nevertheless, the administration's claim that augmented quick-reaction forces not committed to NATO—light Marine and Army combat divisions, naval, amphibious lift, and tactical air forces and mobile strike forces based in the United States—would be adequate to cope with short and intense wars outside the NATO area and would be at the same time economically acceptable may be valid.

The more difficult question is whether, where, when, and how the United States government is prepared to use such forces, given the residual inhibitions against Third-World interventions. Despite high official warnings against Soviet and Cuban interventions in Africa, and strong affirmations of American determination to counter the recent growth of Soviet military power, the United States is not on the threshold of an assertion of American power comparable to the Kennedy period— too much has changed. The growing disposition to define American security interests broadly and to express various degrees of anxiety over real and projected threats to them is not accompanied by a commensurate disposition to contemplate the use of American armed forces in peripheral areas. Therefore, if the Soviet Union exercises a modicum of discretion and avoids precipitating major crises, the reassertion of Cold War rhetoric may be little more than rhetorical.

In this event, the gap between strategic concept and operational power to support it could become greater than at any time since the Korean War. Diplomatic manoeuvres, arms transfers, proxy wars, and the interventions of allied and friendly countries may help close the gap; but there will also be a danger that the historic pattern of an unanticipated threat, met by a belated, improvised, overwrought, and inappropriate American reaction, will recur. One melancholy fact seems clear: the U.S. government cannot turn again to increased reliance on nuclear weapons to close this gap.

Fundamentally, the gap arises from the uncertainties of foreign policy, not the ambiguities of military strategy. If the conception of containment that guided American policy after the Korean War and reached its peak in the mid-'60s still prevailed, the United States, following the logic of limited-war doctrine, would be generating and projecting American armed power even more energetically than during the Kennedy period. Chastened by losing a war and conscious of the new complexities of coping with Soviet power, however, the United States is caught between the lessons of Munich and Vietnam. Consequently, although the strategy of flexible and controlled response by conventional means has never been more widely accepted, its utility as an instrument of policy where the prospect of local wars is greatest has never been more in question since it became an integral part of American strategic thought.

5

The Evolution of
Strategic Nuclear Doctrine

by Henry S. Rowen

Introduction*

Should a President in the event of a nuclear attack be left with the single option of ordering the mass destruction of enemy civilians, in the face of the certainty that it would be followed by the mass slaughter of Americans?

U.S. Foreign Policy for the 1970's,
A Report to Congress by Richard M. Nixon,
February 18, 1970.

Obviously a rhetorical question! Former President Nixon's query came in his first foreign policy report and posed sharply the issue of nuclear options. Evidently no one answered his question because it reappeared in three successive annual foreign policy reports.[1] Not until January of 1974 was it responded to officially.

The answer was "No."

Secretary of Defense James Schlesinger announced that the U.S. was changing its nuclear plans to provide for a greater range of options, including ones that would be a good deal less 'massive' than those that had been available in the past.[2]

Many observers were surprised by the revelation that the U.S. had little flexibility in its nuclear plans. More than a decade had passed since

---

*For much of the material on World War II the author is indebted to Thomas Brown, and for the post-World War II period up to 1963 to William Kaufmann's book, *The McNamara Strategy* (New York: Harper and Row, 1964). The material on the history of nuclear options in the 1960s owes a great deal to Alain Enthoven, former Assistant Secretary of Defense for Systems Analysis. In addition, much material on this subject has been made public through Congressional Hearings and Defense Department reports and statements.

The author is also indebted to Graham Allison and Peter Szanton for assistance and comments in the preparation of this paper. Finally, the perspective on nuclear doctrine has been developed in the course of a project on military doctrines and postures that the author has been carrying out with Albert Wohlstetter, who has provided many useful suggestions and comments.

Eisenhower's strategy of 'massive retaliation' had been abandoned. In 1961, President Kennedy had adopted a policy of having a wide range of military choices. Through the 1960s Secretary McNamara advocated having flexible nuclear plans. One would have thought that President Nixon should have inherited plans for a wide selection of choices from the use of one or a few such weapons on the battlefield, through larger-scale use on military targets, to the option of massive attack on Soviet civil society.

Evidently he did not. Though critics were sceptical about the implication of President Nixon's question, the available evidence is clear that the President had not had a wide range of choice for the use of nuclear weapons. Secretary Schlesinger stated this unambiguously:

> In the past we have had massive pre-planned nuclear strikes in which one would be dumping literally thousands of weapons on the Soviet Union. Some of these strikes could, to some extent, be withheld from going directly against cities, but that was limited even then.
>
> With massive strikes of that sort, it would be impossible to ascertain whether the purpose of a strategic strike was limited or not. It was virtually indistinguishable from an attack on cities. One would not have had blast damage in the cities, but one would have considerable fall-out and the rest of it.

The absence of pre-planned, non-massive nuclear options does not mean, as the Defense Secretary had pointed out, that they could not be prepared in an emergency. But this is a different matter from thinking through, in advance, the problems that might arise, working on how they might be dealt with, and training people in possibly needed operations.

The central question is, why is it, in the third decade of the nuclear era, more than a decade after Kennedy's and McNamara's policy of flexible options, four years after President Nixon's query, a Secretary of Defense said that non-massive nuclear options were only then in the process of being adopted?

The issue of nuclear options is not only of historical interest; it is a matter of considerable current policy relevance. The role of nuclear weapons in U.S. weapons policy in the years ahead is far from settled. If anything, the future of the subject is likely to be a good deal more complex and difficult than the past has been. Anyone who doubts this should reflect on the problem of the role of nuclear weapons in a world in which many countries, perhaps not all politically stable, possess them.

The Nuclear Planning Process

The present process of constructing nuclear plans in the United States dates from August, 1960 when Secretary of Defense Gates created the Joint Strategic Target Planning Staff (JSTPS) and charged it with producing an integrated plan for the use of nuclear weapons possessed by all of the U.S. military commands and for coordinating this nuclear plan with our allies. The Director of this staff reports to the Joint Chiefs of Staff; from the beginning he has been the Commander of the Strategic Air Command. His Deputy has, therefore, always been a naval officer. The JSTPS has provided an integrated plan for the forces of the Commander of the Strategic Air Command (CINCSAC), the Commander of U.S. forces in Europe (CINCEUR), the Commander of U.S. naval forces in the Atlantic (CINCLANT) and the Commander of U.S. forces in the Pacific (CINCPAC); he has also coordinated this plan with those of allied forces under the Supreme Allied Commanders in Europe and the Atlantic, SACEUR and SACLANT.

Until recently, the JSTPS operated under a national strategic targeting attack policy that was prepared by higher military and civilian authorities in 1960. This policy set objectives for the preparation of plans, assigned responsibilities, described the options to be developed, assigned specific tasks to be performed, and identified the forces involved. On the basis of this guidance, the Staff maintained a strategic target list and prepared the Single Integrated Operational Plan, or SIOP for short. The SIOP specified, for several options, the nuclear weapons to be used, the delivery systems, the routes of attack, the timing of attack, and the expected level of target damage to be attained. The options have been characterized in terms of three classes of targets ('nuclear threat', 'other military', and 'urban-industrial') and in terms of the timing of the attack relative to the launch of Soviet forces. (Timing would affect the size and composition of the U.S. forces surviving and available for launch.) The policy also specified the priority to be given to each target class. From 1960 to 1974, the priority in the assignment of weapons was first, to the urban-industrial targets, and then to nuclear threat and other military forces.* The capability of destroying urban-industrial targets was to be assured even with inadequate warning of an attack on American strategic forces and the consequent loss of a sizable portion of them. In short, highest importance has been consistently given to assuring a stipulated level of damage to the Soviet civil society and not to attempting to limit damage to the U.S. or its allies. However, as noted by Secretary

---

*A high 'priority' in this context means 'most important'. It does not mean first in time. Presumably the most time-urgent targets would be military forces, especially nuclear threat ones. Highest priority also does not mean that the greatest *weight of effort* would have to be allocated against urban-industrial targets; rather that the *confidence* of being able to destroy these targets should be high.

Schlesinger in the quotation above, there has existed the option of withholding strikes going directly against cities.

The basic planning process, once overall priorities have been established, is to assign weapons to specific targets. For example, air defences might be assigned to early missile attack because their destruction is important if bombers are to penetrate reliably. The principle of 'cross-targeting' has been employed in order to have high confidence against possible failure, i.e. the assignment of weapons to the same target from forces that have very different vulnerabilities on the ground to Soviet attack and different problems of penetration to target. This process involves multiplying a series of estimated probabilities, e.g. of survival, reliable launch, penetration to target, and probability of target destruction (given a specific bomb or warhead yield and weapon delivery accuracy). Weapons are then assigned to targets to achieve a given level of expected damage or a given level of damage with a certain level of confidence.* The result of this exercise has been the assignment of the weapons in the U.S. nuclear offensive forces (ICBMs, submarine missiles, manned bombers and theatre based forces) to the three target classes.

The countries targeted in the SIOP in the past have been the U.S.S.R., the People's Republic of China, and allies of these two powers in Eastern Europe and elsewhere. A good deal of flexibility has been provided for in the separate targeting of countries—although when the SIOP was first created, plans did not provide for an attack on the U.S.S.R. without also attacking China. This non-separation reflected widely held American beliefs about the monolithism of the Sino-Soviet bloc.

Over the years the number of weapons in both the U.S. and the Soviet forces has increased enormously, as has the number of targets assigned to these weapons, but the number of urban-industrial targets, the most important category as defined by the American political authorities, has increased little. This has made possible the assignment of many more weapons to the lower priority nuclear threat and other military target categories than was possible earlier. So long as the forces survive for launch, the task of producing a high level of urban damage would not be difficult for the U.S. (nor would it be, although with a lag, for the Soviet Union). However, the large increase in the number of warheads deliverable against the Soviet Union and increases in the number, hardness, and mobility of Soviet long-range nuclear forces have resulted in a decline in damage expectancies for this class of targets. And a large and growing part of this force, e.g. submarines at sea, cannot be targeted. There has been no comparable decline in the U.S. ability to deliver weapons against Soviet general purpose forces.

---

*This sequence of probabilities of course assumes a prior one, that the political decision to launch an attack had occurred. As later discussion brings out, the probability that a decision to launch a SIOP attack would be made by the political authorities has come increasingly into question.

Centralizing and integrating nuclear attack planning has meant reconciling the objectives of several U.S. commanders as well as those of other nations, a task of considerable complexity and delicacy. Each can be expected to have his own views about what should be done to meet his responsibilities. Before August 1960, each theatre commander made his own plans for the use of his command's nuclear weapons. In addition, the commander of SAC had a separate nuclear plan for employing the major portion of American nuclear strength. And SACEUR, an allied commander, has long had his own regional plan for the employment of the forces assigned to him, allied as well as U.S.

The directive on nuclear attack policy announced by Secretary Schlesinger in 1974 covered all nuclear weapons, not just those classified as 'strategic'. It differs from the earlier directive not only by providing for less than massive options but, most importantly, by emphasizing the existence of non-targets, i.e. places that it would be in the U.S. interest to preserve from destruction. In the past, there had been constraints, for example, on the amount of fall-out on allied and neutral territory, constraints by SACEUR on collateral damage in Eastern Europe and constraints on damage within allied territory; there was also the city-withhold option. However, on the whole, it had been assumed that collateral damage to places of value to an adversary other than designated targets was a 'bonus'. Now it is explicitly recognized that it might be very much to the U.S. advantage to prevent damage to certain places or things of value in the Soviet Union, e.g. population centres. In short, collateral damage is now being increasingly seen as a 'minus'. There has been no announced change in this policy in the past several years.

The current policy provides an option for attack on urban targets, but with emphasis on targeting selected war-related industrial facilities, not on widespread damage to populations. This distinction in targeting is becoming technically feasible because of the increased accuracy of weapons delivery. High accuracy lowers collateral damage both directly and indirectly. Directly it does this by preventing bombs from missing targets and hitting non-targets, indirectly by making possible the substitution of low-yield weapons for high-yield ones and, in some cases, the use of fewer weapons. In short the linking of 'urban' to 'industrial' targets in the hyphenated phrase 'urban-industrial' does not follow from the laws of physics but from a combination of doctrine and technology specific to a given era. Now both technology and doctrine are undergoing changes.

The new policy also includes the option of assigning weapons to nuclear-threat targets. Most importantly, it includes limited-employment options, e.g. those confined to a region or a specific objective.

Overview

The World War II Experience

The beginning of understanding of later developments is an appreciation of the significance of the experience of both the British and the Americans in strategic bombing in World War II. Although the RAF did not enter World War II with an area bombing doctrine, it soon adopted one. Britain's employment of bombing against urban areas was, in substantial measure, the unintended product of her bombers' inability to penetrate Germany by day and their poor bombing accuracy by night. Poor accuracy contributed to civilian casualties in two ways: first, even when strictly military objectives were the targets, a large number of bombs would miss the target and fall almost at random. (In the early part of the War only about one-fifth of the bombs dropped by the RAF over Germany by night fell within five miles of the target.) Second, the known inaccuracy led to the deliberate selection of targets in the middle of built-up areas so that the large numbers of misses would at least do some 'good'. It was also argued that bombs falling at random on German towns would weaken German morale.[4] This made a virtue out of necessity. These 'industrial area' raids, carried out in the heat of war, were also a response to the German raids against British cities; they were also the product of British frustration in having no other way to strike directly at Germany until the invasion in 1944. Their continuation was possibly dependent on the fact that the Germans could not reply in kind.

The American strategic bombers of the 8th Air Force, using optical means to bomb by day and in good weather, were for some time able to achieve much greater accuracies than the British bombing by night. The Americans attempted to pursue a policy of precision strikes against selected targets, but there was a deterioration in this policy during the course of the war. German air defences made clear weather attacks costly, intelligence limitations kept some targets from being correctly identified, and a desire to co-operate with the RAF led to strikes on targets which were really surrogates for area attacks on towns (e.g. the marshalling yards in Dresden). In the bombing campaign against Japan, a shift in the tactics of the 20th Air Force occurred when General LeMay replaced General Hansell. U.S. area attacks, for example the fire raids on Tokyo, then became a matter of policy.

The upshot was that bombing of the war potential of an adversary, i.e. 'strategic' bombing, by the end of World War II had come to be associated with large-scale civilian destruction—at least as a by-product.

Early Nuclear Doctrine: Continuity with World War II

The policy of strategic bombing was disputed during the War on several grounds: on the payoff from allocating resources to long-range bombers as opposed to other military forces, on the efficacy of area attacks as compared with those against specific war-related factories, and on the morality of area attacks. Later analysis intensified doubts about the policy of strategic bombing. Nevertheless, as American concern with the Soviet threat to Western Europe grew in the late 1940s and early 1950s, a capability of strategic bombing emerged as an essential means of coping with that threat. The belief that the Soviet Union had superior conventional strength in Europe and elsewhere around its borders, along with the knowledge that the United States had clear nuclear superiority, dominated U.S. defence policy for many years. Reliance on the weapon that the United States had a clear advantage in to counter Soviet strength on the ground seemed obvious. The ability to deliver, say, 100 weapons with yields in the tens of kilotons on Soviet major industrial centres that had the majority of its steel, petroleum refining, aircraft and munitions industries was thought to be an impressive deterrent. If the Soviets were to commit aggression none the less, the carrying out of such an attack promised an important advantage—assuming that there was enough strength on the ground to keep the Russians from quickly taking over Western Europe. In short, the nuclear planning task was seen as an extension of strategic bombing in World War II—greatly compressed in time, magnified in effect, and reduced in cost. The task was principally the destruction of critical war-supporting industries in order to affect Soviet battlefield operations, the longer term ability of its economy to support combat, and its will to continue the conflict. The designated ground zeros were almost entirely (1) industrial facilities, (2) 'retardation' targets, e.g. transportation links whose destruction was intended to slow the westward movement of Soviet forces, and (3) counterforce targets, the bases of the small and concentrated Soviet long-range air force. Population damage in this period was viewed largely as a by-product of attacks on industrial and retardation targets.

In the early 1950s the Soviet long-range air force was regarded neither as a major target system nor as a threat to the survival of the U.S. air forces. Here, too, there was an element of continuity with the past; enemy attack on U.S. bases had not been much of a problem throughout most of World War II. However, work done at the Rand Corporation in the early 1950s showed that even a small Soviet long-range air force had the capacity to destroy strategic bases abroad on which the United States were then dependent and even threatened forces in the continental U.S.[5] Although these vulnerabilities were correctable, this work focused attention on what was to be a continuing concern in U.S defence planning, the possibility of the Soviets developing a capacity to destroy the Amercan strategic offensive force by launching a nuclear strike against it. This possibility had implications not only for the survival of the United States' own forces but, more broadly, for the stability of the strategic balance. The existence of vulnerable nuclear forces on both sides would provide an incentive to both to strike first in an ambiguous situation. Concern about vulnerability led the United States to take many actions to reduce the vulnerability of its strategic forces in the 1950s and in the years since then.

A different response to the developing Soviet long-range nuclear threat was a proposal, urged by scientists at M.I.T. and elsewhere, to build a highly effective U.S. continental air defence system. This idea was worked on in the Lincoln Summer Study of 1952 which proposed the construction of a large and costly air defence control system for the U.S. This air defence system was designed primarily to achieve very high effectiveness in defending U.S. cities against nuclear attack by Soviet bombers. Since only a small number of bombs had to get through to these cities in order to do great damage to them, the task faced by this system was formidable. It proved to be infeasible. But as late as the Gaither Committee Report in 1957, even after the development of high-yield fusion weapons and with intercontinental and sea-based missiles in the offing, the advocates of defence proposed a very costly programme of air defences, anti-missile defences and civil defences to protect U.S. industry and population from attack. (The Report also advocated improved protection for the U.S. strategic forces along the lines that had been proposed by Rand.) It is not irrelevant to the current debate about flexible options to observe that many of the enthusiasts for protecting the U.S. population from attack in the 1950s were to shift in the 1960s to the position that populations were the *only* appropriate target for attack in a nuclear war.*

The alternative of using nuclear weapons only or mainly on the battlefield did not seem to exist for many years. Individual battlefield targets did not present large concentrations of military value and they were too numerous to warrant expenditure of the small stockpile of nuclear weapons on them. However, the possibility of having weapons for battlefield use, or indeed limiting their use in this way, was of interest to the Army and to some scientists. Project Vista, conducted at the California Institute of Technology in 1951, was an early effort to develop this concept.

In sum, in the period before the H-Bomb was developed in the early 1950s, U.S. doctrine on the bombing of cities was ambiguous. The use of fission weapons delivered by medium and heavy bombers against the Soviet Union was part of the strategy for the defence of Western Europe. Many of the targets were selected with the intention that they should have an effect, immediate or delayed, on the Soviets' ability to carry on a war; they were also to serve as a deterrent to attack. Attack on targets located in population centres would have caused a good deal of population damage. but the numbers of weapons and their yields were still small

---

*It is also important to note that their indiscriminate enthusiasm for spending money triggered the response from President Eisenhower that their proposals were politically infeasible. A similar misguided inspiration today holds that the failure of the Strategic Arms Limitation negotiations would mean vast added expenditures on arms.

enough for there to be a big difference in the civil damage that would have been produced then and what was to be possible within only a few years.

The possibility of building the H-Bomb produced an intense debate on the uses of nuclear weapons. Many of the opponents saw it as a weapon that could only be used against cities and didn't think it was necessary for that task; fission weapons in larger numbers were good enough for that. Many also opposed attacking cities and favoured having more lower-yield fission weapons for use against military targets. The proponents did not argue that they wanted to make it easier to destroy cities; they were mainly interested in a more powerful and efficient technology. Ironically, both sides in the dispute assumed that these weapons would be usable mainly against cities, and big cities at that. Both sides missed the main impact that thermonuclear weapons were to have for at least the next quarter century: the development of lightweight, medium and low-yield weapons.

However, the development of thermonuclear weapons by both the U.S. and the U.S.S.R. did have consequences for the civil damage that a nuclear war would cause. Between 1954 and 1960, although the number of vehicles in the U.S. strategic force did not change greatly, the total megatonnage in the U.S. strategic offensive and defensive forces increased over twentyfold. (The peak in megatonnage—and in 'effective megatonnage', another index of damage potential—was in 1960.)[6] With yields in the megatons instead of kilotons, the delivery of only a few hundred weapons could destroy a large part of the industrial capacity and, without large-scale civil defences, a large part of the populations of even the largest countries.

The discovery that these weapons could not only be made large in yield but light in weight, i.e. that they would have a high yield per pound and could come in small as well as big packages, made long-range ballistic missiles practical, both land and submarine based. It also meant that the U.S. strategic force, which was concentrated on a small number of airbases in the U.S., and already vulnerable to a co-ordinated 'sneak' attack by bombers, was highly vulnerable to a co-ordinated attack with ballistic missiles.

One consequence of the recognition of this new threat was further vulnerability-reducing changes in the U.S. strategic nuclear posture throughout the 1950s and 1960s. Another was a reinforcing of the notion that a nuclear strike had to be quick and massive rather than controlled and discriminate because strategic bases and forces could not be expected to survive long in a conflict. Still another was that as the Soviet nuclear force grew it became an important target system. And because the Soviets were slow in reducing the vulnerability of their nuclear forces, it was feasible for the U.S. to assign weapons to nuclear threat targets with high damage expectations; this assuming, not unreasonably for some contingencies, given their normal low readiness state, that Soviet forces had not been launched by the time American weapons arrived on target. By the late 1950s, the long-range delivery forces of the U.S. consisted of over 2,000 vehicles, with some vehicles carrying more than one bomb. (About 500 B-52 long-range bombers, 1,485 B-47 and RB-47 medium-range bombers and reconnaissance aircraft, B-58 bombers, and several hundred Snark, Thor, Jupiter, Mace, Matador and Regulus missiles.) This force could cover many more targets than in the late 1940s and early 1950s when there were few bombs available. Moreover, the large area of destruction produced by megaton yield weapons that became operational in the mid and late 1950s meant that attack on military or industrial targets in or on the edge of cities would inevitably produce a great deal of damage to populations. In contrast with the weapons of the late 1940s and early 1950s, it was now virtually impossible to attack specific industrial facilities such as an electric power generating station in a metropolitan area without destroying most of its built-up area and the people in it. Attempts to do precision bombing during World War II had often been frustrated by the need to cope with strong air defences in daylight bombing and poor accuracy in bombing by night or in bad weather. This had produced widespread civilian damage. With thermonuclear weapons, only a few bombs needed to be delivered to destroy each target, but their effects were much more widespread and destructive.

The idea that cities were the natural targets for thermonuclear weapons was reinforced by the low accuracy expected of ballistic missiles. Mid-1950s U.S. estimates were that these missiles would have average miss distances of three to five miles; but such large inaccuracies could be more than compensated for by the large area of damage produced by high-yield weapons against cities. These weapons would also be effective against 'soft' strategic forces such as aircraft on airbases and above-ground, fixed missile sites. But missiles could be put under the sea and put underground and hardened, and alert bombers could be got off the ground on warning. Cities could not be moved.

The major command responsible for conducting strategic nuclear operations was the Strategic Air Command, the descendant of the 8th and 20th Air Forces that had carried out the U.S. bombing campaigns against Germany and Japan. Its wartime experiences were bound to have an important influence on its doctrine.* Shaped by its WWII experience

---

*Characterizing the doctrine of a Command or Service is a tricky business. Within these organizations there are people who have a considerable variety of values, attitudes and expectations—almost as large a variety as is held in American society. Nevertheless, within a Command certain values and operational codes tend to dominate and strongly affect perceptions, attitudes and actions of its members. These are created in large measure by learned experiences and interpretations of experience. Doctrine is, among other things, a codification of learning. However, not everyone in an organization has the same experience or derives the same lessons. Moreover, changes in organizational doctrine have occurred as the result of changes in technology, experiences and leadership. The past yields important information about possible future behaviour, but it is a far from perfect predictor.

and by the views of its long-time Commander, General LeMay, SAC became committed to a high standard of operational proficiency, a high state of readiness, and the concept of delivering a crushing blow against all sources of the opponent's strength: military, industrial, and governmental controls. The SAC view of strategic bombing was that (1) the Soviets could be deterred from engaging in virtually the entire relevant range of hostile acts, including small non-nuclear attacks, through the threat of large-scale nuclear attack; (2) the side that 'prevailed' militarily would dominate in the post-war period—therefore, Soviet military forces were important targets; and (3) urban-industrial facilities and government controls should be hit because their destruction would cripple the Soviet ability to wage war and the ability of the Soviet regime to maintain control.

The SAC doctrine was clearly consistent with the overall defence policy of the Eisenhower administration. The principal threats to U.S. security were seen as the danger of nuclear war and the danger of excessive military spending forced by competition with the Soviet Union. Having a strong nuclear posture was seen as a way of coping effectively and economically with these dangers. It was also consistent with the 'massive retaliation' doctrine enunciated by Secretary of State Dulles (although this doctrine was not regarded by him as an alternative to having more flexible means for dealing with small contingencies). The Eisenhower administration had adopted a policy of main but not sole reliance on nuclear weapons. Given the available technology and prevailing operational concepts, the existing policy was one, in effect, of planning on inflicting massive civil damage.

The Emergence of Alternative Doctrines in the Late 1950s

Although the belief that thermonuclear weapons meant that nuclear war would involve massive and indiscriminate damage to civil societies was widely shared by the end of the 1950s, cities were proposed as the only nuclear targets by some U.S. Navy officers and scientists. Although earlier, in 1948, the Navy had attacked the Air Force's B-36 programme in part on the grounds that the B-36 was designed for the mission of delivering nuclear weapons on cities, the invention of the Polaris submarine missile system produced a shift. Many of the scientists who had opposed the build-up of strategic forces, had fought the development of the H-Bomb, and had favoured strong air defence of the U.S., reversed field. The threat to bomb cities shifted from being bad to being good. It was argued that these missiles could be aimed at cities and launched in a deliberate and controlled way. One variant of this general view was that the strategic force need only consist of a small (called a 'finite') number of these missiles in contrast to having strategic vehicles for use against Soviet military forces as well as industrial and urban targets. On this view, aiming at long-range air force bases, missile sites, etc. was especially bad because it meant threatening a force vital to the Soviet Union; this would cause it to expand its strategic force; this, in turn, would threaten the United States and drive up the size and cost of the U.S. strategic forces; *ad infinitum.* The result would be an 'uncontrollable' arms race as the two sides reacted to each other, all at progressively higher levels of forces and budgets.* Moreover, the concealment, mobility, and therefore assumed high degree of protection of the Polaris meant that *it* did not present to the Soviets a target which would stimulate them to increase their strategic forces and expenditures.† The funds saved by adopting this strategy could then be spent on the traditional forces, i.e. aircraft carriers and other forces which were still needed.

A very different doctrine was developed during the 1950s at Rand and by some Air Force officers. The context of this work was the need for assuring a protected power to retaliate. Within this context, some of the work done emphasized controlled response—but not against cities. It held that a policy of planning for nuclear strikes that had a reflex, 'spasm' character, especially against cities, was irrational and unnecessary, indeed suicidal. Instead, attacks on urban targets should be withheld and any such attacks, if carried out at all—which seemed to many analysts highly undesirable—should be conducted in a deliberate and controlled way. The importance of the military outcome was stressed both in terms of the ability to diminish Soviet military strength and to limit its capacity to do damage to the U.S.

The U.S. Army's view of nuclear weapons was ambivalent. It naturally wanted to make use of these modern weapons; and, as the weapons stockpile grew and as low-yield, light weapons were developed by the weapons laboratories, a considerable variety of short-range weapons were developed and bought. (And some not of short range; the Army's Jupiter ballistic missile had a nominal range of 1500 miles.) The Army explored many ways in which nuclear weapons might be used on the battlefield, either in conjunction with an all-out nuclear campaign or as an alternative to it. The results were not encouraging. The tactical problems of manoeuvre, communications and command on the nuclear battlefield appeared formidable—not to mention the difficulties of keeping troops motivated in a nuclear engagement and of limiting collateral damage to civilians in the combat area. Moreover, there has been no assurance that the Soviets would play the preferred game of limiting nuclear weapons to low yields; for example, they might decide to try to blast through the 7th Army in Germany with high-yield weapons. The Army was divided on this matter, but on balance concluded that non-

---

*This theory assumed, unrealistically, that the adversaries did not have available effective means to reduce their forces' vulnerability as an alternative to costly multiplication; also that there were no binding constraints on available budgets.

†It could, however, result in the Soviets shifting efforts to anti-submarine warfare forces. The net effect of this shift might be no reduction in Soviet military spending or even an increase.

nuclear capabilities should receive most emphasis. Nevertheless, the Army acquired a large number of nuclear weapons; it did so partly because the Eisenhower administration had adopted a policy of placing primary emphasis on nuclear capabilities and partly as a hedge against the possibility that battlefield use might actually occur.*

Despite the emergence of these alternatives, U.S. nuclear strategy by the late 1950s and until 1961 was dominated by the concept of the 'Optimum Mix', the planned massive response by SAC to a Soviet attack abroad or against the U.S. by attacking a combination of high priority military, industrial, and government control targets. This strategy was incorporated into NATO's MC 14/2 which called for a nuclear response to any Soviet intrusion, even local, if it persevered.† This strategy prevailed to the end of the Eisenhower administration despite increasing evidence, displayed vividly in Sputnik and ICBM tests, that the Soviets were building a strong capacity to attack the U.S. It persisted despite growing doubts within the administration about the continued wisdom of the Eisenhower basic national security policy of placing main but not sole reliance on nuclear weapons.‡

The Expansion of Options in the Early 1960s

The Kennedy administration made reduced dependence on nuclear threats its major defence policy initiative. This shift was undertaken on two grounds: (1) strengthening deterrence by having more credible means of response to the more probable, i.e. smaller and non-nuclear, kinds of contingencies which were anticipated; (2) having an alternative between suicide and surrender, if deterrence failed. This meant more emphasis on non-nuclear forces. Moreover, deeper investigation into Soviet conventional strength led to re-evaluation of that strength *vis-à-vis* that of the NATO countries; the result was a considerable deflation of the Soviet side.[7] The task of providing a strong non-nuclear defence to

---

*During the course of the 1950s, nuclear weapons were made available for many missions including air defence, anti-submarine warfare, tactical aircraft delivery, carrier-based aircraft. Allied forces in NATO had been provided with U.S. nuclear weapons under a 'two-key' arrangement which kept them in U.S. custody. By 1961, over 3,000 nuclear weapons had been deployed to Europe for use by U.S. and allied forces. By the late 1960s, the total had risen to 7,000.

†In the late 1950s, SACEUR, then General Lauris Norstad, introduced the concept of a 'pause' after a Soviet intrusion and before the unleashing of the full power of the West. The concept of the 'pause', although never very clearly defined, recognized the possibility that deterrence could fail, that mistakes or accidents could happen and that responsible governments had to have some alternative to rapid commitment to a devastating nuclear war.

‡This was a doctrine that could only be undermined by growing Soviet ability to inflict damage on the U.S. The major effort made in the 1950s to build a continental air defence system to exact a very high attrition level against long-range Soviet bombers was never very promising. The prospect of *effective damage-limiting* through active defence was greatly reduced with the advent of ICBMs because, in the 1950s, effective ABM defence seemed distant at best. The conclusion that damage-limiting through active air defence was unpromising led to sharp and continuing cuts in the 1960s and 1970s. These technological developments were much less damaging to more modest possible goals for active defence: the defence of strategic forces or defence against small nuclear powers or accidental or unauthorized small attacks.

Growing Soviet capacity to attack the U.S., of course, undermined even more the doctrine of attacking only Soviet cities.

Europe, instead of seeming hopelessly impossible, came to appear to many U.S. planners (but by no means all—and certainly not to all Europeans) to be attainable. There were important NATO weaknesses, such as inadequate stocks of ammunition, which if not remedied could be fatal, but the prospect for an effective non-nuclear defence in many contingencies seemed to be far from hopeless. However, there were still uncertainties and there were some contingencies that almost certainly could not be met at the non-nuclear level. Therefore, deterring non-nuclear attack in some areas and deterring first Soviet use of nuclear weapons in all important areas still required a U.S. nuclear threat.

The upshot was no reduction in nuclear weapons abroad. On the contrary, the number in Europe was increased substantially during the 1960s. This build-up occurred for several reasons: (1) The existing policy was one of adding to theatre nuclear stockpiles; a positive effort was needed to reverse it. (2) A policy of defending Europe at the non-nuclear level could not be carried out by the U.S. alone. European co-operation was necessary and the Europeans were suspicious of U.S. motivations in emphasizing non-nuclear forces and, more importantly, they were unwilling to spend money to upgrade their conventional forces. (3) The Kennedy administration, faced with European suspicions about its intentions and eager to win support for a build-up of conventional forces, was unwilling to lend support to those on both sides of the Atlantic who charged that this policy was really one of reducing the U.S. commitment to Europe (what later came to be called a 'decoupling' of the U.S. from Europe). A change in policy to hold down or to reverse the flow of U.S. nuclear weapons to Europe would have been held by some to signal a dangerous reduction in U.S. commitment to Europe's defence. (4) Although the JCS did not have a sound basis for proposing the continued build-up of nuclear weapons in Europe, Secretary McNamara was not armed with powerful arguments to oppose it.* He went along with the increases because he did not think that increasing tactical nuclear weapons made much of a difference one way or another and saw no good grounds for making trouble with the JCS and the Europeans on this issue.

The other key defence initiative taken by the Kennedy administration was the strengthening of the U.S. second-strike, long-range nuclear capacity. Both the Polaris and Minuteman programmes were speeded up and the alertness of the bombers increased. These decisions were motivated by concern for the vulnerability of the U.S. strategic force, not by consideration of targeting. They were accompanied by the retirement of the rest of the B-47 force and the phasing out of Snark, Mace, Matador, Thor, Jupiter, and Regulus missiles, the stopping of B-52 and B-58 production, and the cancelling of the B-70,

---

*The standard fiscal argument wouldn't work well in this case since most of the cost of these weapons was in the budget of the Atomic Energy Commission.

Skybolt and the nuclear powered aeroplane. There were also large cuts in air defences.[8] As a result, the budget for strategic offence and defence forces soon began to shrink both in constant and current dollars during the rest of the 1960s and into the 1970s.[9] However, the programmed force provided a large strategic nuclear force secure for some time into the future against advances in Soviet offensive forces. The combined effect of these changes was to reduce dependence for survival of the U.S. strategic forces on warning and quick response. The B-52s still depended on warning and alertness for their survival but the sheltered Minutemen, and especially Polaris missiles, did not. These changes helped to provide a technological basis for a strategy other than a massive nuclear response.

The importance of having an ability to respond to an attack deliberately and selectively was perceived by Secretary of Defense McNamara.[10] For one thing, there was the possibility of a Soviet nuclear strike limited to the U.S. strategic forces; or the possibility of limited nuclear use by the Soviets against U.S. or allied troops in Europe or elsewhere; or the contingency of a large-scale Soviet attack on Europe, a contingency for which the U.S. had continually and from the very start said it would use nuclear weapons if non-nuclear means were insufficient; or the possibility of accidental or unauthorized launch of nuclear weapons. On this last possibility, there was no reason to believe that the Russians were casual about control over nuclear forces; on the contrary, they appeared to have tight, centralized control. Nevertheless, circumstances might conceivably arise in which some nuclear weapons might be launched other than through a deliberate Politburo decision. The point was not that contingencies of this sort seemed likely but that if they were to occur and the U.S. had only the choice of a massive nuclear response or doing nothing, the results would be catastrophic.*

Consistent with this view, a change in nuclear planning was made in the early 1960s. Basic U.S. options were developed that differentiated more clearly between attacks directed against military targets and against cities. However, although this meant a shift away from Optimum Mix, essentially a single option approach, as Secretary Schlesinger has pointed out, these were still large options, i.e. they involved thousands of weapons. The principal objective remained deterring Soviet attacks, on allies as well as the U.S., by the threat to carry out large-scale nuclear operations, including attack on urban-industrial targets. A second objective was to attempt to limit damage directly, if deterrence failed, by attacking Soviet nuclear forces, by active defences and civil defences (but

---

*By the late 1950s, the idea that the U.S. strategic forces should ·be well protected and used in a controlled way had gained wide acceptance. But there were large differences in targeting concepts, described above. Meanwhile, the operators had to work with the equipment on hand which wasn't very compatible with these notions of controlled use. Many of the warheads had multi-megaton yields, missile accuracy was poor, manned bombers and unsheltered missiles, if not launched quickly, risked destruction, and low-level penetration of bombers meant ground or near-ground bursts which produced enhanced fall-out.

the last were difficult to sell to Congress). The indirect, and potentially much more powerful, way to limit damage was to increase the adversary's incentive to limit damage to the U.S. by withholding attack on his cities. This concept was basic to the option of withholding urban attacks.

Despite his continued endorsement of the importance of controlled response as long as he was in office, the emphasis in McNamara's statements on nuclear forces and doctrine shifted after 1963 to that of Assured Destruction. This doctrine held that a nuclear exchange would, with high probability, result in over 100 million fatalities in both the U.S. and the U.S.S.R. and that attempts to limit damage through active and passive defences could be readily defeated by improvements in offensive forces. The principal test of adequacy of the U.S. strategic force came to be the ability of the programmed force to produce civil damage, even against a greater than expected threat. The damage criterion settled on by McNamara for determining the size of the strategic force was the destruction of 20-25 percent of the Soviet population and 50 percent of its industrial capacity.[11] The programmed forces decided on in the early 1960s readily met this test—so readily that it seemed evident that the forces were more than adequate. The primary purpose of the Assured Destruction capabilities doctrine was to provide a metric for deciding how much force was enough: it provided a basis for denying Service and Congressional claims for more money for strategic forces. It also served the purpose of dramatizing for the Congress and the public the awful consequences of large-scale nuclear war and its inappropriateness as an instrument of policy. (However, it was never proposed by McNamara or his staff that nuclear weapons actually be *used* in this way.)

Assured Destruction was symmetrical. It implied that limiting damage to the U.S. population against large direct nuclear attack was infeasible or too costly. Nevertheless, direct damage-limiting continued to be asserted as an objective for strategic offensive and defensive forces. However, analyses of the cost of protecting populations as against the costs of destroying them—assuming that the enemy sought to kill people as distinct from regarding population damage as a by-product of attack on military targets—showed the defence to be at a cost disadvantage. A country would have to spend a good deal more on defence than offence, e.g. a factor of three times, at each level of damage. This unfavourable ratio, the high costs of such a defence, perhaps along with the political obstacles to persuading the Congress to support a nationwide fall-out shelter programme, led McNamara and President Johnson to conclude that damage-limiting on a large scale should not be pursued. In a special message on defence to the Congress in February, 1965, Johnson said that the United States should be alert to the possibility of limiting destruction, but that a comprehensive damage-limiting programme would be costly and uncertain in effectiveness. He also said that defence expenditure would comprise a declining proportion of a growing GNP with the resources freed going to meet other needs.*

There were serious problems with the doctrine of Assured Destruction. For one thing, there was a continued affirmation of the U.S. intention to use nuclear weapons for the defence of Europe if needed. But many Europeans—and Americans—continued to believe that Europe, or important parts of it, could not be reliably defended at the non-nuclear level. And it was becoming decreasingly credible that the United States would commit suicide in the event of an attack on Europe. Would that attack be deterred if America's only nuclear response to it was a suicidal one? To be sure, McNamara continued to mention, albeit briefly, the case for flexible nuclear response and the objective of limiting damage (but the U.S. had visibly cut back on active air defences, civil defences, and had no plans for anti-missile defence of populations).

Increasingly what was being communicated to the American people, the Europeans, and the Russians, was the prospect of 100 million dead Americans and a similar number of dead Russians (and also of dead Europeans) if a nuclear exchange were to occur. McNamara sought to resolve the conflict between this doctrine and American commitments to allies by persuading the United States' NATO allies to have sufficient non-nuclear strength not be to be dependent on the threat of first use of nuclear weapons. Although his arguments were substantively powerful, they were not highly persuasive to the Europeans and, in any case, they left unsolved the problem of what to do if the Soviets used these weapons first. Any use of nuclear weapons by the Soviets (or the Chinese for that matter) that left the United States with a stake in the continuance of society faced the U.S. with the need for having a non-suicidal response capability and policy.

The process which led Secretary McNamara to support the development of a wider range of nuclear options and to back off, but not reverse, the policy of Assured Destruction deserves a closer look.

Secretary McNamara's interest in nuclear planning was engaged from the outset of his term of office. In an early briefing on the existing nuclear plans, it was pointed out to him that they did not offer a choice between

---

*Damage-limiting was not abandoned altogether. It might be feasible under favourable circumstances. The most important of these were cases in which a mutual interest in survival produced mutual restraint. But for such cases, given the high weapon yields projected in the strategic forces, fall-out protection was important. Studies showed such protection to be highly cost-effective, but the combination of low confidence in the prospect of restrained behaviour along with the political costs of trying to get fall-out shelters, prevented the Johnson administration from advocating them.

Earlier, a large fall-out shelter programme had been advocated by the Gaither Committee in 1957 as part of a large programme of strategic offence and defence, and had been rejected by President Eisenhower. In 1961, there had been a brief period of interest in shelters during the period of greatest concern over the escalation of the Berlin crisis.

The principal exception to the movement away from the objective of direct damage-limiting during the 1960s was the argument used in 1967 to justify building a 'thin' ABM system, justified mainly as an anti-Chinese defence, designed against a small, technologically unsophisticated nuclear power but not against deliberate large attack by the Soviet Union. The alternative of a 'thick' ABM defence against the Soviet Union was explicitly excluded.

attack on urban-industrial targets and attack on military forces. Moreover, they did not provide for the flexibility to attack some communist countries without attacking others. As a result, McNamara directed Alain Enthoven, who created and headed the Office of Systems Anlaysis in the Office of the Secretary of Defense, to work with the Joint Staff to develop a greater range of options. This resulted in new planning guidance.

It distinguished more clearly among the three tasks described in Section I: attack on (1) nuclear threat targets, (2) other military forces and (3) urban-industrial targets. It also provided options for refraining from attacks on particular countries and for withholding direct attack on cities. However, the tasks all involved large attacks, and civilian damage would have been very heavy. Furthermore, there was not a clear distinction between 'urban' and 'industrial' targets, a distinction that had in reality almost disappeared in the 1950s with the advent of high-yield weapons.

Secretary McNamara also argued the need for nuclear flexibility in a number of major statements. An important occasion was the NATO meeting at Athens in May of 1962. This message was repeated in a public speech in June in Ann Arbor in which he said:

> . . . the mere fact that no nation could rationally take steps leading to nuclear war does not guarantee that a nuclear war cannot take place. Not only do nations sometimes act in ways that are hard to explain on a rational basis, but even when acting in a 'rational' way they sometimes, indeed disturbingly often, act on the basis of misunderstandings of the true facts of the situation. . . The U.S. has come to the conclusion that to the extent feasible basic military strategy in a possible general war should be approached in much the same way that more conventional military operations have been regarded in the past. That is to say, principal military objectives, in the event of a nuclear war stemming from a major attack on the Alliance, should be the destruction of the enemy's military forces, not of his civilian population. . . In other words, we are giving a possible opponent the strongest imaginable incentive to refrain from striking our own cities.[12]

In subsequent annual posture statements he reiterated the need for flexibility:

> Furthermore, it is possible that the Soviet's initial strike might be directed solely at our military installations, leaving our cities as hostages for later negotiations. In that event, we might find it to our advantage to direct our immediate retaliatory blow against their military installations, and to withhold our attack on their cities, keeping the forces required to destroy their urban-industrial complex in a protected reserve for some kind of period of time.

Accordingly, we should plan for the 1965-67 time period a force which could: 1. Strike back decisively at the entire Soviet target system simultaneously; or 2. Strike back, first, at the Soviet bomber bases, missiles sites and other military installations associated with their long-range nuclear forces to reduce the power of any follow-up attack—and then, if necessary, strike back at the Soviet urban and industrial complex in a controlled and deliberate way. Such a force would give us the needed flexibility to meet a wide range of possible general war situations.

(FY 1966 Posture Statement)

In talking about global nuclear war, the Soviet leaders always say that they would strike at the entire complex of our military power including government and production centers, meaning our cities. If they were to do so, we would, of course, have no alternative but to retaliate in kind. But we have no way of knowing whether they would actually do so. It would certainly be their interest as well as ours to try to limit the terrible consequences of a nuclear exchange. By building into our forces a flexible capability, we at least eliminate the prospect that we could strike back in only one way, namely, against the entire Soviet target system including their cities. Such a prospect would give the Soviet Union no incentive to withhold attack against our cities in a first strike. We want to give them a better alternative. Whether they would accept it in the crisis of a global nuclear war, no one can say. Considering what is at stake, we believe it is worth the additional effort on our part to have this option.

(FY 1964 Posture Statement)

NATO should not only have an improved capability to meet major non-nuclear assaults with non-nuclear means and forces prepared for that option, but it should also achieve a true *tactical* nuclear capability which should include a broad, flexible range of nuclear options, short of general nuclear war and the means to implement them.

(FY 1966 Posture Statement)

The reaction to this policy initiative was not encouraging. Senators Russell and Margaret Chase Smith attacked the 'no cities' doctrine as a policy of weakness, a policy which revealed to them a lack of resolve. Senator Russell was an opponent of flexibility, but was also no advocate of Mutual Assured Destruction; he said that if there were only two people left in the world both of them should be Americans. Politicians on the left-side were no more supportive. Some saw nuclear flexibility as legitimizing nuclear weapons and making nuclear war more likely. Many of these people advocated a policy of planning to bomb populations as a means of stabilizing deterrence.

Among allies the reaction was mixed. Some favoured the policy for the reasons McNamara gave. Many of those who most enthusiastically supported the concept of having national nuclear forces opposed it because the utility of such forces depended on the argument of population bombing. Most of the allies, however, wanted to keep a U.S. nuclear commitment to Europe, a preference which cut *against* population bombing. But some were confused by McNamara's concepts and suspicious of U.S. motives.

The response of SAC and the JSTPS to this initiative was a mixture of support in recognition of the importance of the military outcome of a conflict and concern with the operational difficulties to be met. Moreover, although the SIOP planning process was a capabilities plan and not a requirements plan, it was not unconnected with the process of generating requirements for delivery systems. Because McNamara's early formulation did not distinguish sharply between capabilities planning and force requirements, the Service responses varied on this point but was largely addressed to the subject of requirements. For example, in 1963, General LeMay testified as follows:

Many people unfortunately measure the effectiveness of a proposed deterrent force by counting the number of enemy citizens to be brought under attack.

As you know, it doesn't take much of a nuclear force to destroy a large number of enemy cities. But the destruction of cities *per se* does not protect U.S. and allied lives.

Only the destruction of his military forces can do this. Therefore, an entirely different force capability is required to destroy those weapon systems posing a threat to U.S. and Allied populations.

The reaction of the Soviets to the American discussion was first to deny that limitations in war were possible, including the distinction between non-nuclear and nuclear conflict. Later, Soviet commentators shifted to the position that conflicts might be held to the non-nuclear level. But the possibility of a limited nuclear conflict was rejected in the Soviet literature during the 1960s.

In balancing these reactions, it seemingly appeared to McNamara that nuclear flexibility was being read as a policy of nuclear restraint and was being widely interpreted as implying that the U.S. could fight, win and survive a nuclear war and that the nation should therefore spend much more money on strategic forces—money that would have to come out of conventional force budgets. This prospect interfered with the task, seen as much more important, of building up non-nuclear strength. Moreover, the likelihood of nuclear war had seemed to recede. Planning of nuclear options seemed increasingly remote from the key defence issues. McNamara, therefore, began to re-emphasize the central importance of continuing to a high-confidence capability of inflicting great civil damage on the Soviet Union.

McNamara, while increasingly talking about Assured Destruction, apparently retained the view that any actual U.S. use of nuclear weapons should be controlled and restrained. He apparently also came to believe that the task of pre-planning nuclear options was a hopelessly difficult one because the contingencies in which weapons might be used were so unpredictable that nuclear planning could only be done when the contingency arose. The main task was trying to assure that major conflicts did not occur and trying to cope with any that might break out without the use of nuclear weapons.

As a result, planners, who had limited enthusiasm for limited options, read McNamara's Assured Destruction signals as meaning that they did not have to develop a wider range of options. The resulting employment doctrine was not one of flexible options; nor was it really a Mutual Assured Destruction one either (and still less was it the mini-variant, Minimum Deterrence). What the United States had was a strategic force far too large to be justified by that doctrine and with military forces as the planned targets. In sum, the nuclear planning process experienced no important change from the early 1960s until the mid-1970s. The assignment of weapons to a growing target list went on in accordance with the political direction established in the early 1960s.

Nuclear Doctrine After 1968

President Nixon's strategic doctrine, labelled Strategic Sufficiency, was put forward in several annual 'State of the World' reports. [13] It meant (1) having strategic forces strong enough to inflict the damage needed to deter strategic attacks on the United States and its allies and strong enough to face an aggressor contemplating less than all-out attack with an unacceptable risk of escalation; (2) also having forces strong enough to keep the U.S. allies from being coerced. It contained themes that had been put forward by McNamara earlier: there should be no indiscriminate mass destruction of civilians as the sole response to challenge; the ability to use force in a controlled way helped deterrence; if war came, a way was needed to prevent escalation; there was to be no policy of launching missiles on warning. But nowhere in his public statements did President Nixon state that actions had been taken that were consistent with the position he was asserting. He was hardly in a position to do so because the JCS had not been given directives to develop flexible options before 1974. Such flexibility as there was, which consisted mostly of some contingency plans outside the SIOP, had been prepared on the initiative of the JCS and the major commanders.

Strategic Sufficiency as described by Nixon's Secretary of Defense, Melvin Laird, centred on four objectives: (1) having a second-strike capability adequate to deter an all-out surprise attack on U.S. forces; (2)

assuring there was no incentive for the Soviet Union to strike first in a crisis; (3) preventing the Soviet Union from having greater ability to do urban-industrial damage to the United States that the U.S. could do to it; and (4) being able to defend against small attacks or accidental launches.[14] The concept of Strategic Sufficiency also included having forces adequate to prevent allies as well as the U.S. from being coerced by designing strategic nuclear forces that could enhance theatre and allied nuclear forces and also offer alternatives to resorting to mass urban and industrial destruction. This version of the doctrine repeated familiar themes: the importance of a second-strike capacity, reducing first-strike incentives, protection against small attacks, the need for flexible options, the contribution of strategic forces to defence of allies. It also echoed the theme of Assured Destruction (while explicitly rejecting it) in stating as an objective of the U.S. the ability to do more civil damage to the Soviet Union than *vice versa* (objective 3 above). On balance, while there was a tilt toward a policy of flexibility and discrimination, it was hardly a clear shift in policy.

James Schlesinger's arguments for flexible options were similar to those used by Robert McNamara; the differences largely reflect changes in the military situation from the 1960s to the 1970s. He stated two purposes: to help the credibility of deterrence and to help keep conflict at a low level if it were to occur. However, in contrast to the early 1960s, the objectives of limiting damage to the U.S. by having the capacity physically to deny the Soviets the ability to kill U.S. civilians was rejected. Schlesinger emphasized that it was beyond the U.S. capability to eliminate the Soviet force entirely, not least because of the large, untargetable submarine component. He also argued that a policy of flexible options did not require any change in the American force structure; i.e. the U.S. did not need new forces or new technology in order to be more flexible in employment.*

Schlesinger's emphasis in the development of nuclear options was on contingencies of special concern to the United States' allies, e.g. the deterrence of major attack on Western Europe and an improved ability to

---

*Some confusion was caused by Schlesinger also announcing the development of a new large warhead for the Minuteman, a warhead which had some transient military use in attacking some military targets, such as Soviet hardened missile silos. (Its value was transient because improvement in missile accuracy was increasing missile effectiveness without the need of larger warheads; improvements in accuracy also helped make possible large reductions in collateral damage.) He justified this proposal in terms of perceptions of the U.S.-U.S.S.R. strategic balance; the Soviet missile force had a much larger payload capacity and larger warheads than did the U.S. one. The proposed large warhead should, he argued, be considered in the context of the Strategic Arms Limitations Talks, a context within which the U.S. was trying to get agreement to reduce missile numbers and total payload. The U.S. was willing to trade away this addition to its counterforce capability in SALT, but needed some currency to trade with. This warhead provided such coin. It had nothing to do with flexible options. Nevertheless, the coincidence of these two policy pronouncements caused some confusion in press reporting and hostility among those opposed to nuclear flexibility anyway.

He argued that the U.S. strategic force should have some ability to destroy hard targets, even though he preferred to see both sides without major counterforce capabilities. He also favoured a programme of fall-out shelters and population relocation for the contingency of attack limited to military targets.

respond to such an attack in a non-suicidal way. As in the 1960s, strong non-nuclear capabilities were seen as essential but smaller nuclear options were also needed for deterrence and for defence. As an example of a class of targets whose destruction might assist the defence of Europe, Schlesinger mentioned the Soviet oil refining industry, an industry whose output was arguably essential for a successful Soviet attack on Western Europe. Clearly, having the ability to destroy targets such as refineries while preserving non-targets such as people requires precision in attack. In fact, improvements in accuracy have permitted reduction in warhead yields so that such attacks are becoming feasible. (The change from early ballistic missile accuracies is striking.) Another contingency mentioned by Schlesinger was the possibility of a Soviet attack limited to U.S. ICBMs and SAC bomber bases; if the Soviets chose to limit collateral damage, the resulting U.S. fatalities could be held to a small fraction of the fatalities produced from direct attack on U.S. cities. In 1975 testimony, he compared the population damage alone from a Soviet SIOP-type of attack wherein American fatalities would be around 95-100 million from prompt effects plus fall-out with the fatalities from more discriminate attacks.[15] An attack on ICBM silos, SAC bases and ballistic missile submarine bases was estimated as producing 5-6 million fatalities; one on ICBMs alone, about 1 million; and on SAC bases alone, about 500,000 fatalities. In short, discriminate attacks were becoming feasible.* This did not mean that contingencies such as these were considered at all likely or that such discriminate nuclear capabilities would in fact be used. On the contrary, these were described as remote possibilities. But these capabilities, it was held, improved deterrence—and could make a large difference in the event of deterrence failing.

Finally, on the subject of obstacles to implementation of a policy of limited options, Schlesinger mentioned the triple problem of command and control, limitations in existing hardware, and the 'mental approach' of the planners. Surmounting this last obstacle apparently required significant changes in operational techniques to develop the kinds of options desired; the variety of constraints implied by the improved guidance seemed to present difficulties for the planners and operators. Under any circumstance, it is difficult to think through and to anticipate specific contingencies in which small nuclear options might be used. (And of course, it is very much harder to think of realistic contingencies in

---

*In order for the Soviets to pursue a selective nuclear policy, it was estimated that they would need (1) to be able to deliver a certain number of nuclear weapons of medium or low yield with precision; and (2) to practise restraint in a conflict, for example, by choosing targets so as to limit collateral damage. On point (1), the Soviets were improving the accuracy of their weapons. The Defense Department reported several years ago that they had achieved or would soon achieve ICBM accuracies of 500 to 700 metres. As for warhead yields, the constraints imposed by having missiles mobile, e.g. in submarines, and of adopting MIRVs were producing a trend towards smaller warheads in a significant part of the Soviet force. Moreover, the use of air bursts rather than surface bursts would both increase blast effects against military targets and reduce collateral damage from fall-out. On point 2, although restraint in a nuclear conflict is by no means assured, it would be powerfully motivated by self-interest; there is little in the record of the behaviour of Soviet leadership to suggest that it has a taste for suicide.

which massive use of nuclear weapons would take place.) Detailed planning for an actual contingency done in the middle of a crisis is not likely to be done well. However, much needed to be done in advance to develop materials and techniques applicable to a wide range of situations. Without this preparation, the alternatives available in the crisis were (and still are) likely to result in a poorly executed attempt to be selective, too massive a use of force, or, most likely, governmental paralysis.

The Importance of Flexibility and the Barriers to its Achievement.

High officials have often asserted the importance of having nuclear flexibility, but it is evident from the foregoing discussion that this has not been seen as an urgent need. An important operational test was the absence of a Presidential directive to this end before 1974. This flexibility was not seen as urgent because of the widely shared belief that major war would not occur. The Soviets would not attack areas vital to U.S. interests and, in particular, they would not use nuclear weapons first. This belief was less firmly held during the crises of the early 1960s; however, most of the time having nuclear options was regarded as sound policy, not a compelling matter. Sound policy implied that even a small probability of nuclear war called for realistic military and political choices other than the use of massive nuclear attacks. However, other, more immediately pressing matters, e.g. building up non-nuclear forces or coping with Vietnam, absorbed most of the attention and energies of the higher civilian and military officials. In short, the demand for such a policy has not been high.

There have also been costs. The shift in Secretary McNamara's position in 1963 illustrated one kind of cost, pressures for additional forces and budgets. Another was the amount of high-level time and effort needed to work out such policies with operational staffs. Flexible nuclear options was not a policy which the members of the JSTPS or JCS organizations advocated. They perceived difficult problems in carrying out controlled and discriminate strikes. Furthermore, such strikes placed constraints on them that they wanted to avoid, and the doctrine of the overwhelming massive strike still had a strong hold. Moreover, some of these operators might have perceived limitations that made flexible option policy appear dangerous and unreliable in ways that politicians might not recognize. Military commanders want to be given well-defined tasks to perform, and the authority and resources needed to carry them out. They do not want to be committed to large tasks without adequate authority and means. From an operator's viewpoint, a nuclear exchange in which the politicians try to mastermind the conflict while keeping the commanders from carrying out what they regard as necessary military operations could be a frightening prospect. (On the other hand, a massive nuclear war conducted without political guidance and constraints is an even more frightening one.)

Organizational factors also played a role in determining the institutional limits of designing a policy of nuclear flexibility. Take, for example, the impact of centralizing nuclear planning in 1960 at the headquarters of the Strategic Air Command (SAC) in Omaha. SAC was primarily dedicated to the operation of manned bombers. The problem of reliably delivering a few weapons with a small number of manned bombers against an intact Soviet air-defence system could be formidable. Moreover, the environments in which SAC (and the submarine missile force) operate differed from those of the theatre Commands. The latter were perhaps much more aware of political factors and constraints than was SAC. But actual contingencies arise in particular places. For example, years ago, political factors led SACEUR to introduce constraints on the employment of nuclear weapons in Europe. And over time, some theatre commanders have come to believe that nuclear weapons have no significant role to play in their area. On the other hand, to have left nuclear planning entirely decentralized would have been inefficient and hazardous, especially in view of the vast increase in Soviet long-range delivery capabilities. Furthermore, SAC, and more recently CINCLANT and CINCPAC with their submarine missiles, have controlled most of the nuclear assets. Putting the globally oriented Command with the largest forces in charge may have cost something in political sensitivity and tactical nuance, but centralized control has made it possible to plan to apply forces in a co-ordinated manner from a broader perspective.

Technological limitations have also been an important obstacle to the development of flexible nuclear options. Decision-makers in the 1950s made technological choices on warhead yields and delivery systems which severely constrained the operators' choices in targeting strategy in the 1960s. This constraint is becoming less binding as R&D and procurement choices in the 1960s provide the operators of the 1970s with a wider range of options.

Finally, there has continued to be a conceptual gap. Plausible examples of contingencies in which nuclear weapons might be used by a country in the expectation of a 'favourable' outcome have been in short supply. This may be because such contingencies do not exist, or it may reflect a failure of imagination on the part of analysts. It happens that governments usually buy military capabilities with only a general idea about their future uses. Weapons often end up being used for purposes quite different from those initially intended. Nuclear weapons may prove no exception. One of the things that has inhibited thought on this subject is the belief that nuclear war is impossible. But nuclear contingencies are—

although one hopes, extremely remote—not impossible. In developing policies of nuclear flexibility, the required intellectual task is one of thinking about nuclear contingencies that might arise, seeing how such contingencies might be prevented from occurring, determining the possible objectives of the adversaries in such contingencies, and then examining how mutually observed constraints might be arrived at and preserved during a conflict. The purpose of such planning is to lower the likelihood of nuclear war while trying to protect one's vital interests. One of these interests is the survival of society if nuclear weapons are ever used. Another is the maintenance of support to allies in the face of threat. Neither objective is promoted by a doctrine which makes the use of nuclear weapons virtually suicidal. Indeed such a doctrine is arguably more likely to lead to erosion of political will, and every military challenge would or could produce the response of desperation—in either direction. Thinking soberly about possible limited uses of nuclear weapons—perhaps by one's adversaries—is, on this view, conducive to stability.

The task of implementing a flexible options policy has remained formidable. The sustained attention of senior officials is required and this commodity is always in short supply. Implementation requires continued monitoring, the solving of a number of difficult conceptual and operational problems, and perhaps developing some new hardware.

None of this, of course, assures that if the U.S. implements a discriminate nuclear and non-nuclear policy, other nuclear powers will build the forces which would be consistent with a policy of discrimination. Nor does it assure that the participants in a nuclear engagement would behave with restraint and that civil damage to the participants would be less than catastrophic. But to the extent that it is implemented by the United States, flexible nuclear policy reduces the likelihood of being faced with the choice of holocaust or surrender. And to the extent that it is *not* implemented by the Soviet Union or other nations, they are increasing the likelihood that they will be faced with such a choice. Despite the bargaining advantage the U.S. might possess in such a situation, Americans should favour their adversaries as well as themselves having alternatives to massive destruction.* In this regard, it is a matter of no small importance that recent changes in the character of the Soviet nuclear force are increasing their capacity to carry out flexible and discriminate nuclear operations.

---

*On one issue, controversial a decade ago, there is near consensus now within the U.S. It is that the nuclear forces and deliverable warheads of both the U.S. and the U.S.S.R. are in excess of reasonable levels. Having small, flexible nuclear options today is not nearly as likely to generate strong support for increasing nuclear forces as was feared a decade ago. The main factor working now for increases in the U.S. strategic forces is the increase in Soviet strategic forces. The SALT negotiation process has focused attention on certain indices of strength such as numbers of missiles, numbers of MIRVs, throwweight and the like which only very imperfectly measure the effectiveness of these weapons in realistic contingencies. Ironically, SALT has intensified pressures for the U.S. to match the Soviet's higher level in several of these indices.

6

CRISIS DIPLOMACY

by Coral Bell

Crisis diplomacy is at least as old as diplomacy itself. It might even be regarded as logically an elder brother to routine formal diplomatic contact, since sovereign states and their rulers, from ancient Egypt onwards, have no doubt been more conscious of the usefulness of signals and parley (the essence of the activity) with either potential adversaries or potential allies during periods of conflict than in times of calm, when the internal affairs of the society tend to take precedence over dealings with outsiders. However, this analysis will be concerned only with the crises of the nuclear age, since 1945. The term 'crisis diplomacy' will be used more or less interchangeably with the perhaps more usual term 'crisis-management', with the reservation that the word 'management' is somewhat misleading for the activity concerned. It carries too many overtones of calm, judicious consideration of the allocation of resources with a view to best long-term advantage. Crises, almost by definition, do not permit much of those luxuries. On the evidence, the decision-makers normally have to juggle with the situation in a spirit of controlled desperation, and under a fog of uncertainty. So crisis diplomacy or crisis bargaining seem more accurate phrases for what actually tends to happen.

The first thing that may be said about the crisis diplomacy of the first thirty-five years of the nuclear age is that none of the many crises of that period has resulted in nuclear war. A rather high proportion have resulted in hostilities of some sort, but most of the wars that have eventuated have been relatively short, and have by one means or another been kept limited in area and participants. On the face of it, this seems to indicate an almost improbable level of success for crisis-management over the period. In fact if those thirty-five years (1945–79) are compared with the equal stretch of history just prior to them, 1911–1945, the improved level of success seems misleadingly great. That miserable earlier epoch, which may be regarded as covering the twilight and death of the old European system of crisis-management, produced twelve years of world war—unlimited hostilities between the powers of the central balance—as well as many minor wars. The thirty-five years of the nuclear age to date have produced no sustained direct hostilities between the powers of the central balance, though they have of course produced two long-lasting conventional or semi-conventional limited wars, Korea and Vietnam, as well as a wide assortment of short local conventional wars, especially in the Middle East and South Asia, and a great many internal wars, insurgencies and counter-insurgencies, and minor military operations. In effect one set of conventions of crisis-management had broken down or become inoperable by 1911, and was not effectively re-created after 1918, whereas in the period since 1945 a reasonably workable set of conventions of crisis-management has evolved, largely by precedent. This set of conventions is not particularly new or original: it has a good deal in common with those that were used in the century before 1914. And it is by no means infallible: there is always the chance that it will fail at the next crisis. Nevertheless, it has had its successes, and these successes have, on the evidence, been connected with the existence of nuclear weapons, so that there is a sense in which it can be called a system specific to the nuclear age. An optimistic judgement, looking back over the ways the system has worked, might hold that nuclear weapons have deterred not merely nuclear war, but also perhaps large conventional wars in theatres vital to the central balance, and that they have provided also a permanent incentive to active crisis-management by the great powers in crises of local balances, as in the Middle East, where there is a possibility of great-power involvement. On the other hand, it has clearly been shown that their existence does not restrain lesser modes of hostilities, and there is some evidence that the system may at times have operated to make local minor wars more probable.

I shall use the term 'conventions' to mean *not* the multilateral treaties sometimes called by that word, but just what it conveys in ordinary parlance: expected and understood signals (as in the conventions of bridge), or rules of behaviour with no particular moral or legal backing, sanctioned chiefly by prudence and custom, and stemming from a particular society. The last point is important. The conventions of diplomacy, like the conventions of Soccer, are international, but stem from European origins. That has perhaps caused some difficulties, but on the whole fewer than might have been expected. The reasons will be examined in more detail later.

Nature and Incidence of Crises

To understand how the system works, and why its effectiveness has to date been limited, we must first look at the nature of war-bearing crises. Any conflict, whether in international or in other relationships, is liable to produce crises. On its derivation, the word just means turning-points or decision-points. A crisis may be defined for our purposes as a tract of time in which the conflicts within a relationship rise to a level which threatens to transform the nature of that relationship.* The threatened transformation which people usually have in mind when they talk of international crises is from peace to war, but there is an important category which I will call intra-mural crises of alliance systems, where the threatened transformation is from alliance to rupture. Crises may arise either in the central balance of power, or in local balances of power. Moreover, the most prolific source of wars in the period we are examining has been crises not in international relationships proper, but in colonial relationships (all the 'wars of national liberation') or in the breakdown of a domestic political relationship.

In sum, we have six main categories of potential war-bearing crises to consider:

First: *Adversary crisis of the central balance,* potentially productive of central war, either nuclear or conventional, as between NATO and the Warsaw Pact, or between the Soviet Union and China, e.g. Cuba crisis of 1962, or Sino-Soviet crisis of 1969.

Second: *Adversary crisis of a local balance,* productive of conventional wars (usually short, for reasons which will be looked at presently), e.g. Middle East war of 1973 or Sino-Indian war of 1962.

Third: *Intramural crises of alliances,* or spheres of power (central or regional) potentially productive of local military repression or punitive strike, e.g. Czechoslovakia 1968 or Hungary 1956 as intramural crises of the Warsaw Pact, and the Egypt-Libya punitive strike of 1977 as an intramural crisis of the Arab League.

Fourth: *Crises of attempted reunification or secession,* a category very productive of war in the period under scrutiny: e.g. 1971 Bangladesh as a successful secession attempt, Biafra as an unsuccessful one. The Korean war may be classed as an unsuccessful war of attempted reunification and the second phase (post 1959) of Vietnam as a successful war of reunification.

---

*There are a number of alternative definitions of crisis used by other writers in the field. 'A crisis normally implies a deliberate challenge and a deliberated response, of a kind which both sides hope will change the course of history in their favour. . . The crisis period covers the formulation of the challenge, the definition of the issue, the decision on the appropriate reaction to the challenge, the impact of such a reaction upon the adversary and the clarification of his response' (Alastair Buchan, *Crisis Management,* 1964, p.21).

'A set of *rapidly* unfolding events which raises the impact of destabilizing forces in the general international system or any of its subsystems substantially above normal (i.e. average) levels and increases the likelihood of violence occurring in the system' (Oran Young, *The Intermediaries,* 1967, p.10).

'A crisis is a situation with four necessary and sufficient conditions, as these are perceived by the highest level decision-makers of the actor concerned: (i) a change in its internal or external environment which generates (ii) a threat to basic values with a simultaneous or subsequent (iii) high probability of involvement in military hostilities and (iv) a finite time for their response to the external value threat' (Michael Brecher, *Towards a Theory of International Crisis Behavior* in *International Studies Quarterly* [XXI, 1977]).

These definitions, while admirably lucid, are obviously devised for adversary crises only, and I would maintain that intramural crises are also of great interest and importance in forwarding analysis of crisis relations in general, so I have chosen a wider and less specific definition.

Fifth: *Crises of colonial or post-colonial relationships,* usually arising from a failure of the metropolitan power to devolve authority as fast or as far as the local nationalists wish. The original 1946 crisis which began the first phase of the Vietnam war was of this variety, and so were the Algerian war, the Angola and Mozambique campaigns, and many others.

Sixth: *Crises of domestic political consensus,* as for instance Ulster since 1968, Lebanon since 1974, or Ethiopia 1975–6.

It is a point of considerable significance, when one is considering the origin of hostilities, that only the first three of these categories of war-bearing crises are fully international. The others all have a domestic or quasi-domestic element to them, and this has tended to exempt them, at least in their early stages, from the attentions of international crisis diplomacy. If one is thinking of the present system as a rudimentary technique of war-prevention, one has to recognize that more than half the crises from which wars have originated in the period we are concerned with have been from areas of political life normally ruled out of its jurisdiction. Whether anything can be done about this is a question which will be considered later.

Another point that should be borne in mind is that when we look at an individual historical episode usually called 'a crisis', for instance October 1973, we often find that it is in fact several crises almost inextricably intertwined with each other. October 1973 was obviously and primarily an adversary crisis of the local balance of power, between Israel on the one hand and Egypt and Syria on the other. It threatened at one point to grow into an adversary crisis of the central balance, between the United States and the Soviet Union. It also precipitated an intramural crisis of NATO, as the West Europeans were hit by the Arab oil blockade. One might call such episodes compound crises.

This many-stranded aspect of most major crises is important to note, because diplomatic success in their management is helped by the recognition that different strands will respond to distinctive diplomatic techniques. The Suez crisis of 1956 was also a many-stranded one: an adversary crisis of the local balance between Israel and Egypt, as well as a post-colonial crisis in the relation between Britain and France on the one hand, and Egypt on the other, and an intramural crisis of NATO because of its affect on American relations with Britain and France. One might say that the greater level of success of American crisis diplomacy in the 1973 episode than in the 1956 one was the greater skill of the then Secretary of State in sorting out these separate strands in the knot of crisis, and dealing with them one by one.

Criteria of Success in Crisis Diplomacy

We have now to attempt to establish some criteria by which crisis diplomacy or crisis management may be classed as successful or unsuccessful. At first sight, it might appear that only one criterion is necessary: whether or not war was averted. But this clearly will not do, for it would oblige us to class as a success for crisis-management the Munich crisis of 1938. War was certainly then averted for a time, but only to be precipitated a year or so later, arguably on worse terms for the Western powers. So if Munich was a success, it was a success for Hitler, a crisis-manager of demonic talent, whose techniques have not even yet received much objective scrutiny.

That brings up the obvious point that when we ask whether a particular episode of crisis diplomacy has been a success, we must also ask 'a success for whom?' But it is subsequently possible to go beyond this question and ask whether it was a success for the society of states as a whole: whether it served the ends of peace or justice or stability. It will not always be possible to *answer* those questions within our time-frame, but it is possible to ask them.

Aside from that question, there are four main criteria of success we can apply to the diplomacy of most adversary crises:

(1) Has the probability of war between the chief adversaries been increased or diminished, over the short term and the longer term?

(2) What has been the effect on the power-position of either?

(3) Has the underlying conflict which produced the crisis been moved toward resolution?

(4) Has any contribution been made to the conventions and techniques of crisis-management?

However, these criteria are applicable only to adversary crises, either of the central or of local balances. There is also, as was mentioned before, the important category of intramural crises of alliance systems for which different criteria must be suggested:

(1) Was the ability of the alliance to function maintained or impaired?

(2) What was the influence of the crisis settlement on the degree of satisfaction of the members with their positions within it?

(3) What was the impact of the settlement on the credibility or 'credit' of the dominant member of the alliance, either within the system or outside?

It should be borne in mind that the intramural crises of one of the major alliance systems, the Warsaw Pact, are as great a potential source of war (at one remove so to speak) as direct adversary crises of the central balance. If for instance dissent within Rumania or East Germany reached a point at which demands to throw off the embrace of the Soviet Union were met by Moscow sending in the tanks, as in Czechoslovakia in 1968, and if the constraints on Western policy which have been effective in 1953, 1956 and 1968 proved weaker (perhaps because of new and inexperienced crisis-managers in Washington or Bonn), an intramural crisis of the Soviet sphere of power could very rapidly become an adversary crisis of the central balance. There is one haunting historical precedent for such a transmutation: July–August 1914 was initially an intramural crisis of the Austrian sphere of power, but was rapidly transformed by imprudent crisis-management in Vienna, Berlin and St Petersburg into an adversary crisis of the central balance, and then into the war which effectively destroyed the European society of states, the great power centre of the world for several centuries.

It may reasonably be judged a matter of some credit to Western policy-makers that the intramural crises of the Western sphere of power have on the whole been managed with far more skill and success than those of the Soviet sphere of power, and that therefore far less disruption has been produced in Western alliances than in Soviet ones. The first intramural crisis of the Soviet power sphere, that over Yugoslavia in 1948, was so handled by Stalin as to result in total breach for many years, not fully healed even now. The intramural crises occasioned by dissent in East Germany in 1953, Poland and Hungary in 1956 and Czechoslovakia in 1968 were settled by harsh military repression: the alliance continued to function, but the modes of settlement can hardly have reconciled the peoples concerned to their place in the alliance, nor did it redound to the credit of the Soviet Union as dominant member. The crises of the Sino-Soviet alliance were even more ill-handled by the Russians, so that they had progressed (or rather deteriorated) from intramural crises (starting about 1956) to sharp adversary crisis, carrying the risk of nuclear war, by 1969.

Nothing in the Western sphere of power has been as mismanaged as these. France's discontent with its status in NATO, as signified by de Gaulle in 1958, was perhaps too casually brushed off by Eisenhower and Dulles, and led to France's ending its *formal* military commitment to NATO (but not its sense that its own military objectives marched with those of NATO). The Cyprus crisis, an endemic intramural problem for NATO, has reduced the willingness of Greece and Turkey to collaborate with each other and with the U.S. for NATO purposes in the Eastern Mediterranean. But aside from these, there has been a lot *less* in many NATO crises than has met the eye, and other American alliance-systems—with Japan, with Australia and New Zealand, and with the Philippines—have rubbed along comfortably enough without defections and without much friction. SEATO was a different story: a misconceived enterprise which died not so much from an intramural crisis as from the ending of its *raison d'être*.

The classification and terminology I have thus far used might naturally be disputed by those strongly concerned with one conflict or another. The Middle East hostilities of 1948, 1956, 1967 and 1973, for instance, which I have labelled 'adversary crises of a local balance', would obviously be seen as wars of aggression by the adherents of one side or the other, as indeed would be most wars by the partisans of particular sides. But I have consciously sought terms which are as neutral as possible, in the interest of deriving generalizations which will be applicable to most cases.

One other preliminary point should be noted: the sometimes paradoxical relationship between crisis-management and conflict-resolution. Though crises grow out of conflicts, some apparent successes for crisis-management may actually have the result of helping to perpetuate a conflict. Usually this eventuates from formal mechanisms which preserve the position of the *weaker* party and enable him to hold his ground well enough to prepare to fight another day. Moral feeling may well demand such mechanisms, but there is no doubt that they prolong the conflict by, in effect, preventing the victory of the stronger side. The very elaborate efforts of U.N. crisis-management over Kashmir, from 1948 to 1971, probably had this tendency. In effect they prevented the conclusive defeat of Pakistan for twenty-three years (until the balance of power swung decisively against her after the Bangladesh war) and one may ask whether that was, in fact, of benefit to the peoples of Kashmir, or to Pakistan, or to the Indian sub-continent, or to the society of states as a whole. It was a gesture demanded by moral and political feeling at the time, but, like other moral gestures in international politics, not unmixedly useful in its effects. The best crisis-management, as Dr. Kissinger has observed, is that which uses the crisis constructively, to nudge the underlying conflict towards a settlement. But that must be rare: usually the pressures of events and feelings at the time militate against it.

Crises since World War II

(Asterisk indicates substantial or fairly substantial hostilities)
Year
1946 Azerbaijan, Indo-China I*
1947 Greece*, Turkey, Kashmir*
1948 Berlin I, Czechoslovakia, Middle East I*, Indonesia*
1949 Malaya* (insurgency)
1950 Korea*, Chinese intervention in Korea*
1951 Abadan
1952 Kenya*
1953 East Germany (riots), Morocco, Tunisia
1954 Indo-China II*, Algeria*, Guatemala*
1955 Cyprus I*
1956 Hungary*, Poland*, Middle East II*
1957 Syria-Turkey
1958 Lebanon-Jordan-Iraq, Quemoy-Matsu, Berlin II
1959 Indo-China III* (Laos)
1960 Congo*, U-2
1961 Laos, Berlin III, Cuba I* (Bay of Pigs), Goa
1962 Cuba II (missiles), China-India*, Yemen*

1963 Malaysia-Indonesia* ('Confrontation')
1964 Cyprus II, Tongking Gulf, Panama, Mozambique*
1965 India-Pakistan*, Dominican Republic*
1966 Rhodesia*
1967 Middle-East III*, Cyprus III
1968 Czechoslovakia, *Pueblo*
1969 Biafra*, Sino-Soviet, Ulster*
1970 Jordan*, Cuba III (Soviet base)
1971 Bangladesh*
1972 Cyprus IV
1973 Middle East IV*, Chile*
1974 Cyprus V*
1975 Portugal, Indo-China IV*, Angola*, *Mayaguez*
1976 Spanish Sahara*
1977 Ethiopia*, Somalia*, Zaire*, Cambodia-Vietnam-Thailand

This list is not intended to be exhaustive, but to include those episodes which the author believes to have had some discernible effect on international politics. The crisis was not necessarily contained within the year to which it has been assigned, but made an impact on international consciousness then.

Likelihood of Hostilities in relation to Category of Crisis

A point of considerable interest, looking at the list of post-war crises, is that direct adversary crisis of the central balance (Berlin, Cuba, U-2) has not often produced hostilities. Even adding crises that are almost in that category (Azerbaijan, Quemoy-Matsu) there is still little actual loss of life. The crises with really heavy ensuing 'body counts' have been the crises of a colonial relationship (Vietnam I, Algeria, Morocco, Tunisia, Indonesia, Angola, Mozambique, Rhodesia, Kenya) or the crises of local balance (the four Middle Eastern campaigns, those of the Indian subcontinent, Ethiopia-Somalia) or the crises of secession (Biafra, Bangladesh, Congo) or reunification (Korea, Vietnam II) or crises of domestic consensus (Lebanon, Ulster, Cyprus). Intramural crises (East Germany, Hungary, Poland, Czechoslovakia) have brought Soviet troops into action, and one intramural crisis, the Dominican Republic, involved the use of American troops.

Admittedly, the two American interventions in wars of reunification (Korea and Vietnam II) produced very heavy casualty lists. The object of the interventions,† maintaining the southern regime against its external and/or internal enemies, was secured (to date) in the first case, Korea,

---

† I am conscious that the optimum or hoped-for objectives of the U.S. government in Korea and Vietnam included several elements: to uphold the U.N. (in Korea), defeat aggression, contain Chinese expansionism and so on. At one stage in Korea it included reunification of the country. Maintaining the southern government in each case was at best a minimum objective, successfully adhered to in Korea but finally abandoned in Vietnam.

but lost in the second. These episodes were of course interpreted in Washington at the time of each initial crisis as 'challenges by proxy' on the part of the communist powers, and the American interventions were based on that premise.

If accepted, such an interpretation would make these interventions indirect wars of the central balance, though with the paradoxical result that the communist powers would be credited with the ability to fight such wars of the central balance without their own troops being involved, except for the Chinese intervention in the Korean case. The author would however hold that though the Washington interpretation of the time was in each case plausible, it was certainly mistaken in the Vietnam case and possibly so in the Korean case. But whatever view one takes of the correctness of the interpretations on which the two Washington interventions were based, the decision to interpret each crisis as a challenge by proxy meant that it in fact became a 'test by proxy', with painful and long-lasting results especially for both America and Vietnam in the second case. Therefore one might say that though direct and unmistakable adversary crises of the central balance have tended to be settled almost without hostilities, through a system of coercive diplomacy, these two indirect or 'proxy' challenges (if that indeed is what they were, and the American interventions make little sense without this possibility) produced long hostilities and heavy casualty lists.

One change which may be regarded as hopeful, if one is assessing the future war-bearing potential of the nuclear age, is that the category 'crisis of a colonial relationship', which produced many of the longest and bloodiest wars of the entire period to date, has now more or less exhausted itself with the ending of the colonial system. The guerrilla war in Rhodesia might be considered a late variant of this category. Unfortunately, however, the ex-colonial world appears likely to be prolific in the three other varieties of crisis which all also have shown high capacity for precipitating hostilities: crises of local balances, crises of secession and reunification and crises of domestic consensus. There are visible on the horizon two potential reunification crises (Taiwan and Korea), one possible secession (and succession) crisis (Yugoslavia), a number of potential intramural crises of the Warsaw Pact in Eastern Europe, various potential crises of local balances in the Middle East, Africa and South-East Asia including some between pairs of communist powers (as Cambodia and Vietnam). Any of these could be compounded by ill-considered crisis-management into an adversary crisis of the central balance, though such a process would be far more likely over East Asia (a new Korean reunification bid), or the Middle East, or Yugoslavia, than elsewhere.

It would be over-optimistic to argue that conventions of crisis-management are well-established between the powers of the central balance, but they are undoubtedly better established in that relationship than in other areas of possible crisis, and that helps to account for the relatively low incidence of hostilities through such episodes.

All crises evoke and are influenced by sets of signals. To some extent they are managed by sets of signals, though that must seem an excessively bland phrase for the many cases where hostilities eventuate. But hostilities must of course themselves be regarded as signals, and the way in which they go, if they do arise, must be sometimes interpreted as the final decisive signal which in time changes the political will of one or other of the parties. The hostilities in Vietnam in early 1968 (the Tet offensive), or at least the way they were interpreted in the United States, constituted the signal which decisively changed the course of American policy in Vietnam, and that episode is a good example of the way the signal conveyed by or read into a military action can differ from its actual 'battlefield'* meaning. But in most cases, for purposes of analysis it seems more useful to regard signals as a substitute for, or an effort to avoid, major hostilities. By signal I mean a threat or offer communicated, or intended to be communicated, to one or more of the parties to the crisis. The signal is not necessarily or even usually a diplomatic note, or other verbal expression of intent. As Dr. Kissinger once remarked, in some ways words are the least effective of signals. The strongest, and sometimes the most effective, is the movement or alerting of military forces. The American strategic alert during the 1973 Middle East crisis was an intentionally loud, strong signal; so also perhaps were the Russian gestures immediately before, which seemed to purport the possible airlifting of Soviet troops to Egypt. The *Mayaguez* incident of 1975 was possibly of more significance as a U.S. signal (to the North Koreans rather than the Cambodians) than as a simple rescue mission. Perhaps the most difficult and delicate area of the crisis-manager's task is the choice of ambiguous or unambiguous signals, or some 'mix' of them. This question of ambiguity will be considered in more detail later.

The Contemporary Crisis-Managers

The crisis diplomacy of the contemporary society of states is determined almost exclusively by the chief decision-makers of the powers (Presidents, Prime Ministers, Chairmen of Politburos, Secretaries of State & Defence, Foreign Secretaries, Chiefs of Staff, heads of intelligence services). The 19th-century function of the career diplomat in this role has vanished. This again is mostly a side-effect of the nuclear

---

*The 'battlefield' meaning of the Tet offensive was of heavy costs to the forces which looked to the north, in the course of spectacular but short-lived seizures of a number of towns. As a 'signal' received and interpreted in Washington, however, what it meant was that the political, moral and prospective manpower costs of the war were greater for America than any objectives which might be received could warrant. Thus one may say that Tet was far more successful as a signal than as a military operation for General Giap. For an account of the reasons, see *Big Story: How the American press and television reported and interpreted the Tet offensive of 1968* by Peter Baestrup (Westview Press, 1977).

age. The stakes are now too high for anyone but the effective chief decision-maker and his closest advisers to be allowed to play for them.

Western knowledge of the decision-making process within the Politburos of China and the Soviet Union is so much less detailed than knowledge of the equivalent process in Washington that there is probably considerable danger in reading too many parallels from the known process to the two relatively unknown ones. Nevertheless Soviet decision-making seems to have been at least as much in Khrushchev's hands in the 1962 Cuba crisis, or Brezhnev's in the 1973 Middle Eastern crisis, as American decision-making was in the hands of the Americans in power at the relevant times. The same appeared to be true of China in the period of Mao Tse-tung and Chou En-lai: foreign policy decision-making of any serious kind was closely reserved to them. This appears to be logical: autocratic systems, whether the autocracy is personal (as was the Shah's) or military (as in many Third World countries) or party (as in communist countries) imply by definition that decision-making is monopolized by a small tight group, or by one man.

That phenomenon has a useful side-effect for crisis-management. It makes almost irrelevant an objection frequently put forward, that since the present world-wide society of states can never be as homogeneous as the old European society of states, it could therefore never develop a similar set of conventions of crisis-management. Nations or electorates do not make the decisions on these life-or-death occasions: the speed of events precludes consultation. It is a *very* small set of individual decision-makers, all in high political or military office, who do so. And the members of this true international 'jet-set' seem often in many ways— education, life-style, experience, temperament, ability—more like each other than each is like the average member of his own society. One would say for instance that Kissinger and Chou En-lai and Sheikh Yamani and Brezhnev were more like each other than Kissinger was like a Middle Western farmer or Chou a Central China peasant or Yamani a Bedu or Brezhnev a Soviet factory worker. This is really not so very dissimilar to the 19th-century European situation, when decision-makers were all members of a small international aristocracy, only then entry to the decision-making group was often by accident of birth, whereas now it is almost always by some kind of political talent. (This is on balance an improvement. Looking back at the crisis-management of 1914 which produced the First World War, one would say that the three men whose power to affect decision was based solely on accident of birth—the Kaiser, the Czar and the Emperor of Austria—were not influences making for a rational outcome.)

Each member of this little 'global village' of decision-makers is in contemporary circumstances very readily in touch with the others: minutes away by 'phone or a day by plane (Castlereagh was about ten days' arduous travel from Metternich). With the proliferation of 'summit meetings', the level of personal acquaintance is probably actually greater than in the nineteenth century. And, paradoxically, the circle of decision-makers for any particular crisis may even be *smaller* in the late twentieth century than it was in the nineteenth, because the number of what one may call 'activist' powers of the central balance (i.e. those actively playing for their own hand, who have numbered as many as ten in the past) has sharply declined.

For any given crisis, there are normally two 'echelons' of policy-makers involved: the local or 'focus of crisis' powers (Arabs and Israelis, for instance, or Greeks, Turks and Cypriots, or Indians, Pakistanis and Bangladeshis or Angolans, South Africans and Portuguese) and the 'central' group, usually only Americans and Russians, though Chinese, French, British, German and other policy-makers may on occasion have the power and the will to affect decisions. The way the central and the local decision-makers have interacted in a set of crises of the last three decades—Quemoy-Matsu 1958, Cuba 1962, Middle East 1973, Cyprus 1974, Angola 1975, Zaire 1977/8—offers illumination of the varieties of this crucial relationship, and the degree to which the central powers exert leverage over the local powers or vice versa.

Two-person Games and N-person Games

The Cuba missile crisis of 1962 is often used as a model for crises and crisis-management.* In fact it was from a remark of McNamara's after the event, 'There is no longer any such thing as strategy, only crisis-management', that the present analytical and academic interest in the subject dates. This is rather unfortunate, because Cuba was in several ways quite untypical of crises in general. It appeared to approximate to the form of a 'two-person game' readily susceptible to analytical and mathematical techniques. The two 'players' were readily identified as Kennedy and Khrushchev, so the locus of decision-making seemed clear and well-defined, a sort of brightly illuminated central stage of the world, with a game of diplomatic chess resulting in a gracefully sustained victory for the more attractive of the two 'players', and an interesting cast of supporting characters, many of whom wrote books about it afterwards. I am not saying that this is how the crisis *was*, only that this is how it *looked* to many Westerners. Most crises are much more sprawling, shapeless and indeterminate than Cuba '62. They are much less well illuminated, and (most important) they tend to be 'N-person games' rather than 'two-person games', which makes them less susceptible to current analytical methods. (Of course, Cuba 1962 would have been at least a three-person game if Dr. Castro had had his way, but his leverage vis-à-vis both the super-powers was small and he could have increased it only by physically seizing the Russian missiles from the Russian soldiers and technicians.

*For instance in Graham Allison, *The Essence of Decision* (Little, Brown, 1971).

That, however, would have alienated Mr. Khrushchev, and sharply strengthened the latter's common interest with President Kennedy, which certainly would have put a complex spin on the crisis-management. And it would not necessarily have done Dr. Castro much good, since his forces had not yet been trained to use the weapons.)

If there is a game usable as a metaphor in the more typical cases, it is certainly not chess, since that is said to be a game which is not susceptible to either bluff or cheating, and in which the (two only) players are equal save in skill. None of this is true of crises. Perhaps poker offers some analogies, especially if envisaged as for five or more hands in the traditional Wild West saloon, with the guns coming into play when the fall of the cards is unpropitious, and the final outcome as much dependent on quickness on the draw as finesse in the shuffle. The Cyprus crisis of 1974 is closer to this normal mode than Cuba '62. It offers a useful illustration of asymmetry and dislocation in decision-making during crisis, which is historically frequent enough.

In the Cyprus case there were six individuals or groups involved in the decisions that produced the ultimate outcome. First, Archbishop Makarios, whose decision to seek the removal of the Greek officers from the island provided the starting point of events. Next, the faceless anonymous leadership of 'Eoka B', which responded by deciding to mount a *coup* against him. Then the disintegrating junta in Athens, under the leadership of Brigadier Ioannides, who decided to sponsor the *coup* and allow Nicos Sampson to be the figurehead of the intended new regime. Then the complex American decision-making machinery, including the Secretary of State, the departmental officers, the Ambassador in Athens, the C.I.A. 'station' there, and the Pentagon. Then Mr. Ecevit and his government in Ankara. And finally the British government, since the decision to do nothing is also a decision that affects outcomes, as indeed was almost equally illustrated in the American case. There is no way in which these decision processes were alike, except that in three of them the normal machinery of decision-making was out of kilter. In Washington, the Cyprus events coincided with the dramatic last three weeks of Mr. Nixon's decline and fall, which absorbed a good deal of the Secretary of State's attention. In Athens the decaying junta simply fell apart under the impact of its own failure: there was literally no-one to take decisions until Mr. Karamanlis was installed. In Cyprus also, once the Archbishop had fled the island, there was a period without any rational interlocutor. In Ankara, on the other hand, there was a coherent and determined, if opportunist, policy, and the military capacity to put it into effect. So the Turks were able to seize thirty-six percent of the island, enforce a ruthless population transfer, and settle down for the eventual negotiations with most of the 'bargaining chips' in their hands.

One of the most interesting things about this crisis is a sidelight it offers on the way detente redistributes diplomatic leverage as between super-powers and middle powers in crisis diplomacy. The leverage which the dominant powers have over their middle-power allies is perhaps inevitably less in a period of detente than in a period of cold war. In effect, the middle power can defy its great and powerful friends, because its great and powerful enemies have ceased to seem so menacing. It needs its allies less. So the American political pressures which were effective in preventing Turkish military operations against Cyprus in the crises of 1964 and 1967 were no longer so effective by 1974. Ioannides, who had sponsored the *coup* in apparent confidence that these pressures *would* again be effective, was destroyed by his own miscalculation. (Admittedly Washington was at this time distracted by the final phase of Watergate and President Nixon himself on the brink of fall, so there could be no equivalent of the Johnson letter in the 1967 crisis, but I think the point about reduced American leverage would have been demonstrated even if this had not been the case.) The only means óf pressure the Americans had was the refusal of future weapons supply, and against this (when it was finally imposed by Congress, not the Administration) the Turks could and did successfully bargain the American bases. But paradoxically, what may be regarded as the ineffective crisis-management of 1974 may be deemed in the upshot to have nudged along the process of conflict-resolution rather more than the 'successes' of 1964 and 1967, in the sense that it forced or allowed more real change in the underlying situation.

There is an even more important point to note about diplomatic leverage in the relation between dominant powers and their middle or small-power allies, which seems to differentiate the nuclear age from earlier periods in matters of crisis-management. In nothing are the three dominant powers more alike than in a steely determination not to let their essential national interests fall into the hands of minor (or even major) allies. The stakes are too high for them to let anyone else call the bids. One can demonstrate this by comparing the relative impotence of Cuba in the 1962 crisis with the roles played by Serbia in the 1914 crisis or Poland in the Anglo-Russian diplomacy of 1939. Since in a crisis situation it is usually the national interest of the minor power that is 'on the block', there is a normal and logical probability that the power concerned will be the most intransigent, and will feel morally justified in its stand. A Serbian nationalist will still maintain that the Serbian nationalists of 1914 were right, even though their efforts helped to destroy a world. But whereas Serbia could determine the choices of Russia in 1914 and Poland impose a veto in 1939, Cuba could not determine the policy of the Soviet Union in 1962, nor Egypt do so in 1973. Nor, in my view, could even as important an ally as West Germany necessarily impose choices on the United States in some future crisis. This factor, which one might call 'nuclear egotism' on the part of the dominant powers, may not be conducive to maintaining unimpaired the interests of their respective allies, but it *is* conducive to maintaining the peace. For it reduces the possible causes of central war, by making it likely that the dominant powers will only engage in major direct hostilities with each other when they are convinced that their *own* vital interests are in danger, not to forward the marginal interests of an ally. (Though what the nuclear power deems marginal might of course be seen as rather more than that by the ally concerned.)

There was a good example of this in the Quemoy-Matsu crisis of 1958, which also offers illustrations of the connection between adversary and intramural crises, and of the uses of ambiguous signalling. By early September 1958 it had become apparent that the government in Peking was intending a bid to take over the islands, which (unlike Taiwan itself) are only a few miles from the mainland (four miles at the narrowest point). The American administration of the time had consciously or unconsciously succeeded in sending ambiguous signals about its reactions in the event of such a bid, President Eisenhower making various mild and conciliatory statements which seemed to indicate a wish to avoid conflict, and Mr. Dulles making tougher statements which seemed to indicate a determination to hold the islands, using the Seventh Fleet if necessary. These ambiguous signals were directed towards a Sino-Soviet alliance which, though only eight years old, had already begun to crack under the stress of the Lebanon-Jordan crisis a few weeks earlier, and various other blows.

When the crisis signals are ambiguous in this fashion, the adversary decision-makers may 'select' those elements most congruous with their respective estimates of their respective national interests. That apparently was what happened in this case: the Chinese 'selected' the milder Eisenhower signals, and demanded Soviet nuclear backing for their own push forward, saying that the imperialists would prove 'paper tigers'. The Russians 'selected' the tougher Dulles signals, and since unlike the Chinese they were quite conscious of the level of American nuclear advantage, they refused to back their ally, retorting that the 'paper tigers' had 'nuclear teeth'. The Chinese could only acquiesce at the time, but in their polemics with the Russians some four years later they disclosed some details of these events, implying that the Russians had proved cowards who would give them no assurances until the prospect of hostilities had ended. So, in effect, differentiated or ambiguous signalling in an adversary crisis of the central balance produced an intramural crisis in the alliance to which those signals were directed, and caused apparently irretrievable damage to that alliance. In the following year, Khrushchev made his journey to America, and the Sino-Soviet relationship seems to have passed its point of no return. But the most interesting lesson of the crisis was the demonstrated Soviet reluctance to take risks in the interests of what was then its major ally, and in some respects is now its most embarrassing adversary.

The same problem of the interests of the allies or protégés of the dominant powers at moments of confrontation between them was illustrated in quite a variety of permutations in the Middle East crisis of 1973. The Soviet Union here had two pivotal allies to consider—Egypt and Syria—and by implication the Arab world as a whole. The Americans had Israel plus their oil-dependent vital allies in NATO and Japan and also, prospectively, the Arab world to consider. Retrospectively, the American crisis-management strikes one as boldly imaginative, resourceful and successful, and the Russian as rather cautious, pedestrian and unsuccessful.* One of the more machiavellian interpretations of Dr. Kissinger's role would have him deliberately delaying the re-supply operation to Israel in the first week of the war in order to secure that the outcome should be nearer to stalemate or 'honours even' than to an Israeli victory on the scale of 1967. Whether that interpretation is true or not, the United States apparently came out of the crisis, and the diplomacy of the succeeding six months, to considerable advantage. It not only restored its position in the Arab world (except Libya) to a better footing than at any time since 1948, but also, despite some abrasive episodes, emerged in a strengthened position vis-à-vis its West European and Japanese allies, since the degree of their vulnerability and dependence on U.S. leverage in oil matters was abundantly illustrated. If the U.S.-Israel connection conformed to the normal diplomatic pattern, one would say there was also enhanced U.S. leverage in that relationship, but the special strength of the 'friends of Israel' lobby in U.S. politics is such that one must hesitate to be categoric on that point.

The Soviet Union, on the other hand, suffered a considerable diplomatic defeat, not only failing to make gains in the Arab world or the 'Third World' generally in the wake of the crisis, but in fact losing much of the influence, with Egypt especially, that it had spent almost twenty years and a great deal of money in building up, and in due course seeing its fleet excluded from Alexandria.

The cases of Angola and Zaire illustrate, by contrast, the way in which the internal political moods or pressures within the state may reduce its effectiveness in external crisis almost to vanishing point, and the degree to which middle or small powers can 'stand-in' for a dominant power where these circumstances provide it with the appropriate opening. The issue in Angola was, according to Dr. Kissinger, 'not a direct threat to our security but the long-term danger of allowing Soviet surrogate forces to intervene globally to tip the scales in local conflicts'. But unfortunately it

---

*In some ways this seems to have been more nearly a 'single-layer' crisis-management on the American side than Cuba was, for in 1962 the Cuba decisions were worked out not by Kennedy himself but the 'Excom' group, by a sort of collegiate decision-making process for at least seven or eight more or less equal voices. Whereas in October 1973 Mr. Nixon was already preoccupied by Watergate, the Chiefs of Staff seem to have been kept firmly in the background, and even Dr. Schlesinger to have been a consultant rather than a decision-maker. So it was primarily Dr. Kissinger with a few close State Department aides.

erupted at the end of 1975, when the U.S. Congress was still in such a state of trauma from Vietnam and Watergate that it in effect tied his hands by voting to cut off all funds for operations in Angola. The Soviet Union thus had a sort of victory by default, though the use of Cuban rather than Russian forces may be taken as a sign of Soviet caution even in these inviting circumstances. In the case of the apparent danger to Zaire from Angola a few months later, the American mood seemed basically still of reluctance to risk any initiative, but by that time France and Morocco were ready and eager to take over what earlier had been the U.S. role in sustaining the Western-oriented government of President Mobutu.

These illustrations of the way in which crisis tends to arise from a confluence of incompatible, 'asymmetrical' decision-making processes, quite liable to disruption from various causes, are intended to dispel any illusions that crisis-management has become or is likely to become 'scientific'. Science supposes the ability to abstract general laws from particular observations. To abstract requires simplification, and to simplify processes which are in fact complex is necessarily to falsify them. At its best, crisis-management can aspire only to the status of a craft demonstrating acquired or traditional skills, and its successes have derived from historical imagination, intellectual creativity, a capacity for reading the fine print in the other side's signals and a flair for endowing one's own signals with nuance and (where useful) drama. Its progress has been by precedent, but even precedent is by no means an infallible guide. The capacity to know the moment for innovation must also be there.

The Conventions of Crisis

With these reservations always firmly in mind, it is nevertheless possible to sketch a set of conventions which seem to have been established, reiterating that conventions denote only expected behaviour and understood signals, not laws, moral norms, or enforceable rules.

1. That communications with the adversary must and will be maintained, and should rather grow closer and more intensive as the confrontation sharpens than be diminished or broken off. The final 'crystallization' of this convention came during or just after the Cuba missile crisis of 1962, with the decision to establish the 'hot line', direct teletype communication between the chief American and the chief Soviet decision-makers. This development tended to make intermediaries of the traditional sort unnecessary to the main diplomatic process, and also tended towards the exclusion of allies, though some of them (and possibly the Chinese) also now have 'hot lines' to Washington. The first serious use of the Washington-Moscow direct link was during the 1967 Middle Eastern crisis, by Kosygin to President Johnson. By the time of the 1973 crisis, the level of communication between Moscow and Washington was so high

that it may be said to have amounted to consultation; the modes used included Kissinger's journey to Moscow, and his day-by-day conversations with the Soviet Ambassador in Washington. This intensity of communication did not, however, obviate the need for the very loud signal constituted by the U.S. strategic alert of 24 October 1973. This was a signal that certainly reached, and was calculated to reach, many ears other than those of the Russians: for instance the Israelis and the Egyptians (to reinforce their consciousness of the potential dangers of the situation) and the West Europeans (to dispel the suspicions of a Soviet-American 'condominium' which had been generated there). How far there was any serious Soviet intention of moving troops to the area is still a moot point: President Nixon in the television interview of May 1977 implied that the Egyptian proposal had been for two divisions each of American and Soviet troops and presumably the Brezhnev letter indicated the Soviet intention of moving its forces unilaterally if the Americans refused the bid, as they did. The full details of the crisis are not as yet available, but its exemplification of the principle of maintenance of communication with the adversary is beyond doubt.

2. That one should not seek to win too much, since the other side cannot afford to lose too much. The most difficult and dangerous calculation in crisis diplomacy is that of estimating the degree to which the adversary's decision-makers are willing to accept defeat on an issue, which means estimating the level at which they value a position. In the 1962 Cuba crisis, one might argue, the danger of nuclear war arose because Khrushchev had originally miscalculated on this point, failing to realize that Soviet missiles installed in Cuba would be seen as an unacceptably large psychological defeat in Washington. What he perhaps omitted to take into account was the non-rational element in the Washington reaction, the American historical and emotional stake in the Monroe Doctrine weighing far heavier than the rather marginal change in the immediate strategic balance.* In the 1973 crisis, on the other hand, in which the Soviet Union actually did sustain, in the outcome, very sweeping losses in diplomatic influence, amounting to the whole of its previous ascendancy in the Arab world except Libya, the defeat was so gradual, disguised and *sub rosa* that there was only a brief moment of crisis confrontation. Comparing the two cases, one might say that the 'insider's' calculation of loss will probably always contain emotional elements not perceived or not estimated at their true weight by most 'outsiders'.

It is logical to assume that the side which feels itself to have the most at stake will be prepared to make the higher 'bid' in terms of cost and risk.

*If one reads the full text of Khrushchev's first letter to Kennedy, which is not yet published, the degree of his personal regret, alarm and consternation at this error emerges very strikingly, and undoubtedly it was that which enabled the Washington crisis-managers, 'Excom', to treat his letter as the true signal from the adversary, rather than the formal Politburo letter which was received later and theoretically ought to have had the greater validity.

The Soviet sphere of influence in the Arab world was about eighteen years old in 1973, dating it from the first Egyptian arms deal of 1955. But it was a fairly troublesome, unsatisfactory and unstable one, as the expulsion of Soviet officers from Egypt in 1972 had demonstrated to the Soviet leadership. There would thus probably have been difficulty for any Soviet 'hawk' at the time in making a case that the previous Soviet degree of influence was of sufficient advantage to the Soviet Union to warrant the risks of confrontation with the United States. The American sphere of influence in Latin America has no doubt also been quite troublesome, unsatisfactory and unstable, but it had a kind of historical sacredness in American eyes, being almost a century and a half old in 1962.

The demonstrated effect that the higher the estimate (always subjective rather than objective) of the national stake involved, the higher the willingness to take risks and the greater the chance of a successful outcome, applied also in Vietnam. It was an 'unlimited' war for the Vietnamese, in the sense that their own national identity, as far as the effective decision-makers on either side were concerned, was staked upon it. It was, however, a 'limited' war for the United States: what was at stake was not survival, nor identity, nor substantial national assets, nor even a stable and valued sphere of influence: only a fragment of diplomatic prestige and credibility. The level of costs the U.S. was willing to bear to avoid that loss was large but limited, and was exhausted by 1974. The conscious or unconscious 'signalling' of this fact was quite correctly read by the decision-makers in Hanoi as meaning that their final offensive, originally intended for 1976, could be advanced to 1975 without serious risk.

The conscious or unconscious signalling of refusal to bear costs or risks in an issue was also the decisive factor in the Angola crisis at the end of 1975. In this case the source of the crucial signal was the American Congress, which insisted on voting at the end of the year entirely to cut off funds to the operation in Angola. The Secretary of State had struggled hard to throw at least a protective shadow of ambiguity over the American reaction by a C.I.A. operation, and by some channelling of funds to the Western-oriented factions, UNITA and the FNLA. For a time his signals seemed to induce a certain hesitancy in Soviet decision-making. The flow of Cubans and matériel to the MPLA faltered for a few weeks in November. But the post-Vietnam revulsion in Congress was too vociferous to be drowned by conflicting signals from the Administration. The Congressional votes of December and January unmistakably conveyed 'no contest' to Moscow: the Cuban operation went ahead at full steam again, and the MPLA were installed in government within three months. What was gained in the way of power-advantage by the Soviet Union may not necessarily prove very substantial or permanent, but as an example of victory-by-default (Congress-enforced default) it was quite striking. Again the point is that the Russian reading of the Congressional signals that Western influence in Angola was not a matter for which America would take risks (or even let the Secretary of State make much effort) was quite accurate.

One might make the generalization that accurate reading of the other side's signals, and a flexible set of low-risk options to enable one to take advantage of the opportunities they indicate, is a key to at least short-term success in crisis diplomacy. The option of using 'proxies', demonstrated by the Soviet Union with the Cubans in this encounter, is one for which the West has no immediate equivalent. Though one case is hardly enough to establish a convention, it may be that some convention about the use of 'proxies' may need to be evolved. A possible convention would be that small states in Cuba's situation vis-à-vis the troubles in Angola and elsewhere in Africa should be regarded entirely as autonomous agents, responsible for their own acts and bearing *themselves* the costs and risks involved. That would be enough to deter most small powers from such adventures: the costs to Cuba of Angola already seem quite substantial, and could conceivably be more so, and the Russians are not necessarily likely to be so pleased with the outcome as to feel the technique would have advantages elsewhere.

3. That one must 'build golden bridges behind the adversary to facilitate his retreat'. No situation could be more dangerous in the nuclear age than to box one of the nuclear powers into a corner from which its decision-makers can see no way out save general war or unacceptable humiliation. This is the point at which the meaningless conference, the bogus quid-pro-quo, and the anodyne U.N. resolution all find real usefulness, as face-saving devices to be pressed upon the adversary with all diplomatic skills available. The removal of the U.S. Jupiter missiles from Turkey (they being obsolescent and due for removal anyway) in the aftermath of the 1962 crisis was one such expedient. The institution of the Geneva conference at which the Soviet Union could be co-chairman, in the aftermath of the sweeping American gains in the Middle East during the 1973 crisis, might be deemed another. This again is a clear contrast to the crisis-management of 1914, when either Serbia or Austria would have had to accept an unacceptable humiliation.

There will always be voices within the circle of decision-makers of the 'victorious' power, and among articulate opinion in that country, which will denounce such expedient gestures as 'appeasement' or as unnecessary concessions to the *amour-propre* of the other side, or of its decision-makers. Devices of this sort, however, are useful in the preservation not only of the system as a whole but of the domestic political position of individual decision-makers who have shown a willingness to accept a set-back philosophically. There is a sense in which Khrushchev's experience in the 1962 crisis was encapsulated into Brezhnev's reactions in the 1973 crisis, and if the system of conventions is to be strengthened and grow, these successive experiences must as far as possible constitute *a learning-curve for the decision-making elite as a whole,* not just for one individual decision-maker. That is the only manner in which the system could become stabilized, established and long-lasting as was the case with the nineteenth-century one.

4. That contingency plans, which inevitably will exist, and the strategic priorities which are assumed to be inherent in them, must not be allowed to dictate the manner in which the crisis is managed. *Political ends must maintain ascendancy, not military means.* Everyone concerned with the Cuba crisis was familiar with the baneful influence which the Schlieffen Plan (first devised by the German General Staff about the turn of the century) is said to have exercised over the German crisis-managers of 1914. Whether this baneful influence is a historical fact or not, its 'memory' was certainly an important check on any tendency to allow an undue weight of decision to rest on the shoulders of the military in 1962. Indeed, political considerations took precedence over military ones even at the tactical level. For instance, there was a 'preferred line', as far as the U.S. Navy was concerned, for the American warships which were to stop the vessels making for Cuba during the operation of the 'quarantine': the line which would keep them out of the range of the Mig aircraft based in Cuba. But this line would have allowed little time for the decision-makers in Moscow to change their minds before the moment when the ships must be stopped. It was therefore decided (on the suggestion of the then British Ambassador in Washington) to take the naval risk of a different line, closer to Cuba, in order to allow more time for reflection in Moscow. The assumed possible danger from the Migs never came to anything, and the extra time so bought may have been important.

The advice tendered by Chiefs of Staff must obviously be a major influence on the chief decision-maker in any serious crisis. If he is a former military man himself, that may help him to resist (or know how far to discount) alleged military necessities. President Eisenhower, for instance, was in a good position professionally to resist advice pressed on him by Admiral Radford and General Curtis LeMay at the time of the 1954 Vietnam crisis. President Johnson, on the other hand, was less well equipped to judge, and seems indeed to have misconceived, the nature of the military prospects in Vietnam during the 1968 crisis of the war. The military as an element in the group of crisis-managers must perhaps have a professional tendency to base their advice on a 'worst-case' analysis. On the other hand, it should not be assumed that they will always opt for military solutions: they may be more conscious than the civilians of what the strategic vulnerability of their own forces will be, once the tanks begin to roll.

During the first Berlin crisis, for instance, several of the policy-advisers in Washington and elsewhere were of the opinion that the Russian 'bluff' should be called with an American tank column (even left-wing persons like Aneurin Bevan in Britain expressed this view). It was the Joint

Chiefs of Staff, and General Marshall as Secretary of State, who were adamant against such a move, undoubtedly on the basis of professional understanding of the real strategic disadvantages faced by the West if the Russians proved *not* to be bluffing. Many Western contingency plans existed against various possible Berlin moves by the Russians in 1961, but it was perhaps fortunate that none of them envisaged the actual event, the wall built across the city. The lack of a plan for that particular contingency caused a hesitancy in Western reactions, which no doubt helped allow the wall to become a fixture. But seventeen years later, the wall may reasonably be seen as less a problem than a solution: a Russian solution to the intramural crisis in the affairs of their East European satellite, which had been occasioned by the tendency of so large a part of the population to 'vote with their feet' for life in the West. Whatever one's sympathy for the East Germans constrained to live in the Soviet sphere, the probability that a Berlin crisis would be the flashpoint for World War III has seemed much less in the years since the wall was built than it did before that time.

5. That local crises will be met in local terms, and that even a true crisis of the central balance will be met at least initially in *conventional* terms. This is really the direct opposite of the ostensible doctrine enunciated by Mr Dulles in 1954, of 'massive and instant retaliation at places and by means of our own choosing', which appeared to imply that a Chinese bid in South-East Asia or Korea, or a Russian bid in Somalia or Mozambique, might be requited by reprisals against Peking or Shanghai or Kiev or Vladivostok. In that form the doctrine was totally incredible from the first, and it is somewhat of an injustice to Mr. Dulles's understanding of international politics to assume he was not aware of this. There are several passages in the same speech which indicate that he did not expect it in fact to obviate all future Western losses. What he apparently hoped was to increase the level of uncertainties facing Russian (and particularly Chinese) decision-makers, so as to deter any propensity to undue risk-taking on their part. One can hardly say, however, that he was successful even in this more modest endeavour: Chinese policy in Indo-China was not modified and Khrushchev, who was to dominate Russian policy-making for the next ten years, undoubtedly pursued more risk-taking policies (Congo, Berlin Wall, U-2, Cuba) than either Stalin and the collegiate leadership before him or Brezhnev after him.

The importance of the local conventional balance in military terms and also the balance of local political forces, has been almost continuously illustrated in every crisis since 1945. It is only in very special cases, with a symbolic value recognized on both sides—for example Berlin—that the strategic nuclear balance can be said apparently to 'override' the local conventional balance. Even for the NATO forces of the central front, often misrepresented as being hopelessly and irretrievably weaker than the Warsaw Pact forces they face (when over most of the period in fact they have only been marginally so), the necessity has always been apparent of building a viable theatre-balance. The 'massive and instant retaliation' doctrine might conceivably be usable in crisis diplomacy, *either* by a power which was so strong that the threat could inhibit any challenge, *or* paradoxically, by one so weak that it visibly had no other means of resistance. In the latter case, however, the decision-makers of the power concerned would probably also have to cultivate an image of being prepared to die as a community rather than yield: what might be called a 'Masada' stratagem.

In more normal cases, for middle powers especially, enough local military capacity to hold ground until the processes of international crisis-management could take effect may well prove the crucial factor. The business of reversing a military *fait accompli* (as in Cyprus after the Turkish invasion) offers great difficulties. The capacity rapidly to reinforce a threatened line, or a potential 'co-belligerent' (for instance Yugoslavia) with matériel, or conceivably forces, would appear vital to maintaining the credibility of this convention, as far as the dominant powers are concerned.

The deployment of tactical nuclear weapons in the European theatre does not reduce the importance of the conventional-forces balance there for ruling-out 'pre-emptive options' which might otherwise be thought worth chancing in crisis situations. Tactical nuclear warheads provide a sort of reinforcement of the conventional forces' role in rendering unattractive any such opportunist moves. Their existence means that the adversary forces need to be kept dispersed in order to avoid presenting 'high-yield' targets, and that in turn means that operations in the nature of massing for attack would be clearly signalled (some analysts say by as much as a month), thus providing extra warning time for diplomacy to get under way. So they may be considered to have a peace-time function as part of the mechanism of surveillance, as well as the battlefield function usually ascribed to them. How long the interval for negotiation would be between the first conventional clash and the military demand to use tactical nuclear weapons would obviously depend on the forces-balance in the area concerned, and the general political relationship between the powers: that is, on whether detente or cold war prevailed.

7. That the other side's sphere of influence requires a special wariness and restraint when touched by intramural crisis in the way of dissent. The first exemplification of this convention was Mr. Dulles's extreme caution in the 1953 East German riots, though he had just campaigned for the Republicans on a platform of 'liberation' in Eastern Europe. He adhered to that principle again in 1956, despite the urging of some of the bolder spirits in the C.I.A. for a 'spontaneous' general uprising. And President Johnson maintained a similar caution during the Czech events of 1968.

One of the uncertainties imported into American foreign policy with the advent of the Carter administration was whether this convention would continue to hold. Probably it will, yet the President's claim that promoting the observance of human rights has become a major objective of American foreign policy could easily be misinterpreted by hopeful spirits in Eastern Europe (or anxious ones in Moscow) as a promise that the contrary would be true. If developments like those of 1953, or 1956, or 1968 precipitated a new intramural crisis of the Warsaw Pact with dissidents demanding human rights on the Western model and more freedom from the oppressive Soviet embrace, the United States administration might have a lot of difficulty keeping intact its credibility on the one hand or the European peace on the other.

8. That the powers will not allow their signals to each other to become infected with excess or misleading ambiguities through consultation with allies. This is really a convention necessary for the Western side rather than the Soviet Union to observe. No-one in Washington seems likely to calculate that the decision-makers in Moscow will modify their choices in the light of representations from Bulgaria or even Poland. But the nature of the Western political and logistic situation is so different that it is more possible to imagine Soviet decision-makers counting on French or German or Italian complications obstructing U.S. action in some future crisis. This would particularly be possible if the French or Italian governments were coalitions including the Communist party, as might be the case within a few years. There was a foretaste of this kind of difficulty in the 1973 crisis, in the obstacles placed by the West German and other governments in the way of the U.S. resupply operation to Israel.

The speed of events in many crises operates usefully to prevent the problem becoming acute—and, in fact, to exempt allied heads-of-government from the burden of choice. President de Gaulle said after a briefing by Kennedy's envoy during the Cuba '62 crisis 'I was glad to be informed: I would not wish to be consulted.' The known necessity for speed operated not only to preclude the sharing of responsibility for decision, but also to rule out any possible Russian calculations that the misgivings of allies would prevent decisive American reaction. There are potential crisis-areas, however, especially Berlin and Eastern Europe, where the only effective action would be allied action, and where therefore this useful simplifying of the adversary choices would not take place. Possibly the known existence, ahead of the crisis, of a unified diplomatic 'command structure', parallel to the unified military 'command structure', is a useful hedge against such calculations.

9. That surveillance by contemporary means is legitimate, and will not be 'blinded' (short perhaps of the near-advent of direct hostilities). The nuclear age, or at least the period since 1960, might almost better be called the age of surveillance. The powers of the central balance have of course always watched each other like hawks by means of traditional espionage, and one would not assume that branch of international endeavour to have in the least diminished. But progressively since the

early 'sixties it has been supplemented by photo-reconnaisance and even more advanced techniques, based on satellites, very high flying aircraft, radar and sonar arrays, seismographic installations, upper-air analyses and so on. The powers able to afford a decisive amount of this very expensive hardware, and the very large intelligence services needed to interpret the evidence it collects, are at present only the United States and the Soviet Union, though China and some other countries are beginning to acquire a small capacity in satellites.

Surveillance, however, has a slightly double-edged quality as regards crisis-management. The Cuba crisis of 1962, for instance, could well be classed as the first crisis of the age of surveillance, in that it was the evidence picked up by U.S. photo-reconnaissance (U-2, not satellite) of the Soviet missile installations that precipitated the crisis. (However, if the evidence had not been picked up then, and the installations had been completed, there would almost certainly have been a still more dangerous crisis at some later date, and very possibly a war.) Similarly, in the 1973 crisis, the most direct signal of the imminence of attack (though Israeli intelligence discounted it) was the launch of the Soviet satellites two days before.

The possession of satellite-gathered information is a very substantial advantage to the dominant powers vis-à-vis allies, clients and others. It is said, for instance, that the United States supplies Peking with more detailed information than the Chinese can gather for themselves of the deployment of the Russian forces behind the border areas, and that this useful service is one of the reasons for Peking's relative tolerance of the U.S. ties with Taiwan. In turn, some allies of the U.S., for instance Turkey and Australia, provide bases essential for retrieval of material of this sort, and that gives them a form of diplomatic leverage, useful in crisis-situations, as probably to Turkey in 1974–75, in the wake of the Cyprus crisis. More importantly, this vast invisible net of surveillance is essential to the viability of SALT and other arms-control efforts. Under the euphemism 'national means of inspection' it receives almost formal recognition in the A.B.M. and other agreements. It may seem rather unlikely, as was hinted earlier, that this convention could survive the apparent near-approach of major hostilities between the powers of the central balance. Satellite-based surveillance could theoretically be 'blinded' by the use of 'killer' satellites which would put the observation satellite out of action. But for either power to do this would be such an enormously strong signal of impending attack that it would seem to invite a pre-emptive strike. One could, however, imagine a satellite-blinding, *pre-announced,* being used as a demonstration-effect in some tense situation.

10. Possibly a convention is also emerging that arms-control efforts should take special account of the needs of crisis-management in two arenas. On the one hand, as between the powers of the central balance,

there should be sought restraint on, or elimination of, those forces which might conduce towards pre-emptive strike in crisis. 'Soft' land-based missiles are in this category because of their vulnerability. SLBMs, land-mobile missiles, 'hardened' missiles, and cruise missiles do not share the same disadvantage. As regards conventional forces, the fear of surprise strike can be somewhat diminished by measures such as are being promoted under the Helsinki Final Act to secure notification of troop movements and the inviting of observers from the adversary coalition to manoeuvres. There is also some stabilization possible through the reduction of tank armies and forward-based quick-reaction systems.

The other aspect of crisis-management that could be advanced through arms-control measures concerns crises of local balances. As was mentioned earlier, the wars stemming from such crises (the most important of which have been in the Middle East and South Asia) have already tended to be short because the contemporary battlefield (even when local and conventional) consumes ammunition and spare parts at a truly formidable rate. Unless the army concerned can secure an air-lift of supplies from its great-power arms-supplier, it might face defeat through depletion of stores in a fortnight. The Israeli dilemma in the first week of the 1973 war offered a vivid illustration of the scope this provides for the great-power patron to push the local powers towards cease-fire, and to shape the settlement. The zeal with which some powers have set about acquiring very advanced weapon-systems from the half-dozen suppliers who alone are able to provide them has thus made the governments concerned more susceptible to this form of pressure than they were in the days when they fought with rifles.

The Future of Crisis Diplomacy

There are various other established precedents in crisis that one might see as probably hardening into conventions: for instance a tacit agreement that neither side will interfere with the other's air-lift to a client, strikingly exemplified during the 1973 crisis, when the U.S. air-lift to Israel and the Soviet air-lift to Syria went through more or less the same air-space with no incidents. This example illustrates the way that conventions evolve: it might at present be classed just as a maxim of prudence, based on obvious mutual interest. But if it holds for another crisis or two, then it could be seen as an established convention. Indeed any of the propositions I have called conventions, it may be objected, could be regarded instead as maxims of prudence. But the one tends to crystallize out of the other in ordinary social usage, as well as in international and political life. The conventions of a constitution are really formalizations of prudential practices that have been found to make it workable. One might see an analogy in the highway code as it has evolved since the beginning of the automobile age. The first motorists inherited some conventions from the previous age of horse-drawn traffic, and these were amalgamated with prudential maxims arising from the new technology to become, first, the understood conventions of early motorists, and, later, enforced traffic rules. The final stage of crystallization into agreed and enforceable law is perhaps not to be expected in international politics, so the penultimate stage of conventions must be looked to as the most valid source of restraint in helping to avoid disaster.

It is important to note, however, that the conventions I have sketched probably hold at present only for the powers of the central balance. This is not necessarily because of cultural differences between the decision-makers concerned and those of local balances, though that may be a factor. It is rather that the central balance powers have a common interest in seeing themselves as managing an ongoing system in which they must bear in mind what their situations might be, vis-à-vis the prime adversary, in the next crisis but three. The local power, by contrast, tends to define the existing crisis of the moment in moral terms ('We are the victims of aggression') rather than in diplomatic terms ('We are involved in a local-balance crisis with such-and-such a neighbour'). Its decision-makers will often tend to see any crisis as a life-or-death matter. The Israelis certainly do so, and perhaps with justification: they say the Arabs can afford to lose many rounds in the battle, but they cannot themselves afford to lose even one.

Thus, of the six categories of war-bearing crises distinguished earlier, it may prove that only the first two will be responsive to this mode of restraint. A third group, crises of colonial systems are perhaps now exhausted as a category, unless a new imperial age arises (a prospect by no means to be dismissed, but perhaps sufficiently distant to warrant neglecting it for the moment). The other three categories—crises of local balances, crises of secession and reunification, and crises of domestic consensus (which overlap partially but not entirely with the previous category)—all seem likely to persist as a source of hostilities, and the casualties and destruction which go with them.

Central balance powers can do something to restrain and shorten such hostilities by their arms-supply policies. Regional organizations like the O.A.U. and the Arab League can operate to supply mediators and guarantees, though they have not been conspicuously successful in this role to date. The U.N. could play a bolder role in restraining military action during the development phase of crises. (Its record to date has not been impressive, save perhaps in what might be called the 'tidying-up' phase, *after* the resolution of the crisis.) But it remains the case that political or economic action to resolve the conflicts and remedy the grievances from which the crises arise is the only long-term process likely to be effective, and that is too large a subject for this essay.

With all its limitations, one may yet say that in crises and potential crises of the central balance, from Azerbaijan on for more than thirty years, the existing system of understandings and signals has operated as a kind of safety-net against disaster. Although that particular kind of crisis has been neither the most frequent, nor the most productive of hostilities, it undoubtedly has the greatest potentiality for general ruin: universal cataclysm as against local cataclysm. So there is every reason to maintain and develop the system, and ensure if possible that its infrastructure continues in good repair.

I have argued elsewhere* that the infrastructure concerned consists of four main elements: the exchange of hostages, surveillance, a common strategic ideology and a preponderance of power on the side of the *status quo*. It will be obvious that the first two of these continue. Neither of the two super-powers has as yet any plausible mode of 'withdrawing its hostages': that is, erecting a credible shelter system for its cities and people. There are occasionally reports in the Western press of the Soviet civil defence systems' alleged capacity to do this, but the evidence has not yet been convincing to the Western intelligence community. Surveillance also obviously persists, growing every year in universality and intensity, and perhaps in acceptance and legitimacy.

More questions might be raised as to the third and fourth elements in the system: a common strategic ideology and a preponderance of power on the side of the *status quo*.

Looking first at the latter, the alarms which were raised in 1975–76 about the alleged prospective military predominance of the Soviet Union perhaps had more to do with the political battle in those years in the United States than with actual analysis of the existing balance of forces, whether it was the central nuclear balance, or the European theatre balance, or the naval balance, that was under consideration. The inevitability, and even the necessity, of such alarms needs to be conceded. Forces-balances which are not only complex, and wrapped in secrecy, but subject to rapid destabilizing change by technological breakthrough, will necessarily be susceptible to conflicting interpretations, even as between people within the intelligence community. And these conflicting interpretations will always be usable for political purposes, as the 'missile gap' allegations of 1959–60, and the 'Russians-at-the-Rhine-in-48-hours' allegations of 1975–76, were to various parties in the nomination and election processes of those two Presidential campaigns. At the time of writing, in the late 'seventies, the consensus in the strategic community maintained that there was still a considerable preponderance of power on the side of the *status quo,* interpreting that to mean the West and its fellow-travellers, and that this preponderance was not merely strategic, but also reflected the greater productivity of Western agriculture and industry, the greater liveliness and variety of its political and intellectual life and the greater skill, on the whole, of its

---

*See the author's *The Conventions of Crises* (O.U.P. 1971), p. 52 seq.

diplomacy. As to the future balance of forces, there were voices to warn that five years hence the advantage overall might lie with the Soviet Union: that such predictions have been presented regularly almost every year since 1949 does not, of course, preclude the possibility that some day they might prove true.

There remains the final and difficult question of a common strategic ideology. The concept does not assert *identical* strategic doctrine on the two sides, still less identical tactical doctrine. There have in fact always been considerable differences between the two sides on such matters as the use of tactical nuclear weapons. And of course the 'strategic missions' of the two sets of forces in the European theatre are not identical, the Western forces needing to hold the present line as far East as possible, and the opposing forces presumably to push as rapidly as possible into NATO territory during the first few days of hostilities. These differing strategic missions are reflected in forms like the respective investments of the two sides in, for instance, tanks as against anti-tank weapons. But the two sets of political decision-makers do need to have roughly the same sort of intellectual appreciation of what the shape and meaning of the potential battle would be, and its impact on their respective societies. Crisis-management, in Schelling's phrase, rests on 'the manipulation of shared risk', and if the strategic appreciation of that risk was quite different on the two sides, an element of radical uncertainty would be introduced into the process. It is possible that some of the new weaponry *could* introduce such a change: that a nuclear war could appear something conceivably to be 'won', instead of something to be deterred, to one set of decision-makers or the other. Western comment, from right-wing sources, had some tendency to attribute such a change to the Soviet Union, but there was little sign of it in the Soviet approach to crisis up to 1978. (Angola is not evidence to the contrary: Congress had specifically insisted on defining that as a 'no-risk' situation for the Soviet Union.) Also, on such evidence as was available, the lead in the advanced weapons technology that would make such a concept feasible, like neutron warheads and precision-guided missiles, was American, not Soviet. Thus the prospects for rational management of the crises of the central balance appeared at least as good, towards the end of the seventies, as when the system had survived its baptism of fire, thirty years earlier.

7

Disarmament and Arms Control
Since 1945

by John Garnett

Not even a supreme optimist could regard the disarmament record since 1945 as a success story. Close to four hundred billion (400,000,000,000) dollars is now being spent annually on armaments, and the magnitude of this expenditure is dramatically indicated by the fact that total annual world military expenditure 'is about equal to the entire national income of the poorer half of mankind . . . the amount of aid given to the underdeveloped countries is a mere five percent of the money spent for military purposes.'[1]

Arguably, the record has not been quite so disastrous as that of the inter-war years when the League of Nations battled painfully and ineffectually with the same fundamental problem. But the slender achievements since 1945 are far outnumbered by the failures, and in the end what has been achieved is of marginal significance. Anyone acquainted with the disarmament efforts of the 1920s and 1930s cannot avoid the feeling that he has heard much of it before, because, although the weapons and technology have changed, the fundamental problem and the arguments surrounding it are depressingly familiar. Behind current arms control negotiators one can almost hear the ghostly voices of Paul Boncour, Lord Cecil, Maxim Litvinov, S. de Madariaga and all those other distinguished statesmen who grappled so manfully with the disarmament deadlock in the protracted negotiations leading up to and including the World Disarmament Conference. Without question the basic conceptual apparatus for thinking about disarmament was articulated well before the Second World War; and although a few interesting new ideas have emerged since 1945, it is quite remarkable how much of the post-war thinking was foreshadowed in that earlier period.

Over the years, the case for disarmament has scarcely changed at all. The main argument has always been that arms races make wars more likely and more destructive than they would otherwise be. The awesome weapons developed since the Second World War may have reinforced the persuasiveness of that argument, but it has always been a major plank in the disarmament platform. Even before the First World War it was recognized that the mere possession of military capability sometimes shaped the will to use it, and that statesmen were made nervous, if not trigger-happy, by the military power of others. One commentator on British naval rearmament put it this way: 'What I fear is that if we have a navy so strong that we can crush all creation, we shall be inclined to try the experiment by crushing it.' It was acknowledged that armaments created and exacerbated political tension. Their acquisition was always liable to inject new uncertainty into explosive political situations because states, always unsure of their position in the arms race, might believe that any military advantage they possessed was likely to be temporary, since sooner or later the other side would catch up and even pass them by making their armaments inadequate or obsolescent. Nervous states would, therefore, be tempted to capitalize a temporary lead by waging war when it was most advantageous to them, largely on the grounds that, since war seemed inevitable in the long run, it should be waged when prospects for success were brightest.

One may detect an element of this kind of thinking in Germany before the First World War, when, realizing the dangers of having the Schlieffen plan upset by the Russian railway development scheduled for completion in 1917, and the dangers of allowing the power of the German fleet to be more and more effectively counterbalanced by the implementation of British naval plans, the German General Staff, already resigned to the inevitability of conflict, favoured war sooner rather than later.[2]

Moreover, even a state which at a particular point in time finds itself disadvantageously placed in an arms race may none the less feel impelled to wage war if it seems that the weapons gap is likely to widen rather than close with the passage of time. From the point of view of the weak state, and all things being equal, the conclusion of a war fought with slightly inferior armaments is likely to be more satisfactory than that of a war fought with vastly inferior armaments.

The Japanese were not unaware of this point when they decided to attack Pearl Harbor in 1941. In debating whether or not to prolong diplomatic negotiations, navy minister Shimada acknowledged that if the negotiations failed, Japan would 'be forced to open hostilities at a great operational disadvantage, caused by the delay'[3]. The decision to attack 'was supported with all kinds of figures indicating that Japan could not hope to keep up with American production of armaments or aircraft, coupled with the frequent repetition that "each moment of delay will place us at a greater disadvantage".'[4]

In the post-war world it soon became apparent that these traditional hazards of an arms race were further complicated by the peculiar and exacting requirements of the mutual deterrence strategy which lay at the heart of East-West security. In 1959 Albert Wohlstetter described the nuclear balance as 'a delicate balance of terror',[5] quite likely to be upset by unrestrained competitive rearmament. If mutual deterrence was to be achieved and maintained, he argued, a high degree of effort was required from each of the parties concerned. Both must seek to deploy and maintain that quality and quantity of weaponry which enabled them to threaten unacceptable damage even after a surprise attack, but neither must, through a policy of unrestrained rearmament, unduly alarm the other by suggesting offensive, first-strike intent. In other words, the maintenance of stable mutual deterrence required a certain amount of intelligent restraint on the part of both sides in their armaments policies. Only by channelling the arms race along mutually accepted lines, through some kind of arms control, could this particular hazard of unrestrained arms competition be avoided.

The problems of strategic stability became particularly acute in the late 1960s when it appeared that the rough strategic parity which had emerged in superpower relations was threatened by certain technological developments, notably anti-ballistic missiles and multiple re-entry vehicles. The deployment of anti-ballistic missiles was regarded as highly destabilizing because it threatened to undermine the effectiveness of retaliatory strikes. The uncontrolled deployment of ABMs jeopardized the entire posture of mutual deterrence by raising the possibility that one side might effectively defend itself against a punishing blow from the other by acquiring the capability to destroy incoming missiles. Unless controls could be agreed upon, it was feared that the arms race would accelerate rapidly, as each side tried to acquire offensive weapons capable of 'saturating' or cancelling out the new defences.

In 1972, a treaty limiting ABMs was signed. ABMs were not prohibited, but the restrictions agreed upon were such that in future neither side could hope to defend a significant fraction of its population or industry. In this way a new twist to the arms race was avoided, and, by agreeing to live in a state of mutual vulnerability, the two super-powers helped to preserve mutual deterrence.

Developments in 'offensive' technology have also threatened the stability of the nuclear balance, and whilst the SALT I Interim Agreement on Offensive Missiles may reasonably be regarded as a minor step towards controlling offensive systems, the major problems associated with the deployment of multiple, independently targeted re-entry vehicles were left to the SALT II negotiations. MIRVs are dangerous because multiple warheads, with an accuracy and yield sufficient to give a high probability of destroying hardened missile sites, raise the prospect of 'first strike' capability and a new massive round of rearmament. It is too early to say whether the very considerable problems of controlling MIRVs will be solved, but the attempt finally is yet another example of super-power determination to avoid the hazards of unrestricted rearmament by channelling the arms race along mutually accepted lines.

Any arms race, involving, as it does, the amassing and improving of weaponry, inevitably means that any particular war will be fought with those weapons. In so far as any improvement in the quantity and quality of armaments implies an improvement in the capacity of both sides to destroy and kill, there is truth in the age-old argument that an unrestrained arms race makes the event of war more destructive. Since the Second World War the acquisition of nuclear, biological, and chemical weapons in large quantities reflects a modern tendency to amass weapons which, by their very nature, cannot easily be used in a discriminating, merciful, and selective fashion. A war in which large numbers of these weapons are used is likely to be much more destructive of life and property than a war in which fewer weapons are used. In that sense the traditional argument that arms races increase the destructiveness of any particular war which may occur has gained strength since 1945.

However, it is worth pointing out that an arms race is not necessarily concentrated on the most destructive weapons. In some cases the most fierce competition may be channelled into producing small weapons, defensive weapons, and accurate delivery systems which make it possible to discriminate between military and civilian targets. The present trend of the East-West arms race suggests that its continuance will not make war any more devastating than it already is. Indeed, some of the most important recent innovations in weapon technology have made possible less rather than more destructive weapons.

Since the early 1960s, for example, much of the effort expended in the research and development of nuclear weapons has been directed towards the miniaturization of warheads and the production of low-yield weapons. 'Mini nukes', relatively 'clean' and with weapons yields in the ton rather than the kiloton range, are one obvious example of a trend towards less destructive armaments. Though they may be regarded as undesirable for other reasons, their use in war may bring the possibility of fewer rather than more deaths and less rather than more collateral damage.

Similarly, in the conventional field, the development of precision guidance techniques intended to improve vastly the single-shot kill probabilities of particular weapons has made surgical targeting with small warheads a practical possibility for the first time. The possibility of reducing collateral damage has been further improved by refinements in conventional missiles which offer enhanced destruction capability with reduction of unwanted blast effects. It is now arguable that whereas the widespread use of the military hardware developed during the 1950s and 1960s almost certainly threatened the wholesale destruction of urban centres within the battlefield area, the hardware of the late 1970s and

1980s holds out the possibility—and one would not want to put it higher than that—of survivable war even in areas as densely populated as Western Europe.

Recent improvements in the accuracy of long-range missiles and in flexible targeting techniques have made it possible for the United States to amend significantly its deterrent posture in the direction of less rather than more violence. In 1974 Secretary of Defense James R. Schlesinger announced a new doctrine of flexible nuclear options which, amongst other things, might limit the chance of uncontrolled escalation if war occurred.[6] The new strategy distinguished between civilian and military targets and by emphasizing counter-force targeting envisaged the possibility of nuclear exchanges which avoided the wholesale and indiscriminate slaughter of entire populations.

When strategic policies, and the weapons which implement them, are devised primarily with the intention of deterring war and, via such doctrines as that of controlled response, of making war somewhat more civilized and humane than it would otherwise be, it is unfair and misleading to suggest that an arms race inevitably implies greater rather than lesser destruction.

Some Dangers of Disarmament and Arms Control

The alternative to an arms race is some kind of disarmament or arms control. Disarmament means the reduction or elimination of weapons, and it is an aspiration which has had a long, if unsuccessful, history. Of course, even the most ambitious plans for disarmament do not envisage a world which is totally without arms and from which the possibility of violence has been abolished. Such a world is almost impossible to imagine, let alone create. It would bear so little resemblance to the present world order that speculation about it is irrelevant. In practice, most disarmament supporters have accepted the qualification to the cause of complete disarmament which was first established by Article VIII of the League of Nations, . . . 'the maintenance of peace requires the reduction of armaments *to the lowest point consistent with national safety.*' Even that relatively modest objective has proved elusive.

Arms control is a much less ambitious goal, and, since it has been articulated only in the last twenty years, a relatively new idea. It merely implies co-operation between potential enemies to establish qualities and quantities of weapons likely to reduce both the chances and ferocity of war, and to control the development, deployment and use of weapons along mutually acceptable lines.

In arms control schemes, attention is focused on *managing* weapons; in disarmament schemes, attention is focused on *reducing* weapons. Another way of expressing this difference of emphasis is to say that 'Disarmament seeks safety from arms, while arms control seeks safety through arms.'[7] But the two approaches overlap in the sense that while it is possible to think of proposals for arms control which do not involve disarmament, and proposals for disarmament which do not involve arms control, it is also possible to think of schemes which fit *both* categories. Any agreement involving the supervised and controlled dismantling of weaponry would be an example of both disarmament and arms control.

Because of this overlap it might appear that disarmament and arms control are really both varieties of the same thing and that the latter is merely a less ambitious form of the former. This is a misleading perspective, in the sense that those who believe in the more radical forms of disarmament operate from a quite different intellectual position from that of the more modest arms controllers. In essence, the disarmers are *revolutionaries*; at heart, they wish to abolish military power and to abandon many of the traditional practices of inter-state relations. In contrast, the arms controllers are *conservatives*; they believe in evolution rather than revolution, and instead of seeking a transformation of the international system, they merely want to make it work properly. They are interested in the kind of marginal tinkering which may enable us to stagger through the next fifty years more or less the way we have staggered through the last fifty years. It is perhaps a moot point whether it is more realistic to believe, as the arms controllers do, that in the long run military power can be successfully managed, or to believe, as the disarmers do, that it can be dramatically reduced or abolished.

Though, as we have seen, an unrestrained arms race is not without its dangers, these alternatives of disarmament and arms control, or at least certain forms of them, also entail risk, and the purpose of the following pages is to point out that statesmen should be wary of merely exchanging, via arms control or disarmament, one kind of insecurity for another.

Even an ostensibly successful disarmament treaty should be appraised cautiously since it may have consequences which are quite the reverse of those intended by the men who drafted the treaty. For example, a disarmament agreement may simply register the obsolescence or unimportance of whatever is being restricted by its terms. It has been argued that the partial test-ban treaty of 1963, far from halting the development of nuclear weapons, simply recognized the growing irrelevance of atmospheric testing for current research and the continuing significance of underground testing for developing new generations of small warheads. In effect, by signing the treaty, the two super-powers formally agreed not to do something which they did not really want to do anyway, while preserving the right to forge ahead in those areas of nuclear weapons research which really interested them. The arms race was neither halted nor even slowed: it was merely re-channelled, and from the point of view of peace and security the test ban treaty may even have been counterproductive. As Thomas Schelling has put it, 'once the testing goes underground and the weapons become invisible, the milk gets clean, the geiger counters stop clicking, people may stop worrying, and it may become possible to talk rationally and coolly about nuclear weapons again.'[8]

Another reason for a cautious appraisal of even successfully negotiated arms control proposals is that treaties which limit certain categories of weaponry may have the unintended effect of channelling the arms race into categories of weapons not yet forbidden, and stimulating research into new weapons. It is sometimes argued, for example, that the disarmament clauses of the Versailles agreement, far from halting German rearmament in the interwar years, simply altered its course by driving German scientists to develop new weapons not covered by the treaty.

The dangers of reading too much into a measure of arms control are further exemplified by that part of the SALT I agreement which dealt with offensive missiles. The Interim Agreement put a ceiling on the permissible number of strategic nuclear delivery vehicles for each super-power. Superficially, at least, it seemed that the arms race volcano had been capped, and many optimists regarded this treaty as 'one of the most important arms control agreements of the nuclear age.'[9] But in reality the limitations were largely illusory because the Interim Agreement did nothing to control the deployment of multiple re-entry vehicles. Since this technology has dramatically increased the number of nuclear warheads a single missile can deliver, it has made the numerical limitation on the missiles themselves almost irrelevant. In short, the arms race may have been re-directed but its impetus has hardly been affected at all.

Putting the point in general terms, what this implies is that 'a bargain struck on the basis of the technological characteristics of specific weapons existing at the time of agreement will become inequitable as one side or the other introduces qualitative improvements which have not been ruled out, or deploys alternative systems which bypass the restrictions agreed upon.'[10] The speed of technological innovation in the weapons business has increased enormously since 1945 and the effect of this has been to undermine and even invalidate negotiated arms control agreements. Christoph Bertram has argued that arms control agreements which fix precise quantities of weapons are particularly vulnerable to technological change and their negotiation may actually diminish rather than increase the security of participating states.[11] Just as the 1972 SALT ceilings for strategic delivery vehicles were made virtually meaningless by Soviet MIRV technology, it is possible that a Mutual Force Reduction agreement on the numbers of tanks permitted to NATO and the Warsaw Pact will be similarly undermined by improvements in anti-tank technology. Rapid innovations in weapon technology have introduced a new element of uncertainty and risk into the disarmament business and states need to be wary of reading too much into any agreement which they have signed.

One of the more subtle ways in which technological innovation threatens to undermine arms control arrangements is by prompting the development of new weapons which cannot be fitted into traditional descriptive categories because of their multi-purpose roles. The modern cruise missile is an excellent example of a sophisticated hybrid weapons system which straddles a number of weapon categories in the sense that it may be used tactically or strategically, armed with either a conventional or a nuclear warhead, and launched from air, sea or land based platforms. What is more, its mission may be switched at relatively short notice. The effect of developing multi-mission weapons of this kind has been to negate the value of certain arms control agreements by presenting signatory states with new opportunities, not for *evading* their terms, but for *bypassing* them altogether. After all, there is little point in signing agreements limiting armaments whose function can be taken over by new weapons which are flexible enough to be used for the same purpose.

Perhaps one way of coping with the problem caused by technological innovations is to move away from the counting and comparing game which has dominated disarmament thinking since before the Second World War. Bertram has suggested that it might make more sense to drop the numbers game and to focus attention on the various military missions which military power is designed to serve.[12] What this means is that instead of seeking primarily to limit numbers of weapons, arms control agreements should attempt to constrain capabilities to perform specific military tasks. Instead of worrying about military inputs—men, tanks, missiles, etc.—arms controllers should concentrate on military outputs: surprise attack, pre-emptive strikes, etc. In a nutshell, 'option symmetry' rather than 'numerical symmetry' is the object of the exercise.

In the context of East-West relations, both super-powers have an interest in limiting the opportunities for a surprise nuclear strike against those land-based ICBMs which form a significant part of their deterrent forces. A surprise counterforce strike is a military mission which both the Americans and the Russians appear keen to eliminate. The argument here is that the best way of doing this is by abandoning the quest for detailed quantitive agreements of the SALT variety in favour of mission-controlling agreements which are more resistant to technological pressure and easier to negotiate since they offer signatory states some degree of flexibility in the number and mix of their weapons. Making military missions rather than weapons systems the main subject of disarmament is a very new idea but in a field where new ideas are rare it seems one of the most promising to emerge since the Second World War.

Another reason for treating disarmament and arms control proposals warily is that unless they are very carefully thought out, their implementation, far from enhancing the prospects of world peace, may actually diminish them by upsetting a precarious balance of power. Numerous writers have emphasized the significance of an equilibrium of power in preserving peace. The theory is that when the power of every state, or likely grouping of states, is roughly but effectively counterbalanced by equal power elsewhere in the international system, then aggression is unlikely to occur, or if it does occur, to succeed. Thus, stability, peace, and national security tend to coincide with a balance or equilibrium of power in the international system. When there is a balance of power the incentives to aggression are cancelled by the disincentives. No power, either alone or in combination with others, feels sufficiently strong to inflict its will upon other states with impunity. Hence there are minimal incentives to break the peace when there is a balance of power.

Disarmament and arms control schemes which threaten to upset a balance, no matter how fragile it may be, may provoke the very war they are intended to avoid. The most extreme kind of power imbalance may occur as a result of unilateral disarmament which may be interpreted as a sign of weakness by enemies who confuse the higher, virtuous motives of its protagonists with an incapacity to pay the defence bill required to stay in the race.

A.F.K. Organski, writing about 'the balance of power', has, by implication at least, outlined a possible defence of unilateral disarmament. He claims that 'the relationship between peace and the balance of power appears to be exactly opposite to what has been claimed. The periods of balance, real or imagined, are periods of warfare, while the periods of known preponderance are periods of peace.'[13] The argument is that since the computation of military strength is inherently difficult and a matter of subjective evaluation, states are most likely to make a mistake in their assessment of a particular distribution of power when there is parity between them, and least likely to make a mistake when it is patently obvious where preponderant power lies. When there is a roughly equal distribution of power between rival states it is easy for one side to believe it has the edge on its rivals, and is therefore in a position to wage war advantageously. But when there is an extremely uneven distribution of power, no reasonable statesman can possibly misread the power situation. The very weak behave because they have no power to misbehave; the very strong behave because they are perfectly secure from the threats of the very weak.

Although Organski's argument is worth an airing, it is perhaps reasonable to question the validity of the assumption which underlies it, namely, the view that strong states wage war only in defence of their security. Some would suggest that since the nature of states is not unlike that of tigers, the powerful states would gobble up the weak states all the more quickly for their being weak.

Acknowledgement of the possible destabilizing effect of unilateral disarmament on the balance of power has led to the view that disarmament or arms control schemes should be multilateral, and should be so arranged that an existing distribution of power between participating states is fundamentally unchanged. As it was expressed in principle 5 of the 1961 McCloy-Zorin Agreement on Principles for Disarmament, 'All measures of general and complete disarmament should be balanced so that at no stage . . . could any state or group of states gain military advantage, and that security is ensured equally for all.'[14] More accurately perhaps, disarmament or arms control must not give any one state a military advantage over others *which it does not already possess.*

Attempts to embody this principle in concrete agreements have failed for a number of reasons. To begin with, it has proved impossible to assess or measure objectively a given distribution of power. There is neither agreement as to what should be counted, nor agreement on how what is counted can be compared. These difficulties have made it impossible to arrive at disarmament figures which would effect a balanced, equitable, reduction. Numerous disarmament schemes both before and after 1945 have foundered on these rocks.

In the early 1920s, for example, Lord Esher submitted a very neat plan to the League of Nations which sought to reduce armaments by setting up a 'unit of armament', say 30,000 men, and attributing to each nation a figure or coefficient which, when multiplied by the 'unit of armament', would represent the army allowed to the state concerned. Thus, France would have a coefficient of 6, Italy 4, Britain 3 and hence their respective armies would be 180,000 men, 120,000 and 90,000. The difficulty with the scheme was that it proved impossible to determine a 'unit of armament' which had a reasonable degree of comparability. The power of 30,000 man units could vary enormously depending upon the quality and quantity of military-technological equipment available to them.

More than fifty years later similar problems of measurement and comparison plague the talks on Mutual Force Reductions. The object of the negotiations in Vienna is to achieve 'equal security' and to 'maintain the present degree of security at reduced cost'; but the two alliance systems are finding it extraordinarily difficult both to evaluate the military capabilities of forces and weapons which do not easily lend themselves to comparison, and to agree on which forces should be reduced and by how much. Both the Warsaw Pact and NATO possess enormous military strength, but significant asymmetries in terms of the character of their weaponry and in the numbers and quality of their manpower are making it very difficult to agree a formula for arms reduction. Not surprisingly, working out reductions which will not, in the opinion of both sides, destabilize the strategic situation is proving as difficult in the 1970s as it did in the inter-war years.

A further important reason why it is difficult to negotiate agreements which leave unchanged an existing distribution of power is that some states generally object to that power structure. Only the strong are satisfied with the status quo; the weak would like to change it, and therefore reject arms control and disarmament measures which threaten to freeze permanently what they consider to be an unjust and temporary inferiority.

At the Rome Conference of 1924, called to extend the provisions of the Washington Naval Agreement, Spain refused to accept a level of naval armament commensurate with her low position at that time in the naval power hierarchy. She did so on the grounds that her weakness, a temporary consequence of unparalleled building on the part of other powers both before and during the First World War, would soon be remedied by the completion of her own programme of naval rearmament. De Madariaga relates the wonderful story of how, at the Conference, 'One day the Spanish Admiral accosted the British Admiral at the end of a sitting and declared himself ready to accept the status quo. His British colleague was very much elated. Then the Spaniard added: "But we must discuss one point: the year to be chosen to define the status quo." "Why", said the Englishman, "1921"; "Oh no", said the Spaniard: "I suggest 1588."[15]

Exactly the same sort of reasoning may be discerned in the arguments put forward by NATO negotiators at the current Mutual Force Reduction talks. Since MFR got under way in 1973, a major NATO objective has been to correct the numerical imbalance of ground forces in the Central Region. With this in mind the NATO team has insisted on a common manpower ceiling for NATO and Warsaw Pact forces. In other words, whereas the Warsaw Pact, negotiating from a position of conventional superiority, has sought *proportional* reductions which would leave unchanged the relative distribution of power between the two alliances, NATO has attempted to change what it regards as an unjust status quo in favour of a more equitable balance of power. As the NATO powers have discovered, there is all the difference in the world between accepting a position of weakness which arises out of the natural, competitive order of things, and voluntarily accepting an inferiority which is enshrined in a treaty.

The achievement of arms reduction which does not tempt aggression by unduly disturbing a distribution of power conducive to peace has been further complicated by certain unique characteristics of that variety of the balance of power known as the 'balance of terror'.

Now a 'balance of terror', or situation of mutual deterrence, rests upon each side possessing 'assured destruction capability'. If, through disarmament or arms control, the retaliatory capacity of either side is so seriously impaired that it cannot cause what the other side regards as 'unacceptable damage', then a stable balance of terror is replaced by a highly unstable balance of power in which either side, by striking first, has the capacity to destroy the other's retaliatory force, and hence to wage war without fear of punishment. When states are pursuing security primarily through a strategy of deterrence, disarmament and arms control have to be limited and tailored to meet the peculiar and demanding requirements of the balance of terror. It is for this reason that an unrestrained disarmament programme could have the same effect as an unrestrained arms race in undermining deterrence.

It would appear then that, although there is a relationship between the level of armaments and international stability, it is not automatically true that stability is most assured when the level of armaments is very low. In fact, paradoxical as it may seem at first sight, there is a certain safety in a high level of armaments.

Apart from the argument that a fairly high level of armaments is less likely to undermine mutual deterrence than a very low level of armaments, there is another reason for being wary of drastic reductions. If, in a disarmament treaty, the permissible number of nuclear weapons is set for both sides at zero (or a number approaching it), then even a very small evasion of the agreement, say 10 hidden missiles, may confer a decisive advantage on the evading state. And since such an evasion is very difficult to detect, there will probably be a great deal of international tension even after the agreement has been implemented. Neither side knows for certain whether the other has evaded its obligations, and hence each may be tempted to evade the agreement just in case the other has. This tense situation could be avoided if the permissible number of weapons for each side was much higher. If each side was allowed say 500 weapons, then even a fairly substantial evasion would not be sufficient to confer a decisive advantage. Even twenty or more hidden and illegal weapons would not be sufficient to make surprise attack worth while, because in a situation where both sides have large numbers, even a moderate numerical advantage cannot give an attacker the assured capacity to destroy his opponent's ability to retaliate and punish. Hence it may be concluded that both sides may feel more at ease with disarmament which is less, rather than more, exacting in its demand to reduce nuclear weapons.

All this is not intended as an argument for an arms race. Its purpose is merely to point out that though an arms race is undoubtedly dangerous, certain ill-considered schemes to control it may be equally dangerous. Well-meaning enthusiasts sometimes display a frightening ignorance of the phenomenon they are trying to control or abolish, and it seems sensible to continue this analysis by examining the nature of the arms race and the way in which it works.

The Logic of Arms Races

Arms races have been defined as 'intense competitions between opposed powers or groups of powers, each trying to achieve an advantage in military power by increasing the quantity or improving the quality of its armaments or armed forces.'[16] Not so very long ago it was fashionable to blame their existence on armaments manufacturers. A great deal of energy was spent investigating the activities of these 'merchants of death', and a sinister picture was propagated, particularly by the Left Wing, of rich, powerful, and unscrupulous men, exacerbating, even creating, international tension, and profiting from the arms race and the sufferings of war to which it contributed.[17]

The modern variant of this indictment of private citizens is to blame the current East-West arms race on the American 'Military Industrial Complex', an unholy alliance of 'Big Business' and the 'Armed Services', which, according to its critics, has created a pressure group of such enormous size and power that it is beyond democratic control.[18] Now it may be true that large numbers of people have a vested interest in perpetuating the arms race, and it may also be true that in the past some armaments manufacturers seized every opportunity to increase their business by fomenting rumours of war and urging politicians to rearm; but the causes of international tension and war lie much deeper than the machinations of either individuals or even powerful pressure groups. The causes of international tension are so deeply entwined in the human condition that focusing responsibility in this way is absurd.

Herbert Butterfield, who has probed more deeply than most into the problems of human conflict, was forced to the conclusion that at the basis of all relationships, including international relationships, there is a built-in, unsurmountable obstacle to perfect trust and goodwill. Butterfield has described this obstacle, inherent in all social relationships, as 'the absolute predicament and the irreducible dilemma',[19] and he is careful to point out that this predicament is 'one which we can see would have led to a serious conflict of wills even if all men had been fairly intelligent, and reasonably well intentioned'.[20] This predicament contains the necessary ingredients of conflict irrespective of any special wickedness in any of the parties concerned. 'The greatest war in history could be produced without the intervention of any great criminals who might be out to do deliberate harm in the world. It could be produced between two Powers both of which were desperately anxious to avoid a conflict of any sort.'[21]

What, according to Butterfield, is the basis of this predicament which inevitably mars all human relationships? The basis lies in 'what I should call Hobbesian fear—that you yourself may vividly feel the terrible fear that you have of the other party, but you cannot enter into the other man's counter-fear, or even understand why he should be particularly nervous. For you know that you yourself mean him no harm, and that you want nothing from him save guarantees for your own safety; and it is never possible for you to realise or remember properly that since he cannot see the inside of your mind, he can never have the same assurance of your intentions that you have.'[22]

This passage is one of the most profound in the entire literature of international politics. It explains why all statesmen sooner or later find it necessary to deliver some variant of the following speech created by L.F. Richardson. 'The intentions of our country are entirely pacific. We have given ample evidence of this by the treaties which we have recently concluded with our neighbours. Yet, when we consider the state of unrest in the world at large and the menaces by which we are surrounded, we should be failing in our duty as a government if we did not take adequate steps to increase the defences of our beloved land.'[23] These sentiments have been expressed in many languages, and there is no prima facie reason for doubting the sincerity of the statesmen who utter them. Let us grant that statesmen, and the governments and people they speak for, genuinely want peace and would like to disarm. They dare not do so because, since no human being is able to put himself in the shoes of another human being, they are unable to be absolutely certain that the intentions of other statesmen are as friendly and honourable as they seem to be. A residue of fear and insecurity is thus built into any social relationship, be it between individuals or states, and no amount of protestations of good faith can ever eliminate it.

However, even at this very fundamental level of analysis, it should not be thought that national insecurity and the international tension it gives rise to are only a consequence of the international predicament. They are also a result of the fact that state relationships are forged by an act of will on the part of governments which, by definition, can be changed, and is therefore unpredictable in the long run. Even if, for the moment rightly, a statesman is convinced of the friendly disposition of another state, insecurity remains because the possibility that the friendly relationship will deteriorate is always there. Friendship may be transformed into hatred by a unilateral act of will, and a state which, as a result of allowing itself to be lulled—at the time quite legitimately—into a sense of security, has dropped its guard, may find that it can no longer defend itself against former friends, who, reacting perhaps to an imagined rather than real grievance, or to changed circumstances, are now pursuing policies inimical to the interests of a former ally. Nothing is permanent in international relations, and statesmen, mindful of the possibilities of adverse change and conscious of their responsibilities, must therefore temper friendship with caution so that their respective states never find themselves in a position of vulnerability from which they cannot extricate themselves.

If, to this mistrust which is endemic in any social situation, and which, because it is in the nature of things, implies no dereliction of duty on the part of any individual, we add the mistrust which arises from an appreciation of the frailty of human and state nature, it becomes clear why so many writers have described international relations in terms of inevitable and unceasing conflict. Ambitious and aggressive men, perhaps driven into competing for a more than fair share of the fruits of the earth by a will to power, which, according to one writer,[24] is virtually indistinguishable from the will to live, find themselves thwarted by the similar ambitions of others, and are therefore forced to resort to physical violence as the ultimate arbiter of who is master.

Military capability, based upon armaments, is the means by which violent conflict is waged or threatened, and it is acquired because it is believed to serve this function of preserving and promoting the interests of the state which commands it. The conclusion to be drawn from this analysis is that the existence of an arms race, though partly explicable in terms of the 'social situation' or 'the absolute predicament', is also a result of the fact that armaments play a role in the pursuit of human ambitions. Any adequate explanation of an arms race must acknowledge that, to some extent at least, arms races develop because statesmen see an advantage in using military power to achieve their objectives.

An important point is being made here. The arms race is not a manifestation of human madness, an insane out-of-control suicide race promoted by men who are either wicked or stupid. It is a result of reasoned decisions by sensible men grappling to the best of their ability with the wretched situation in which they find themselves. Those, like Bertrand Russell or Alva Myrdal, who[25] fulminate about 'the reign of unreason' and 'global folly', make the mistake of judging arms races from the detached 'god-like' perspective of a rational, omniscient being looking down on planet earth. To such a being, the arms race, like many other aspects of human behaviour, must look absurd. But criticism from that perspective is as irrelevant to an individual statesman as human criticism of the behaviour of lemmings is to an individual lemming.

The fascinating thing about mutual suspicion in an arms race is that once it has begun it develops a dynamic of its own. Like the multiplier process familiar to economists, it is self-reinforcing, so that suspicion spirals upwards at an ever increasing rate. Those processes, in which a movement on the part of one party induces a movement in the other party, which in turn provokes another movement by the first party, and hence another movement by the second, and so on, have been described by Kenneth Boulding as 'reaction processes.'[26] The most thorough theoretical treatment of these processes has been made by L. F. Richardson,[27] who was concerned to prove that wars often emerge from the process of action and reaction which forms an arms race.

State A, devoid of aggressive intent but naturally suspicious of the reluctance of State B to disarm completely, feels that she must guard against the possibility of aggression by State B, and therefore adds to its armaments. State B, also innocent of offensive intent, uneasily perceives the rearmament of State A, and draws the plausible conclusion that not only was she right in ignoring State A's plea to disarm completely, but that in view of the recent rearmament of that state, her own arms requirement needs revising upwards. State A, her original suspicions about the aggressive intentions of State B now amply confirmed by the latter's rearmament, feels impelled in the interest of security to rearm further in order not to fall behind in the arms race. One round of rearmament inevitably leads to the next, since any degree of rearmament by one side is immediately reciprocated by the other. The rearmament process spirals upwards, and, because neither state can accurately estimate the military strength of the other, in the interests of safety each tends to overestimate the level of armaments it must acquire in order to be secure. This reciprocated error in judgement further exacerbates tension, thereby adding momentum to an arms race which neither side wants and neither side is keen to win, but which neither can afford to lose, and which therefore tends to be run at an increasingly fast pace.

This view that the armaments policies of states are best understood in the context of arms *races* has a long and distinguished history, even though the term 'race' was rarely used before 1900. Richard Cobden believed it in the nineteenth century[28]; Lord Grey believed it before the First World War[29]; Salvador de Madariaga believed it in the inter-war years[30]; and it has been common currency amongst arms controllers since the Second World War. There is clearly something in it. But the view that armaments policies are competitive in the sense of being affected, if not determined, by other armaments policies, is not the only plausible interpretation of a rearmament programme. A persistent, though less dominant, strand in military thought has been the view that force requirements are related to the function they have to perform rather than to the armed force levels of potential enemies. This view is sometimes referred to as 'the doctrine of absolute requirements', and is responsible for the persistent demand in the 1920s of the British navy for seventy cruisers irrespective of the level of naval armament possessed by other powers.

Lord Cecil explained this strand in British naval thought at the first session of the Preparatory Commission for the World Disarmament Conference. 'In the case of the Navy there is no doubt a certain element of—I will not call it competition, but dependence on the size of other navies. That was very carefully considered from the point of view of certain kinds of ships at the Washington Conference, which ended in an agreement which was very warmly welcomed in my country. The Washington Conference, however, only dealt with certain kinds of ships. It is possible that further agreements may be made in respect of submarines and cruisers, but I ought to point out that the number of cruisers in the British Navy is also largely a question of overseas commitments and not of the size of foreign navies, or only very slightly a question of their size.'[31]

In a similar vein it may be argued that a large part of the strategic arsenal of the United States, far from reflecting a series of sensitive responses to Soviet rearmament, was largely determined by the crude requirements of nuclear deterrence. The strategy of 'Mutual Assured Destruction' required the United States to amass sufficient retaliatory power to cause massive, unacceptable, damage in the Soviet Union. With this goal in mind, Mr R. McNamara aimed at acquiring the capacity to destroy between a fifth and a quarter of the Soviet population and one half of its industrial capacity, even after absorbing a first strike against American strategic forces. Though the weaponry required to deliver this retaliatory blow was obviously related to Soviet offensive power, it was more fundamentally determined by American conceptions of unacceptable retaliatory damage which were unaffected by Soviet rearmament policies. In short, to see the build-up of American strategic power solely in terms of a 'reaction process' or 'race' is to miss the point that much of it was acquired to give practical expression to an interpretation of 'unacceptable punishment' which was generated within the American administration and which was quite unaffected by Soviet military policy.

One of the most damaging attacks on the idea that a policy of rearmament implies participation in an arms race has followed the upsurge of interest in 'bureaucratic politics'. Various analysts have convincingly demonstrated that major weapons decisions have been taken largely as a result of 'politiking' within government departments. Paul Hammond, for example, has explained how some of the major strategic weapons purchased by the USA after World War II were bought, not so much for strategic reasons, but as a result of organizational pressures from within the Services.[32] And Vincent Davis, in a very revealing analysis of the naval establishment as a pressure group, has also documented the influence of organizational pressure on weapon procurement. He makes the point that during World War II 'Air force officers . . . . sometimes seemed incapable of distinguishing between their dedication to country and their dedication to proving the validity of their Douhet-Mitchell strategic ideology.'[33] Later on, in the 1950s, when the Air Force felt threatened by the advent of the missile, the same organizational parochialism manifested itself. 'In the controversy over the proposed B-70 bomber, the willingness of the Air Force men to relabel this plane a reconnaisance aircraft after it had been denied to them as a bomber seemed to say: "We feel that we must have this aeroplane regardless of what it is called and what it may be used for." '[34]

Although it is fashionable to speak of the 'strategic' dialogue between the United States and the Soviet Union, and to seek explanations of their armaments policies in terms of reciprocated reactions to each other's behaviour, the drift of this analysis is to suggest that decisions about weapons are taken, not as a result of rational analysis by statesmen sensitive to every move the enemy makes, but as a result of a much more sordid process of organizational bargaining. In short, though it is customary to speak of the arms *race* between the United States and the Soviet Union, an appreciation of the importance of 'bureaucratic politics' may lead us to consider the possibility that there is no race—just two clumsy military bureaucracies, each doing its own thing.

Albert Wohlstetter has recently directed further carefully researched criticism at those who have persistently regarded the super-powers as being engaged in an arms *race,* a mortal contest in which each provokes the other into endless rearmament.[35] The United States, so the conventional wisdom goes, has consistently overestimated the Soviet threat, and in so doing has talked itself into the unnecessarily high defence expenditure necessary to meet that exaggerated threat. The Soviet Union, doing its own 'worst case' analysis, has compounded the error, and by reinforcing original American mis-perceptions, has fuelled an endlessly spiralling arms race.

But, as Wohlstetter points out with some exasperation, the facts simply do not support this popular view of the arms race. In the 1960s, far from overestimating Soviet 'offensive deployments', the Americans actually underestimated them, and instead of spending more and more money on 'winning', American strategic expenditure went down 'not simply as a percentage of GNP but in real terms.'[36] The point is a simple one. 'To justify the term "race", any side that is racing has at least to be increasing its strategic budgets and forces. Even if the increase does not proceed at an increasing rate, for the name "race" to make any sense at all, there would have to be at the very least an increasing trend.'[37] The facts clearly demonstrate that not only were the Americans falling behind in the 'race', they were actually moving backwards; and, as Wohlstetter says, 'If that doesn't do lethal damage to the arms race metaphor, nothing will.'[38]

Whatever conclusions are reached on the vexed question of whether particular arms races are really *races,* the analysis of arms race dynamics in terms of 'reaction processes' remains a revealing one. It suggests that political tension exists because states hold images of mistrust about each other's intentions, and it implies that this mistrust may be endemic in the situation in which states find themselves. It further suggests that although these images of mistrust may be quite unjustified in the sense that they do not accurately mirror the real situation, it is still possible for them to reinforce each other in such a way that a single misinterpretation on the part of one state could lead to a fantastic spiral of miscalculations culminating in a war no-one wanted and a conflict with no real-world foundation. This kind of arms race has been compared to the story of King Arthur's last battle, before which, at a peace conference, the drawn sword of one of the knights about to kill a snake which had bitten him was misinterpreted as a sign that the battle had begun, whereupon the knights fell upon and virtually annihilated each other.

However, although a study of inter-state relationships reveals the possibility of a fascinating and unstable process of mutual interaction based upon an initial misunderstanding, it should not be thought that this process necessarily militates against friendly inter-state relations. A misconceived imputation of friendship on the part of one power could initiate a reaction process leading to increased friendship. This could happen because State A's image of State B partly determines, and is partly determined by, State B's image of State A. If State B behaves in a friendly way towards State A, the latter will tend to return that friendship. Perhaps the same general tendency which moves individuals to live up—or down—to other people's expectations of them, also exists between independent sovereign states.

It is worth pointing out, however, that a misconceived imputation of friendship is not nearly as common as a misconceived imputation of hostility. The reason for this is simply that the consequences of mistaking enemies for friends are much more dangerous than the consequences of regarding friends as enemies. We all know what happened to Little Red Riding Hood, and her narrow escape provides us with a clear warning of what may happen to those who fail to recognize their enemies.

Notwithstanding this point, however, and taking note of the reaction process which forms the inherent structure of any arms race, Charles Osgood has developed from it the idea that in a bilateral arms race, if one side would disarm to a very small extent (that is to say, if one side would, for a moment, behave towards the other as if it were a friend rather than an enemy), then this may provide an opportunity for reversing the arms race by breaking into the reaction process.[39] The argument is that if one side would unilaterally reduce its armaments by a very small amount, certainly not enough to affect adversely its overall security, this would reduce tension by favourably modifying the other side's image, and would encourage that side to make a similar small reduction, which would, in turn, modify the first side's image in the direction of increased friendship. Once this dynamic process of reciprocated action got under way, its momentum would lead, step by step, to a disarmed world, in which there existed a minimum of tension.

The theory is an attractive one but it seems to assume that, in an arms race, the only significant tension is that which is induced by armaments themselves. As we have already seen, armaments are to some extent a *result* as well as a *cause* of political tension. Osgood's theory is concerned with reducing that tension which is exacerbated by the existence of armaments, and, as a means to this end, unilateral disarmament measures are appropriate. But unilateral gestures do not affect the more fundamental images of mistrust which are a prerequisite for an arms race in the first place. This mistrust cannot be diminished by unilateral measures of disarmament because it has nothing to do with the existence or non-existence of weapons. Arms are a consequence, not a cause, of this tension. In other words, although 'graduated reciprocation in tension reduction' may reduce that part of arms race tension which is generated by the arms race itself, it cannot lead to disarmament in those instances where an arms programme is a reasoned response by states to the situation in which they find themselves.

Osgood seems to think that an arms race is always a self-generating, self-perpetuating, *mistake*. Of course, if an arms race is the result of a series of reciprocated misunderstandings, then it can be abolished by a series of unilateral gestures which will progressively remove tension and restore inter-state relations to their original condition. Unfortunately, probably few arms races are of this type. Most, while admittedly exacerbating tension, are a response to an underlying political hostility which could have many causes, and which is probably unavoidable in a world of sovereign states.

Direct and Indirect Disarmament

It may be concluded from the preceding analysis that those interpretations which regard an arms race either exclusively as a reflection, or exclusively as a cause, of international tension, are inadequate. As Inis Claude has pointed out, 'the truth is that this is a circular problem, in which causes and effects, policies and instruments of policy, revolve in a cycle of interaction and are blurred into indistinguishability.'[40] Arms races are both a consequence and a cause of political tension, and an adequate explanation of arms race dynamics must take this into account.

Recognition of the fact that arms and tension mutually reinforce each other has led to the development of two distinct but compatible approaches to the problem of disarmament. Those who have emphasized the point that armaments are a reflection of an underlying political hostility which could have many causes, have tended to favour those schemes for disarmament which are primarily directed towards removing the international tensions which provoke arms races and make them necessary. A medical analogy is often employed to explain the reasoning of those who favour this 'indirect', 'tensions first', approach to disarmament. Just as medical treatment should be directed towards removing the causes of a disease rather than the symptoms the patient complains of, so disarmament schemes should be concerned with removing the political tension which armaments are symptomatic of, rather than armaments themselves. Support for the 'indirect method' arises out of the perception that the causes of arms races lie deeper than the existence of weapons, and a string of proposals from the 1920s onwards can be directly attributed to this line of thinking.

Even in the post-1945 years the 'indirect' approach has continued to command support. In May 1955, for example, the Soviet Union linked its new disarmament proposals to its traditional objectives of putting an end to propaganda, settling outstanding problems through international negotiation, withdrawing all troops from Germany, liquidating foreign military bases, settling Far Eastern problems and removing barriers to trade. Marshal Bulganin insisted that 'a broad disarmament programme can be carried out only if the "Cold War" is brought to an end and the necessary confidence in relations between states, which unfortunately is now lacking, is established.'[41] During the 1950s, numerous proposals for removing mistrust as a prelude to disarmament were initiated and discussed by the United States and the Soviet Union. It is in this context that the famous 'Open Skies' proposal of General Eisenhower and the various other current schemes to inspect and verify the military power on each side of the Iron Curtain should be located.

The system of 'confidence-building measures' initiated by the Conference on Security and Cooperation in Europe is the most recent expression of this traditional approach to the problem of disarmament. The object of the Helsinki confidence-building measures is to reassure states about the political and military postures of their enemies, to demonstrate that their fears are groundless by undertaking various practical measures such as exchanging military information on troop movements and manouvres. The implicit assumption is that once the uncertainties and misunderstandings are dispelled, the states of Europe will be willing to move to more positive steps of arms control.

Though the 'tensions first' approach has always had its proponents, it has also had its critics. Many people, puzzled by its devious and roundabout attack on the disarmament question, regarded it as an excuse for doing nothing directly to reduce the number of weapons in the world. Others, despairing of the practicability of resolving political tensions without first reducing armaments, became convinced that the reduction of armaments was essentially a prerequisite for the reduction of tension and not a consequence of it. These critics favoured the 'direct' approach to disarmament through the reduction or abolition of weapons. Whilst they recognized that armaments were to some extent a product of international tension, they emphasized the view that armaments were in themselves a major cause of tension, which, therefore, merited reduction irrespective of outstanding political differences, and, indeed, as a step towards the resolution of those differences.

In the twentieth century, from the time of the Esher proposals of 1921 and the Washington Treaties of the same year, through the various proposed treaties for General and Complete Disarmament, to the present talks on Strategic Arms Limitation and Mutual Force Reductions in Europe, the 'direct' method has enjoyed widespread support. It is so simple and so obviously directed to the heart of the problem that it has dominated the minds of the enthusiasts, those men of good will who all too often have regarded more subtle approaches as evidence of lack of sympathy for the disarmament cause.

To those who argue that the theory of 'direct' disarmament is fallacious because it mistakes an effect for a cause, and can therefore be compared to the medical treatment of symptoms rather than the causes of disease, its supporters would simply point out that although armaments are indeed a symptom, they are a symptom which exacerbates the disease, and for this reason they qualify for treatment. As J. Strachey has pointed out for the benefit of those enamoured of the medical analogy, 'In modern medical practice it is . . . . . often indispensable to attack the symptom—say a raging fever—before, or at least simultaneously with, an attack on the causes of the disease itself.'[42]

And in fact it should be clear that the 'direct' and 'indirect' approaches to the problem of disarmament are neither mutually exclusive nor incompatible. The United States recognized this very early on when in 1951 President Truman announced that political settlements and disarmament negotiations should proceed *concurrently*, with progress in either area facilitating progress in the other area.[43]

Problems of Verification and Inspection.

Almost all disarmament and arms control proposals involve a mutual agreement between participating states deliberately to shackle their military strength in some way. But although each of the states involved may be anxious to comply with an agreement, none of them can be sufficiently certain that the others are acting in good faith to do likewise. Nearly all proposals for disarmament between mutually hostile powers raise this problem of how to overcome the lack of trust which possibly caused the arms race in the first instance, and certainly inhibits either side from relying on the integrity of the other to prevent the evasion of agreed limitations. According to some, the existence of this mutual mistrust makes disarmament at once both necessary and impossible. If it could be abolished, arms reduction would become perfectly possible but quite unnecessary.

If we assume from the outset that states will not, or dare not, trust their partners in a disarmament treaty to meet their obligations under it, then the pertinent question is whether some scheme can be devised to make their mutual mistrust an irrelevancy in the issue of whether or not to accept a proposed reduction.

One approach is to devise a system which enables the parties to a treaty to verify or confirm the truth of each other's claims to have complied with the terms of the agreement. Such a system would provide reliable information about the way in which the agreement was being implemented, and would make mutual trust between the participating states quite unnecessary. The idea behind this approach is that states which are unable to trust each other may nevertheless find it possible to trust a verification procedure, and hence to disarm with some confidence that other states are doing likewise.

Statesmen, with no faith in each other, are advised to put their trust in a variety of techniques designed to verify the compliance of all states participating in a disarmament agreement. They range from techniques such as aerial, satellite, and radar reconnaisance and remote-controlled 'black box' devices—all of which can be utilized without setting foot in the territory of the state whose compliance is being verified—to more searching techniques which involve the presence, sometimes in large numbers, of highly trained 'inspectors' in the territory of the inspected state. These latter techniques include budgetary inspection, the inspection of arms and related factories, military establishments and installations, research centres, storehouses, and plants engaged in the production or processing of those materials which are critically important in the production of armaments.[44]

The principle upon which all these physical verification techniques is based is that the search for violations in an arms control agreement is to be pursued in *places,* but there is a different and more controversial principle, namely that verification should be pursued in *people,* that is to say, in the minds and actions of policy-makers and private citizens likely to have knowledge of clandestine evasions of an agreement. Those who favour the use of spies, truth serums, hypnosis, polygraphs, and systematic and regular cross examination as a means of verification, point out that physical inspection techniques are of limited usefulness. They cannot, for example, reveal a deeply buried illegal stockpile of armaments or a very small laboratory producing germs. But a human being with knowledge of that stockpile or laboratory is a vulnerable target to the trained interrogator.[45]

Of course, the whole idea of making reliance on a verification system a substitute for reliance on the good faith of participating states only stands up if in fact statesmen are convinced of the reliability of the verification system chosen. If they have serious doubts about its ability to detect significant evasions, then its existence will fail to provide statesmen with the necessary assurance that their co-signatories are fulfilling their part of the bargain, and hence its existence will fail to provide a basis for agreement.

It should be noted that even if all appropriate available verification techniques were used to supervise an agreement, no state could be absolutely certain that its rivals were not somehow evading their legal obligations. After all, each participating state would be aware of various incentives which might tempt other signatories to default on their commitments. Each state would know that clandestine rearmament, if successful, might be very rewarding. For the state with aggressive intentions, evasions might confer a decisive military advantage. For the state with defensive intentions they might provide increased security. A defensive state, suspicious of its partners, might feel that complying with the terms of an agreement was prohibitively dangerous; in those circumstances it would be tempted to rearm purely as an insurance policy against the bad faith of the other participants. It is possible to envisage an ironic situation in which states which have agreed to disarm deem it necessary to devote enormous effort to evading the spirit and letter of the agreement they have just negotiated.

Evasion techniques might be quite subtle. One may expect guilty nations to provoke false alarms, which, when inspected, prove to be false alarms, thereby reassuring other states of the guilty country's peaceful intentions and good faith. By using this kind of deception the guilty nation will always appear to be the most innocent. The evasion techniques employed by Germany under the Weimar Republic in an attempt to 'neutralize the poison of Versailles' are revealing examples of what, with a little ingenuity, can be done to get round an inspection and control system.[46]

Because of the possibility of ingenious evasion techniques no state can be absolutely confident of a verification system. In 1975 there was considerable concern in the United States that the Soviet Union was evading its obligations under the SALT I Treaty. American fears centred upon a number of suspicions. First, that the Russians were interfering with American attempts to monitor the agreement by 'national technical means'; second, that the SS-19 missile which the Russians were deploying was a prohibited 'heavy' missile; and third, that new and illegal ICBM silos were being constructed. In the end most American fears were assuaged, at least in the sense that the Administration was persuaded that the Russians were keeping to the letter of the SALT agreement even if they were evading its spirit by an idiosyncratic but plausible interpretation of its terms. But the fear of undetected cheating is inherent in any arms control agreement.

Even though each state can be almost certain that its rivals are meeting their obligations, a nagging suspicion inevitably remains. To be sure, if there is inspection of the whole field of military activity, if military expenditure, the armed forces, storehouses, arms factories, etc, are all supervised, then the chances of detecting evasions of an arms agreement are much better than if only one technique is being used. Inspection systems mutually reinforce each other. But a residue of doubt about the reliability of verification inevitably remains, and it is this small uncertainty which assumes enormous significance in the minds of those who believe that even minute risks of incurring great danger are not worth taking.

The supporters of verification think differently. They suggest that the small risks involved in trusting a verification system with low fallibility are completely outweighed by the large risks involved in a continuing arms race. They point out, quite truthfully, that all policies involve risk, and that it is up to the statesman to choose the least risky course available to him. The only reasonable criticism of inspection techniques is not that they involve risk but that they involve greater risks than the continuation of competitive rearmament.[47]

Although questions about verification arise in the discussion of almost all disarmament schemes, it should not be thought that states which reject verification and control schemes do so solely on the grounds of their unreliability. This is an impression sometimes conveyed by those who believe that disarmament is primarily a technical problem, and that once certain technical difficulties have been overcome there is nothing to stand in the way of disarmament. Even if states which were anxious to disarm agreed that a particular verification and inspection scheme was one hundred per cent reliable, they might still object to it on the grounds that it undermined their sovereign status, that it encouraged commercial and military espionage, that it robbed them of the military advantages implied by a 'closed' society, and that it left unsolved the problem of how to discipline an evading state.

Since the Second World War the Soviet Union has, on different occasions, raised all these objections to particular disarmament schemes initiated by the West.[48] Soviet delegates have been particularly firm in their rejection of inspection schemes which allow foreigners to have unlimited access to their country's military secrets. Russia has traditionally regarded foreigners as a contaminating influence, and there is some historical evidence to support the government's view that too many relationships with the outside world undermine the authority of the regime. Any government which allows large numbers of foreigners to circulate at will among its people cannot hope to maintain strict social control or to keep many secrets from the world at large. Understandably the government is reluctant to allow actions which would both diminish its authority over the Soviet people, and perhaps force a certain amount of dirty linen to be washed in public.

Apart from the natural reticence of a closed society to open its doors to outsiders, the Russians have always made something of a fetish out of military secrecy. The fear which the Soviets have of spies is almost pathological, and when combined with an obsession with secrecy which runs deep in the Russian national character, this makes the Russians extremely nervous about accepting an inspection system which would give unparalleled opportunities for subversion and military and commercial espionage.

And of course, strategically speaking, the Russians have more to lose from a comprehensive inspection system than have the Americans. This follows from the fact that the United States, like all democratic societies, finds it difficult to cloak much of its military policy in a veil of secrecy. Because the U.S.A. is an open society, the Russians already know a great deal about its military affairs. New information gained through an inspection system in the U.S.A. would be useful to the Russians, but it would not compare in importance with the increment of knowledge which the Americans would get about Soviet military preparedness from similar inspection facilities in the Soviet Union. The United States has been precluded by its democratic system of government from fully exploiting secrecy as a military weapon, but the Soviet Union has operated under no such disadvantage.

Throughout the 1950s and 1960s all proposals which required the Soviets to accept effective inspection of the whole range of Soviet armoury, even at the very first stage of a phased disarmament programme, were rejected by Russia. Soviet spokesmen pointed out that Western insistence on this point was, in effect, a demand that the Russians give up their military secrets without any guarantee that the disarmament proposals would actually be implemented. The Russians feared that if the West discovered their military secrets in the initial stages of a disarmament programme, it would have no incentive to continue disarming and might even be tempted to make a preventive strike against the Soviet rocket forces, the location of which it had just discovered.

It should not be thought, however, that the Russians were against *all* inspection. They were perfectly willing to allow *disarmament* to be inspected, that is to say, they were willing to allow inspectors to observe the destruction of agreed weapons; but they were not willing to allow the inspectors to have access to their whole military machine. Quite correctly they pointed out that this implied not the inspection and control of disarmament, but the inspection and control of armaments.

An interesting plan to end this East-West deadlock was devised by Louis B. Sohn, whose fundamental ideas were incorporated into United States disarmament policy.[49] What Sohn tried to do was to devise a plan for implementing the principle that the extent of inspection during any stage of a disarmament programme should be related both to the amount of disarmament undertaken, and to the degree of risk to the participating states of possible violations. His scheme was designed to meet the Soviet objection that the West has demanded one hundred per cent inspection without any disarmament, and the Western objection that the Soviet proposals imply one hundred per cent disarmament without any inspection.

Sohn's plan has been amended and developed by a variety of writers. In essence it envisaged a progressive, supervised, territorial demilitarization of the two super-powers over a number of years. In Sohn's words, 'let us assume that there is an agreement to introduce certain disarmament and arms control measures over a six year period..... In such a case, the territories of the United States and the Soviet Union would be divided into six regions, and each year the disarmament measures and the accompanying controls would be introduced to one of these six regions. At the end of the six years all the territory of both sides would be covered, all the agreed disarmament measures would be executed and there would no longer be any limitation on controls.'[50]

However, in spite of various ingenious attempts to devise sufficiently foolproof and politically acceptable inspection schemes to satisfy both super-powers, no satisfactory solution has been found, and by the 1970s the principle of 'on site inspection' had been abandoned in favour of verification 'by national technical means'. For example, both the ABM treaty and the 1972 Interim Agreement on Offensive Strategic Weapons specified that verification of compliance with the terms of the treaties would be carried out by each party's use of 'national technical means of verification ...... in a manner consistent with generally recognised principles of international law.'[51] What precisely is permitted under this fairly loose terminology is not clear; the line between acceptable verification and unacceptable espionage is difficult to determine. In practice the Russians appear to regard satellite surveillance as acceptable and aerial reconnaissance as unacceptable, but it is difficult to discern any principle which enables them so to differentiate between these two varieties of 'national technical means of verification.'

For some kinds of disarmament satellite observation is perfectly satisfactory, but for others it fails to provide sufficiently detailed information to assuage the suspicions of enemies who mistrust each other. It is doubtful, for example, whether the range of a cruise missile or the number of warheads carried by a missile could be verified by satellite reconnaissance. As Christoph Bertram has noted, the sad truth is that 'significant improvements in military forces and weapons are becoming less and less observable.'[52] By undermining the usefulness of satellite observation, technical innovations underline the limitations of 'national technical means of verification.'

Moderate Arms Control

As the very real difficulties inherent in general and complete disarmament schemes became apparent in the 1950s, the idea of massive disarmament began to lose its appeal. By the end of the 1960s one commentator was moved to conclude, 'Disarmament has almost been abandoned as a seriously discussed objective of policy .... Now the politicians scarcely pay lip service to disarmament when addressing their national audiences. The intellectual debate has died out.'[53]

Sophisticated 'arms controllers' pointed out that an uncontrolled arms race and a substantially disarmed world are not the only alternatives available to statesmen. There is a 'middle of the road' possibility, namely, the control of the arms race by a series of measures which, though unable to guarantee peace, may mitigate some of the hazards of an unrestrained arms race without undermining the security, or frustrating the political ambitions, of the states involved.

Since the late 1950s a variety of these modest, but by no means insignificant, arms control proposals have been successfully negotiated.[54] Some of the most important have been directed towards stabilizing the strategic balance between the super-powers. With deterrence in mind, each super-power was encouraged, first, to maintain sufficient 'hardened' retaliatory capability to be able to punish and therefore deter a potential aggressor, but not enough to suggest a 'first strike' posture likely to undermine the effectiveness of his deterrent; second, to avoid building any defensive system which might weaken the punishing power of an enemy's retaliatory strike; and third, to take measures to reassure its potential enemy of its peaceful intentions and ability to avoid accidental wars.

The SALT I Agreements signed in 1972 incorporated an ABM treaty through which the super-powers renounced the option of deploying nationwide defence systems based on anti-ballistic missiles, and an Interim Agreement on Offensive Systems through which both super-powers sought to control the deployment of offensive weapons. The object of the exercise was to try to stabilize mutual deterrence by guaranteeing 'mutual vulnerability'. Though some progress was made towards this goal, it was recognized that further agreement was necessary if the objective was to be fully realized. The United States and the Soviet Union resumed negotiations in November 1972 and, in the ongoing talks, attention has been focused on controlling offensive missiles equipped with multiple re-entry vehicles.

In the early 1960s, and with the idea of improving the stability of their relationship by reassuring each other about their behaviour in crisis situations, the two super-powers instituted the hot-line between Washington and Moscow. This has since been followed up with an Agreement, signed in 1971, on Measures to Reduce the Risk of the Outbreak of Nuclear War. By its terms both the Americans and the Russians agreed to improve their arrangements for preventing the accidental and unauthorized use of nuclear weapons, and to cooperate in reducing the risk that any such incident would be misinterpreted as an act of deliberate war.

Preserving the stability of the nuclear balance has probably been the most important priority in East-West arms control negotiations; but initiatives in this field have not inhibited both super-powers from cooperating with a variety of states in wider measures of arms control. In 1959, the Antarctica Treaty was signed by twelve countries. It reflected an attempt to demilitarize the region and to preserve it for 'peaceful purposes' by prohibiting from it all military bases, manoeuvres and weapons testing. This treaty was followed by initiatives to make Latin America a nuclear free zone, to make illegal the emplacement of weapons of mass destruction in space, and to prevent the installation of weapons systems on the sea bed. All of these attempts were based on the assumption, probably justified, that it is easier to exclude weapons from an environment to which they have not yet been introduced than it is to remove or limit them where they already exist.

One of the most important areas of arms control since the early 1960s has been the attempt to halt or at least slow down the spread of nuclear weapons to new countries. Various attempts have been made, via the Partial Test-Ban Treaty of 1963 (and the Threshold Ban Treaty of 1974), and the Non-Proliferation Treaty of 1968, to make it difficult for new states to acquire nuclear capability. So far no comprehensive test ban has been negotiated, and the best that can be said of the partial test-ban arrangements is that they have made nuclear testing more costly and inconvenient for those who are bound by them. Significantly, neither France nor China has had anything to do with attempts to limit nuclear testing. The Non-Proliferation Treaty was heralded by President Johnson as 'the most important international agreement since the beginning of the nuclear age', but it has been condemned by some as a 'grossly discriminatory treaty' and most observers are sceptical of its potential. In truth, the danger of nuclear proliferation is as acute as ever.

In 1972 an attempt was made to grapple with the problems caused by the development of biological weapons. The Biological Weapons Convention of that year prohibited the development, production and stockpiling of biological and toxin weapons, and provided for their destruction. It did not, however, encompass chemical weapons.

In general, the record is not encouraging and it is easy to agree with Elizabeth Young that 'Up to now arms control and disarmament policies and negotiations have had ...... about as much bearing on the life of nations as a Mafioso's crossing himself as he loads his gun has on his hopes of heaven.'[55] Progress has been so slow that participants are frequently accused of wilfully dragging their feet. Alva Myrdal, after reflecting bitterly on some ten years of negotiations, was forced to the equally depressing conclusion, 'that we have accomplished no real disarmament, that we can see hardly any tangible results of our work, and that the underlying major cause must be that the super-powers have not seriously tried to achieve disarmament.'[56] Those like Mrs Myrdal who query the motives of states ostensibly pursuing the disarmament cause can, with justice, point to the 'gamesmanship' of disarmament conferences and the endless propaganda war which is waged by the negotiators. Joseph Nogee has described the technique whereby 'Every plan offered by either side has contained a set of proposals calculated to have a wide popular appeal. Every such set has included at least one feature that the other side could not possibly accept, thus forcing a rejection. Then the proposing side has been able to claim that the rejector is opposed to the idea of disarmament *in toto*. The objectionable feature may be thought of as the "joker" in every series of proposals.'[57]

What is odd is not that this kind of gamesmanship goes on, but that anyone of Mrs Myrdal's experience should be outraged by it. After all, disarmament talks do not take place in a political vacuum. They are conducted in a world of jealous, mistrustful states pursuing a variety of interests by a variety of means. Inevitably, disarmament negotiations, like all negotiations, are sometimes used to pursue objectives other than those for which they are called. Inevitably, the negotiations themselves sometimes become a vehicle through which wider political differences may be exploited. That does not mean that participants are uninterested in disarmament, only that they are interested in other things as well.

Perhaps it is inevitable that those committed to general and complete disarmament should regard the achievements as minimal and the prospects as bleak. Indeed, the historical record suggests that their pessimism is entirely justified. What is not justified is the rather crude way in which they sometimes attribute responsibility for the failure to disarm. Alva Myrdal roundly condemns the super-powers in much the same way that Philip Noel-Baker did years before when he accused the Americans of failing to take advantage of 'the moment of hope' which presented itself in 1955.[58] Elizabeth Young also puts the blame firmly on the shoulders of the super-powers. 'It would not be unfair to say that during the 1960s the super-powers have colluded in presenting to the world a series of insignificant agreements, and that these have been turned into insignificant treaties at very considerable expense of international time and trouble and breath.'[59] But the main thrust of the present paper is to show that there never was a 'moment of hope', and that when it comes to drastic disarmament, the super-powers, indeed all states, are in a classic 'catch 22' situation. They cannot disarm because of the suspicion which each has of the other, but, equally, they cannot overcome their suspicions without reducing their armaments. Actually, the 'catch 22' model does not do justice to the intractability of the disarmament dilemma. The super-powers find it difficult to disarm because of the suspicion which each has of the other; but, as we have seen, they cannot overcome all of their suspicion even by reducing their arms.

Progress is slow, not because states are ruled by evil or unenlightened men, but because, in a world of sovereign states, the difficulties are virtually insuperable. Senor de Madariaga went to the heart of the matter with his comment that 'the problem of disarmament is not the problem of disarmament. It really is the problem of the organisation of the world community.'[60] Unfortunately, the 'system change' implied by de Madariaga's accurate diagnosis is beyond us. Henry IV's reputed comment on an ambitious scheme for reorganizing the world community is still appropriate. 'It is perfect,' the king said, 'perfect. I see no single flaw in it save one, namely that no earthly prince would ever agree to it.' Hedley Bull has rightly condemned such impractical solutions as 'a corruption of thinking about international relations and a distraction from its proper concerns.'[61] A more constructive approach is to accept military power as a fact of life, and instead of seeking to abolish that which cannot be abolished, to try and manage it successfully so that wars become less rather than more frequent occurrences in international politics. This is the philosophy underlying recent arms control negotiations. For the disarmers it is a philosophy of despair; for the arms controllers it is all there is.

References

Chapter 1 **THE ROLE OF MILITARY FORCE IN THE NUCLEAR AGE**

1. Two extreme statements of the necessary emergence of alternatives to armed force are W. Millis, *A World Without War,* Santa Barbara, Center for Democratic Institutions, 1961, and A. Larson, *A Warless World,* New York, McGraw, Hill, 1963. A brief, balanced discussion is K. Knorr, *On the Uses of Military Power in the Nuclear Age,* Princeton University, Princeton, 1966.
2. cf. K. W. Deutsch et al., *Political Community and the North Atlantic Area,* Princeton, Princeton University Press, 1957.
3. A definitive treatment of this theory is P. van den Dungen, 'Industrial Society and the End of War', PhD thesis, King's College, London.
4. The earliest substantial treatment was B. Brodie ed., *The Absolute Weapon,* New York, Harcourt, 1946. See the chapters by Henry Rowen and Albert Wohlstetter in this volume.
5. Classic statements were B. Brodie, *Strategy in the Missile Age,* Princeton, Princeton University Press, 1959, and A. Wohlstetter, 'The Delicate Balance of Terror', *Foreign Affairs,* Vol. 37, pp. 211 ff.
6. See Robert Osgood's chapter in this volume.
7. cf. J. Kahan, *Security in the Nuclear Age,* Washington DC, The Brookings Institution, 1975, esp. ch. 6.
8. cf. R. Osgood, 'The Military Issues' in Osgood et al., *America and the World,* Baltimore, The Johns Hopkins Press, 1970, pp.189 ff.
9. The classic publication marking this shift was *Daedalus,* Fall, 1960, special issue on 'Arms Control', edited by D. G. Brennan. An effective explosion of the projects for general disarmament was A. Wolfers et al., *The United States in a Disarmed World,* Baltimore, The Johns Hopkins Press, 1966.
10. Robert McNamara's hopes and fears about stability can be perceived in R. S. McNamara, *The Essence of Security,* New York, Harper, 1968.
11. Press Conference by H. Kissinger, Moscow, July 3, 1974, *New York Times,* July 4, 1974; cf. Kissinger, Statement on Angola to Senate Foreign Relations Committee, January 29, 1976, and Address to Commonwealth Club of San Francisco, February 3, 1976.
12. cf. Lynn Davis, *Limited Nuclear Options,* London, Adelphi Paper 121, 1975/6; Laurence Martin, 'Changes in American Strategic Doctrine: An Initial Interpretation', *Survival,* July/August 1974.

219

13. It should be noted that the necessity for some responses more flexible than all-out retaliation became a theme of the Nixon Administration's strategic rhetoric under Henry Kissinger, who seems to have partly originated the trend he later seemed to think was getting out of hand. Cf. Richard Nixon, *A New Strategy for Peace,* February 15, 1970, p.92, and the chapter by Henry Rowen in this volume.
14. James Schlesinger, BBC Radio 4, Analysis, October 24, 1974.
15. A. Beaufre, *Deterrence and Strategy,* New York, Praeger, 1966, pp.46 ff.
16. See L. Gouré, F. D. Kohler, M. L. Harvey, *The Role of Nuclear Force in Current Soviet Strategy,* Coral Gables, University of Miami, 1974; R. Pipes, 'Why the Soviet Union thinks it could Win a Nuclear War', *Commentary,* 1977; the classic Soviet source is V. D. Sokolovsky, *Soviet Military Strategy,* New York, Crane, Russak, 1975 (ed. H. F. Scott), originally published 1968. More recently, A. A. Grechko, *The Armed Forces of the Soviet State,* 2nd edn., Moscow, 1975.
17. cf. R. J. Vincent, *Military Power and Political Influence,* Adelphi Paper 119, 1975; Laurence Martin, 'The Use of Military Force', in *The Future of Force in Modern Societies,* Adelphi Paper 102, 1973.
18. B. M Blechman and S. S. Kaplan, *The Use of Armed Forces as a Political Instrument,* Washington DC, The Brookings Institution, 1977.
19. E. Luttwak, *Strategic Power,* Washington Paper, 38.
20. cf. Vincent, op. cit.: K. Booth, *The Military Instrument in Soviet Foreign Policy,* 1910-1972, London, RUSI, 1973; an interesting discussion is R. W. Tucker, *The Radical Left and American Foreign Policy,* Baltimore, The Johns Hopkins Press, 1971. The most important statements of the optimistic view are those of politicians and publicists. For an example see Frank Allaun, 'The Bang of the War Drum', *Sunday Times,* August 20, 1978.
21. J. Record, *Sizing Up the Soviet Army,* Washington, The Brookings Institution, 1974, pp.40 ff; J. P. Douglass, 'A Soviet Selective Targeting Strategy Toward Europe', Arlington, Va., System Planning Corporation, 1977.
22. See 'Japan Under U.S. Pressure', *Defence Monitor,* November, 1975; Richard Ellingworth, *Japanese Economic Policies and Security,* Adelphi Paper 90, 1972, esp. pp.28 ff.
23. K. Knorr, 'International Economic Leverage and its Uses', in K. Knorr and F. N. Trager, eds., *Economic Issues and National Security,* Lawrence, Kansas, National Security Education Program, 1977, chapter 4.
24. E. Luttwak, *The Political Uses of Sea Power,* Baltimore, The Johns Hopkins Press, 1974, esp. pp.39 ff; U. Nerlich, 'Continuity and Change: the Political Context of Western Europe's Defence', in J. Holst and U. Nerlich, *Beyond Nuclear Deterrence,* New York, Crane, Russak, 1977.
25. Among many discussions of Western conceptions of world order see R. W. Tucker, 'The American Outlook', in Osgood, *America and the World,* op. cit, ch. 2.
26. See *New Conventional Weapons and East-West Security,* Adelphi Paper 144-45, 1977; F. Duchêne, 'The Proliferation of Arms: Motives, Magnitude and Consequences', in *The Diffusion of Power,* Adelphi Paper 133, 1977; J. Digby, 'New Weapons and the Dispersal of Military Power', California Seminar on Arms Control, October 1977.
27. See Robert Osgood's chapter in this volume.
28. A statement of this view important at the time was C. Mayhew, *Britain's Role Tomorrow,* London: Hutchinson, 1967.
29. H. Maull, *Oil and Influence: The Oil Weapon Examined,* Adelphi Paper 117, 1975; cf. Knorr and Trager, op. cit. Part II.
30. For a negative argument see H. S. Dinerstein, *Intervention Against Communism,* Baltimore, The Johns Hopkins Press, 1967.
31. W. Scott Thompson, *Power Projection,* New York, National Strategy Information Center, 1978; J. G. Roche, 'The Soviet's Growing Reach', Paper presented to European-American Workshop, Belmont, November, 1977; A. Hasselkorn, *The*

Evolution of Soviet Security Strategy, New York, Crane, Russak for National Strategy Information Center, 1978.
32. The major source on American attitudes to covert operations is the multi-volume *Final Report of the Select Committee to Study Governmental Operations with Respect to Intelligence Activities*, 1976, esp. Books 1 and 4.
33. See European-American Institute, *Peripheral Contingencies and Western Responses*, Conference Report, November 1977, and two contributing papers: H. Rowen, 'Projections of Power: Far and Near', and Laurence Martin, 'Western Stakes in Peripheral Contingencies'.
34. R. Ellsworth, 'Improvising Change in the Rules of the Global Game; will NATO Play a Role?', European-American Workshop, June, 1976.

Chapter 2 THE NOT SO HIDDEN HAND

Economic Factors in the World Balance since 1945

1. Alec Nove, *An Economic History of the USSR*, pp.356-7.
2. Jürgen B. Donges, 'A Comparative Survey of Industrialization Policies in Fifteen Semi-Industrial Countries', *Review of World Economics*, Institut für Weltwirtschaft, Kiel (Band 112, Heft 4, 1976), pp.626-59.
3. See *The Military Balance 1977-1978*, pages 86 and 87, International Institute for Strategic Studies (IISS) London.
4. Christopher T. Saunders in 'World Economy and East-West Trade' Workshop on E-W European Economic Interaction ed. Nemschak, Vienna Institute of Comparative Economic Studies (1975) shows the following trends in hourly earnings and consumer prices from 1968-1974 (annual compound percentage increases):

	Hourly Earnings	Consumer Prices	Labour costs per unit of Output
W. Germany	10.6	5.2	7.5
France	12.8	7.3	6.0
Italy	16.7	7.9	11.0
Netherlands	13.2	7.5	5.5
U.K.	13.0	8.7	10.5
Japan	20.5	9.6	9.5
U.S.A.	6.6	6.0	4.0

Source: NIESR Review, May 1975, Appendix Table 18 and p.31.
5. B. Guibert, 'La Mutation industrielle de la France', Collections de l'INSEE, Série E31/2, p.15. Some revealing statistics based on data (of the well-known *Fortune* type) for manufacturing corporations employing over 40,000 persons *worldwide* are given in S. J. Prais, *The Evolution of Giant Firms* (Cambridge University Press 1976), p.156.

National Base	No. of Corporations	Worldwide Employment ('000s)	Worldwide employment as % of total manufacturing in the base country
U.S.A.	89	8,050	42
U.K.	30	2,670	34
W. Germany	12	1,590	15
France	12	1,150	19
Benelux	5	800	32
Italy	6	640	11

6. Murray Feshbackh, 'The Structure and Composition of the Soviet Industrial Labor Force', in *The USSR in the 1980s*, NATO Directorate of Economic Affairs, 1978, pp.55-69.

7. Volkhart Vincentz, 'Evaluation of growth prospects, the Soviet 10th Five Year Plan and results from economic models of the Soviet economy' in *The USSR in the 1980s*, NATO Directorate of Economic Affairs, 1978.
8. Wolfgang Michalski, 'Industrial Raw Materials' in *OECD Observer*, July 1978.
9. *The Times*, London, 4 October, 1978, p.24, 'International bankers weigh debt problems in loans to Third World'.
10. See the Annual Year Books of the Stockholm International Peace Research Institute (SIPRI).

Chapter 3 STRATEGIC INTELLIGENCE: PROBLEMS AND REMEDIES

1. Avi Shlaim, 'Failures in National Intelligence Estimates: The Case of the Yom Kippur War', *World Politics* XXVIII, 1976, p.348.
2. Roberta Wohlstetter, *Pearl Harbor: Warning and Decision* (Stanford, Stanford University Press, 1962).
3. Barton Whaley, *Codeword Barbarossa* (Cambridge, Mass., MIT Press, 1973), p. 244.
4. Ibid., p. 223.
5. Thomas G. Belden, 'Indications, Warning, and Crisis Operations', *International Studies Quarterly*, vol. XXI, March 1977, pp. 185-186.
6. Robert Axelrod, 'The Rational Timing of Surprise', to be published in *World Politics*, vol. 31 (1979).
7. Paul Bracken, *Unintended Consequences of Strategic Gaming*, Hudson Institute Paper, May 2, 1977.
8. Harold L. Wilensky, *Organizational Intelligence* (New York, Basic Books, 1967) pp. 24 ff.
9. Bracken, op. cit., pp. 28 ff.
10. William T. Lee, *Understanding the Soviet Military Threat*, National Strategy Information Center, Agenda Paper No. 6, New York, 1977, pp. 7-22.
11. Ibid., pp. 24-32. See also the papers by Wohlstetter listed in the Appendix.
12. Lee, op. cit., p. 27.
13. Bracken, op. cit., p. 7.
14. Wilensky, op. cit., p. 64.

Chapter 5. THE EVOLUTION OF STRATEGIC NUCLEAR DOCTRINE

1. Richard Nixon, *U.S. Foreign Policy for the 1970s*, Reports to the Congress: February 25, 1971, February 9, 1972, and May 3, 1973; Washington D.C.: U.S. Government Printing Office.
2. James R. Schlesinger, Secretary of Defense, Remarks to Overseas Writers Association Luncheon, International Club, Washington D.C., January 10, 1974.
3. James R. Schlesinger, *US-USSR Strategic Policies*, Hearing before sub-committee on Arms Control, International Law & Organization of the Committee of Foreign Relations, U.S. Senate, March 4, 1974, p. 9.
4. Sir Charles Webster and Noble Frankland, *The Strategic Air Offensive Against Germany 1939-1945*, London: H.M.S.O., 1961.
5. A. J. Wohlstetter, F.S. Hoffman, R. J. Lutz, and H. S. Rowen, *Selection and Use of Strategic Air Bases*, The RAND Corporation, R-266, April 1954, declassified 1962.
6. Albert Wohlstetter, 'Is There A Strategic Arms Race?', *Foreign Policy*, No. 15, Summer 1974 and 'Is There A Strategic Arms Race? (II): Rivals, But No "Race",' *Foreign Policy*, No. 16, Fall 1974.

7. Alain C. Enthoven & K. Wayne Smith, *How Much is Enough? Shaping the Defense Program, 1961-1969* (New York: Harper & Row, Publishers, 1971).
8. Alain C. Enthoven and K. Wayne Smith, op. cit.
9. Albert Wohlstetter, *Foreign Policy* articles, op. cit.
10. William Kaufman, *The McNamara Strategy*, op. cit.
11. Alain C. Enthoven & K. Wayne Smith, op. cit.
12. William Kaufmann, *The McNamara Strategy*, p. 114-15.
13. Richard Nixon, *U.S. Foreign Policy for the 1970s*, op. cit.
14. Melvin R. Laird, *Fiscal Year 1971 Defense Program and Budget*, Statement before a Joint Session of the Senate Arms Services and Appropriations Committee, February 20, 1970, Washington: U.S. Government Printing Office, 1970.
15. James R. Schlesinger, 'Briefing on Counterforce Attacks', Hearing before the Subcommittee on Arms Control, International Law and Organization of the Committee on Foreign Relations, U.S. Senate, 93rd Congress, September 11, 1974, Washington: U.S. Government Printing Office, 1975.

Chapter 7 DISARMAMENT AND ARMS CONTROL SINCE 1945

1. F. Barnaby & R. Huisken, *Arms Uncontrolled*, prepared for SIPRI (Cambridge Mass. & London: Harvard University Press 1975), p.3.
2. For an elaboration of this point, see I. Geiss, *German Foreign Policy 1871-1914* (London & Boston: Routledge and Kegan Paul, 1976), pp.148-149.
3. Quoted in R. Wohlstetter, *Pearl Harbor, Warning and Decision* (Stanford: Stanford University Press, 1962), p.351.
4. *Ibid*, p.352.
5. A. Wohlstetter, 'The Delicate Balance of Terror', *Foreign Affairs*, Jan. 1959.
6. Some elements of the new doctrine were spelt out in a press conference held by the Secretary of Defense on 10 Jan. 1974. Extracts were reprinted in *Survival*, Vol. XVI, No. 2 (1974), pp.86-90. The new strategy is analysed in L. W. Martin, 'Changes in American Strategic Doctrine – an initial interpretation', *Survival*, Vol. XVI, No. 4 (1974), pp.158-164.
7. A. Etzioni, *The Hard Way to Peace* (New York: Collier Books, 1962), p.126.
8. T. C. Schelling, 'The Importance of Agreements', in D. Carlton and C. Schaerf (eds), *The Dynamics of the Arms Race* (London: Croom Helm, 1975), p.74.
9. See, for example, A. J. Pierre, 'The SALT Agreement and Europe', *World Today*, Vol. 28, No. 7, (July 1972).
10. C. Bertram, 'Arms Control and Technological Change: Elements of a New Approach', *Adelphi Paper* No. 146, (London: IISS, 1978), p.2.
11. *Ibid*, p.17.
12. *Ibid*, pp.15-31.
13. A.F.K. Organski, *World Politics* (New York: Alfred A. Knopf, 1958), p.292.
14. For details of the Joint Statement on Agreed Principles, see Keesing's Research Report 7, *Disarmament: Negotiations and Treaties, 1946-1971* (New York: Charles Scribner's Sons, 1972), pp.83-85.
15. S.de Madariaga, *Disarmament* (London: Oxford University Press, 1929), p.91.
16. H. Bull, *The Control of the Arms Race* (London: Weidenfeld and Nicolson, 1961), p.5.
17. See for example, P. Noel-Baker, *The Private Manufacture of Armaments* (London: Victor Gollancz, 1936), Vol. i; F. Brockway and F. Mullally, *Death Pays a Dividend* (London: Victor Gollancz, 1944); John E. Wiltz, *In Search of Peace; The Senate Munitions Inquiry, 1934-36* (Baton Rouge: Louisiana State University Press, 1963).
18. Much of the literature on the Industrial-Military Complex is sensational and alarmist, but, amongst others, the following books deserve serious consideration: C. Wright

Mills, *The Power Elite* (New York: Oxford University Press, 1956); J. M. Swomley, Jr., *The Military Establishment* (Boston: Beacon, 1964); S. Melman, *Pentagon Capitalism* (New York: McGraw-Hill, 1970). Interested readers are also directed to H.O. Lasswell, 'The Garrison-State Hypothesis Today', in S.P. Huntington, *Changing Patterns of Military Politics* (New York: Free Press).

19. H. Butterfield, *History and Human Relations* (London: Collins, 1951), p.19.
20. *Ibid*, p.14.
21. *Ibid*, pp.19-20.
22. *Ibid*, p.21.
23. L. F. Richardson, *Arms and Insecurity: A Mathematical Study of the Causes and Origins of War* (London: Stevens and Sons, 1960), p.14.
24. R. Niebuhr, *Moral Man and Immoral Society* (New York and London: Charles Scribner's Sons, 1932), p.42.
25. See, for example, B. Russell, *Common Sense and Nuclear Warfare* (London: Allen and Unwin, 1959) and A. Myrdal, *op.cit*. Russell is particularly interesting because although he generally underestimates the difficulty of weaning men away from their irrational beliefs and habits, his diagnosis of the human condition is very realistic. J. M. Keynes' comment is very apt, 'Bertie in particular sustained simultaneously a pair of opinions ludicrously incompatible. He held that in fact human affairs were carried on after a most irrational fashion, but that the remedy was quite simple and easy, since all we had to do was to carry them on rationally.'
26. See K. Boulding, *Conflict and Defense: A General Theory* (New York: Harper and Bros., 1962), pp.24-25.
27. L. F. Richardson's thoughts on arms races have been published in two volumes, *Statistics of Deadly Quarrels*, eds. Quincy Wright and Carl C. Lienau (London: Stevens and Sons, 1960), and *Arms and Insecurity, op.cit*.
28. Richard Cobden called the arms race 'the game of beggar-my neighbour'. See W. H. Dawson, *Richard Cobden and Foreign Policy* (London: Allen and Unwin, 1926), p.159. Cobden's views on Anglo-French naval competition during the 1850s are to be found in R. Cobden, *The Three Panics: An Historical Episode* (3rd. Edition, London: Ward & Co., 1862).
29. See Viscount Grey, *Twenty-Five Years, 1892-1916* (8th. Edition, London: Hodder and Stoughton, 1935), Vol. II, pp.259-272.
30. S. de Madariaga, *op.cit*. This book is one of the few books from the inter-war years to survive the test of time. Much of it is as relevant today as when it was published in 1929.
31. Lord Cecil, *Documents of the Preparatory Commission for the Disarmament Conference*, Series II. p.14.
32. P. Hammond, 'Super Carriers and B-36 bombers: Appropriations, Strategy and Politics', in H. Stein (ed.) *American Civil Military Decisions* (Birmingham, Ala: University of Alabama Press, 1963).
33. V. Davis, *The Admirals Lobby* (Chapel Hill: University of North Carolina Press, 1967), p.228.
34. *Ibid*, p.229.
35. A. Wohlstetter, 'Racing Forward or Ambling Back', *Survey*, Vol. 22 (1976).
36. *Ibid*, p.199.
37. *Ibid*, p.192.
38. *Ibid*, p.202.
39. C. Osgood, *An Alternative to War or Surrender* (Urbana, Chicago, London: University of Illinois Press, 1962), pp.85–134.
40. I. Claude, *Swords into Plowshares* (New York: Random House, 1956), p.298.
41. Quoted in B. G. Bechhoefer, *Postwar Negotiations for Arms Control* (Washington D.C.: Brookings Institutions, 1961), p.298.
42. See his comment in *The Control of the Arms Race, op.cit.,* p.213.
43. See B.G. Bechhoefer, *op.cit.,* p.429.

44. For a thorough and comprehensive analysis of these techniques see S. Melman (ed.), *Inspection for Disarmament* (New York: Columbia University Press, 1958).
45. For a detailed examination of these techniques see Lewis C. Bohn, 'Non Physical Techniques of Disarmament Inspection' in Q. Wright, W. M. Evans and M. Deitsch (eds.), *Preventing World War III* (New York: Simon and Schuster, 1962), pp.20-39.
46. For an interesting analysis of evasion techniques employed under the Weimar Republic see E. J. Gumbel, 'Disarmament and Clandestine Rearmament' in S. Melman, *Inspection for Disarmament,* pp.203-219.
47. For an elaboration of this point see L. S. Rodberg, 'The Rationale of Inspection', in S. Melman (ed), *Disarmament: Its Politics and Economics* (Boston: The American Academy of Arts and Sciences, 1962).
48. For a full discussion of Soviet attitudes to inspection, see A. Dallin, et al, *The Soviet Union and Disarmament: An Appraisal of Soviet Attitudes and Intentions* (New York: Frederick A. Praeger, 1964), pp.142-158.
49. L. B. Sohn, 'Phasing of Arms Reduction: The Territorial method' in D. H. Frisch (ed) *Arms Reduction, Program and Issues* (New York: The Twentieth Century Fund, 1961), pp.123-127.
50. *Ibid,* p.125.
51. See Article XII of the Treaty on Anti-Ballistic Missile Systems and Article V of the Interim Agreement and Protocol on Strategic Offensive Missiles. The full text of agreements is reproduced in *Survival,* Vol. XIX, No.4, (1972), pp.192-199.
52. C. Bertram, *op.cit.* p.3.
53. R. R. Neild, *What Has Happened to Disarmament?* (London: David Davies Memorial Institute of International Studies, 1968), p.3.
54. A useful and manageable description of Disarmament and Arms Control negotiations since the Second World War is to be found in J. H. Barton and L. D. Weiler (eds.), *International Arms Control: Issues and Agreements* (Stanford: Stanford University Press, 1976).
55. E. Young, *A Farewell to Arms Control?* (Penguin, Harmondsworth, 1972) pp.13-14.
56. A Myrdal, *op.cit.* p.110.
57. J. L. Nogee, 'The Diplomacy of Disarmament', *International Conciliation* No. 526 (New York: Carnegie Endowment for International Peace, 1960), p.282.
58. See P. Noel-Baker, *The Arms Race: A Programme for World Disarmament* (London: Stevens and Sons, 1958), pp.12-30.
59. E. Young, *op.cit,* p.135.
60. S. de Madariaga, *op.cit.* p.48.
61. H. Bull, *op.cit.* pp.26-27.

INDEX

Abadan, 163
Aegean, 125
Afghanistan, 38, 54
Africa, violence in, 18, 37; Soviet intervention in, 22–4, 28, 45, 47, 54, 127; French campaigns in, 25; political situation in, 38; average incomes, 60; per capita GDP, 68; local actions in, 128; *see also* individual countries
Africa, southern 128
air-lifts, 182
Albania, 48, 78
Algeria, 33; trade, 42; nationalism in, 46–7; and West, 55; 1954–62 war in, 94, 108–9, 160, 163–4
America, Latin, 37–8, 42, 49, 175, 214
Angola, US setbacks in, 8; Cubans in, 22, 27, 73, 173, 176; Soviet strategy in, 23, 73; counterintervention in, 25; and West, 55; as crisis war, 160, 164, 168, 172–3, 175–6, 185
Antarctic Treaty (1959), 214
Anti-Ballistic Missiles, (ABM), 6, 143n, 147n, 181, 189, 213–14
Arab-Israeli wars *see* Israel
Arab League, 159, 183
Argentina, 39
armed force *see* military force
arms expenditure, 187
arms control and disarmament, 5–6, 181–2, 187–90; aims of, 191–3; mission controlling, 194; and power balance, 195–6, 198–206; verification and inspection, 198, 208–13; and mutual mistrust, 200–202, 208, 216; unilateral reduction, 205–6; and reduction of political hostility, 206–7; formal measures for, 214–15
Army of the Republic of Vietnam (ARVN), 113
Asia, 19, 60, 68
Asia, East, 38, 49, 59, 165
Asia, North-East, 4, 129
Asia, South-East, 7, 14, 23–4, 26, 126, 158, 182; *see also* individual countries
Assured Destruction, 146–7, 151–2; *see also* Mutual Assured Destruction
Australia, 54, 162, 181
Azerbaijan, 163–4, 184

Bandoeng Conference, 49
Bangladesh, 159, 163–4
Beaufre, Gen. André, 10
Berlin, 73, 106n, 163–4, 177–8, 180
Bertram, Christoph, 193–4, 213
Bevan, Aneurin, 177
Biafra, 46, 159, 164
biological weapons, 190; 1972 Convention on, 215
Bismarck, Prince Otto von, 45
Boncour, Paul, 187
Boulding, Kenneth, 201
Brazil, 38, 54, 56, 67
Brezhnev, Leonid, 49, 167, 174, 176, 178
Britain, national nuclear force, 13; in Malaysia, 19; retreat from Eastern commitments, 21; industrial revolution in, 32; pre-war pacifism, 33, 78; reduction of forces, 44; in India, 45; economic unrest in, 50–51; industrial output, 62; growth rate, 64; income distribution, 66; and outbreak of war, 73; and German invasion of USSR, 75; World War II bombing policy, 82–3, 136; estimates of bombing casualties, 82–3; and limited war strategy, 96; and Suez crisis, 160; and 1974 Cyprus crisis, 169; and naval limits, 197, 202
Brown, Harold, 121n
Buchan, Alastair, 37
Bulganin, Marshal Nikolai Aleksandrovich, 207
Bulgaria, 66
Bull, Hedley, 216
Burma, 108
Butterfield, Herbert, 199
Buzzard, Admiral Sir Anthony, 105

California Institute of Technology, 138
Cambodia (Kampuchea), 25, 35, 48, 164–5
Canada, 54, 67
Carter, President Jimmy, 5, 121n, 129, 179–80
Castro, Fidel, 168–9
Cecil of Chelwood, Viscount, 187, 202
Central Intelligence Agency, investigated, 25; and Soviet defence, 44, 82; and 1962 Cuba crisis, 76; independent reviews, 87;